Religion, Tradition, and Restorative Justice in Sierra Leone

LYN S. GRAYBILL

Religion, Tradition, and Restorative Justice in Sierra Leone

UNIVERSITY OF NOTRE DAME PRESS
NOTRE DAME, INDIANA

University of Notre Dame Press
Notre Dame, Indiana 46556
www.undpress.nd.edu

Copyright © 2017 by the University of Notre Dame

All Rights Reserved

Published in the United States of America

Library of Congress Cataloging-in-Publication Data
Names: Graybill, Lyn S., author.
Title: Religion, tradition, and restorative justice in Sierra Leone / Lyn S. Graybill.
Description: Notre Dame : University of Notre Dame Press, 2017. | Includes bibliographical references and index.
Identifiers: LCCN 2016058507 (print) | LCCN 2017005371 (ebook) | ISBN 9780268101893 (hardcover : alk. paper) | ISBN 0268101892 (hardcover : alk. paper) | ISBN 9780268101909 (pdf) | ISBN 9780268101916 (epub)
Subjects: LCSH: Sierra Leone—Religion—History—20th century. | Religion and politics—Sierra Leone. | Sierra Leone. Truth and Reconciliation Commission. | Transitional justice—Sierra Leone. | Reparations for historical injustices—Sierra Leone. | Restorative justice—Sierra Leone. | Reconciliation—Political aspects—Sierra Leone.
Classification: LCC BL2470.S55 G73 2017 (print) | LCC BL2470.S55 (ebook) | DDC 201/.7209664—dc23
LC record available at https://lccn.loc.gov/2016058507

∞ This paper meets the requirements of ANSI/NISO Z39.48-1992 (Permanence of Paper).

Dedicated to the Honors Political Science Class of 2010 at Fourah Bay College: Mohammed Dukulay, Lindsay Ellis, Dennis George, Yayah Jalloh, Albert Jusu, Christocia Ebu Kawaley, Sahr Kendema, Manjia Success Kobba, Joseph Mallah, Osman Kabiru Mansary, Sidiru Deen Tejan Moiguah, and Edward Bai Turay.

CONTENTS

Acknowledgments *ix*

Preface *xi*

Abbreviations *xv*

Introduction: Postwar Transitional Justice *1*

ONE Role of the Inter-Religious Council *7*

TWO The Sierra Leone Truth and Reconciliation Commission *31*

THREE Women and Transitional Justice *53*

FOUR Popular Views of the TRC and the Special Court *71*

FIVE Perceptions of Religious Leaders *97*

SIX Traditional Reconciliation Practices *127*

SEVEN Unfinished Business *153*

Conclusion *181*

Appendix 1. The Instrument *203*

Appendix 2. Interviews of Religious Leaders *205*

Notes *209*

Bibliography *263*

Index *285*

ACKNOWLEDGMENTS

I wish to express gratitude for friends and colleagues who read earlier versions of the manuscript, especially Daniel Philpott, Scott Appleby, and John Paul Lederach at the University of Notre Dame. I appreciate the valuable comments of the anonymous reviewers and also those of David Keen, whose critiques I incorporated in this final version. I am especially indebted to Stephen Wrinn, Stephen Little, and Robyn Karkiewicz for shepherding the project to publication.

The book could not have been completed without the generous funding of the United States Institute of Peace (USIP), whose grant afforded me the opportunity to travel to Sierra Leone in the summer of 2007 to conduct interviews. The Fulbright Scholarship Program also supported my work in Sierra Leone in 2009–10. Dana van Brandt, the public affairs officer at the US Embassy in Freetown, and Amy Challe, the Fulbright coordinator, were most helpful in facilitating my research. I also am grateful for the friendship of the other Fulbrighters: Jimmy Kandeh, Zoe Marks, and Niloufar Khonsari.

Two people in particular in Sierra Leone deserve mention. I learned much from the Reverend Moses Khanu, former director of the Inter-Religious Council (IRC), and at the time a member of the Sierra Leone Human Rights Commission. He opened up the archives of the IRC to me and graciously provided me his own written account of the role of the IRC during the war and postwar period. I also am indebted to John Caulker, executive director of Fambul Tok International. I met with him several times between 2006 and 2010 to learn more about the traditional methods of reconciliation his organization fosters. I appreciate all the people who were kind enough to be interviewed; their names are included in the appendix and bibliography.

I would be remiss in not mentioning Abdul Bah, driver extraordinaire, friend, and confidant. Thanks also to my husband, Jamie Aliperti, who read every word of the book multiple times and whose skillful editing improved the prose immensely. I dedicate this book to the students in my Honors Political Science class at Fourah Bay College, whose encouragement and support were unwavering.

PREFACE

When my book, subtitled with the unanswered question *Miracle or Model?*, on the South African Truth and Reconciliation Commission (SATRC) was published in 2002, Sierra Leone had just begun its path to truth and reconciliation, largely on the basis of the South African model, suggesting that the South African case had not been a onetime occurrence but would likely be replicated elsewhere on the continent.[1] The criticisms against the Sierra Leonean TRC, while not unlike those made against its South African predecessor, were moderated by the existence of the Special Court, operating at the same time, and thus met the objections of those who worried that human rights violations would take place with impunity unless there was also punishment. In short, and to simplify many different arguments, critics of the SATRC found its emphasis on reconciliation rather than on justice undesirable.

In particular, secular critics were suspicious of the use of religion and tradition in proceedings they believed should be governed by reason, law, and objectivity. One letter to the *Mail and Guardian* newspaper expressed the common complaint: "I understand how Desmond Tutu identifies reconciliation with forgiveness. I don't, because I'm not a Christian and I think it's grossly immoral to forgive that which is unforgivable."[2] A young woman opined, "What really makes me angry about the TRC and Tutu is that they are putting pressure on me to forgive. . . . I don't know if I will ever be able to forgive. I carry this ball of anger within me and I don't know where to begin dealing with it. The oppression was bad, but what is much worse, what makes me even angrier, is that they are trying to dictate my forgiveness."[3] Anthropologist Richard Wilson complained that, "Commissioners never missed an opportunity to praise witnesses who did not express any desire for revenge.... The hearings were structured in such a way that any expression of a desire for revenge would seem out of place. Virtues of forgiveness and reconciliation were so loudly and roundly applauded that emotions of revenge, hatred and bitterness were rendered unacceptable, an ugly intrusion on a peaceful, healing process."[4]

Were these critics onto something? Did people harbor negative views about the process their leaders had chosen for them to deal with the past? Or was this religious-redemptive model broadly accepted by South Africans, who are also overwhelmingly Christians?

Archbishop Desmond Tutu, the South African TRC's chairman, believes that reconciliation is not just biblically based but is also central to African tradition embodied in the notion of *ubuntu*. In African traditional thought, the emphasis is on *restoring* evildoers to the community rather than on *punishing* them. Tutu's own description of *ubuntu* is enlightening: "*Ubuntu* says I am human only because you are human. If I undermine your humanity, I dehumanize myself. You must do what you can to maintain this great harmony, which is perpetually undermined by resentment, anger, desire for vengeance."[5] *Ubuntu*, then, emphasizes the priority of *restorative* as opposed to *retributive* justice. Critics like Wilson who challenge this view argue that to view African tradition and law as completely excluding revenge is "wishful romantic naiveté."[6]

This debate fascinated me. To what degree were South Africans in particular, and Africans in general, more supportive of restorative approaches? Or was this approach pushed on people by religious personalities like Archbishop Tutu, when it did not actually resonate with their beliefs, understandings, and perspectives? While opinions about the success of the South African TRC are divided, and many people wish it had done more in the way of making reparations to victims, the basic supposition that acknowledging wrongdoing can promote reconciliation is not generally challenged (although most South Africans criticize how few perpetrators ultimately confessed their deeds).

If, in fact, Africans do support more reconciliatory processes, what might this mean for international jurisprudence in Africa, in light of the burgeoning role of the International Criminal Court on the continent? Do Africans prefer reconciliation over justice? Is any such preference limited to the level of the religious elite, or is it more widely shared?

I hope in this book to begin to answer those questions through a case study of Sierra Leone's experience with transitional justice. Through interviewing religious leaders in 2006 and 2007 about their perspectives and preferences, and comparing their views with public polls taken over several years, I concluded that *ubuntu* is alive and well in Sierra Leone—and not merely among Christian and Muslim religious leaders. Both religious and traditional resources exist that push in the direction of a restorative justice approach favoring apology, forgiveness, and reintegration, which is at odds with the dominant paradigm of transitional justice, what Daniel Philpott terms *liberal peace*, favored by Western governments and international organizations such as the United Nations, which emphasizes a retributive justice approach.[7] What this will mean for future prosecutions by the International Criminal Court in Africa is problematic if international preferences are at odds with local values, as they clearly were in the case of Sierra Leone.

ABBREVIATIONS

AFRC	Armed Forces Revolutionary Council
APC	All Peoples Congress
CDF	Civil Defense Forces
ECOMOG	Economic Community of West African States Monitoring Group
IRC	Inter-Religious Council
RUF	Revolutionary United Front
SATRC	South African Truth and Reconciliation Commission
SLPP	Sierra Leone Peoples Party
TRC	Sierra Leone Truth and Reconciliation Commission
UNAMSIL	United Nations Mission in Sierra Leone

INTRODUCTION: POSTWAR TRANSITIONAL JUSTICE

In the aftermath of a brutal, decade-long civil war (1991–2002), Sierra Leone pursued both reconciliation and justice in a two-pronged process. Those persons "who [bore] the greatest responsibility" for crimes against humanity, war crimes, and other serious violations of humanitarian law were tried in the Special Court for Sierra Leone.[1] Others (both perpetrators and victims) were heard by a South African–styled truth and reconciliation commission. Methodist bishop Joseph Humper, chair of the Sierra Leone Truth and Reconciliation Commission (TRC), described the two institutions as "going to the promised land but by different roads."[2]

Different roads, indeed. The Special Court for Sierra Leone emphasized justice through punishment of perpetrators, while the TRC promoted reconciliation between perpetrators and victims through a process of acknowledgment, apology, and forgiveness.

Have these institutions complemented each other, or have their goals and methods been at cross purposes? Which institution has enjoyed more public support? Which one will have the greatest impact? Finally, given the important place that religion holds in Sierra Leone—60% of the population is Muslim, 30% is Christian, and 10% is animist (practitioners of traditional African religions)—what role did religion play in these processes?

This book will first examine the significant role that religious leaders played in brokering the Lome Peace Accord that ended the war. The efforts of the Inter-Religious Council (IRC), an umbrella group of Muslim and Christian leaders established in 1997 as a chapter of the World Conference of Religions for Peace, were crucial. Its members served as mediators, acted as neutral arbiters, and convinced both sides to stay at the bargaining table. Enjoying the confidence and respect of the people, the IRC stood out during the civil war "as the most highly visible and efficient non-governmental bridge builder between the warring factions."[3]

Next, Christian and Muslim religious support within Sierra Leone for a truth commission that aimed at promoting reconciliation will be examined. It was through the IRC-supported Lome Peace Accord that amnesty was granted and a truth commission was authorized. Religious leaders' opinions on the contributions of the TRC, which formally concluded in October 2004 with the publication of its final report, will be probed. For interviews with religious leaders from the IRC, I employed the format of Chapman and Spong, who interviewed religious leaders in South Africa on the efficacy of the SATRC after its conclusion. They sought the views of thirty-three religious leaders as a component of a comprehensive evaluation of the SATRC conducted by the Science and Human Rights Program of the American Association for the Advancement of Science, in collaboration with the Johannesburg-based Center for the Study of Violence and Reconciliation.[4]

Like those interviewed by Chapman and Spong, the interviewees for this book were questioned about their understanding of reconciliation and its relationship to forgiveness, the contribution of the TRC to reconciliation and the value of its work to survivors, the role of religious communities in furthering the goals of the TRC, and the differences between religious and secular approaches to reconciliation.[5] It became clear during the interviews that the question about differences in religious and secular approaches to reconciliation made no sense to the respondents. A more fruitful question would have been whether a religious approach differed from a traditional one. Both religion and tradition provided resources that had the potential to bring about reconciliation, and both are more compatible than antagonistic in their views on acknowledgment, confession, forgiveness, and reparation. Religion in Sierra Leone is marked by syncretism; Islam and Christianity have been influenced by and incorporated into local cultures, and vice versa. For that reason, this book includes a chapter on traditional approaches to conflict resolution in Sierra Leone, exploring in particular the work of Fambul Tok, an indigenous organization that assists localities to conduct reconciliation ceremonies in their communities.

The arguments of scholars who have criticized truth commissions as too Western and not culturally appropriate, and questioned their continued use in postconflict African nations, will be addressed. Tim Kelsall and Rosalind Shaw, for instance, have argued that local understandings of reconciliation in Sierra Leone do not support the kind of truth commission set up by the government. Shaw rejected the notion that truth-telling before a truth commission is healing for victims and questioned the assertion that vocalizing one's pain is an appropriate way to heal one's memories. Noting that the recounting of verbal memories and trauma is part of Western psychotherapeutic practice, Shaw contended that it may not be particularly relevant to West African communities. Her research on memories of the slave trade in Temne-speaking areas of Sierra Leone showed that the past is remembered in tacit forms ("in the landscape, ritual practices, and visionary experience") rather than in verbal form.[6] She believes that healing has taken place locally through a process of social forgetting (similar to the conclusion of Honwana, who argued that reconciliation in Mozambique depended on the willingness of victims to forget, not remember, and certainly not to articulate their suffering).[7] Social forgetting is the refusal to give the violence social reality, to reproduce it through public speech. Shaw wrote that communities seemed less concerned with what perpetrators have said (formal apologies) than with changes in their behavior, a "cool heart," which after all defines true repentance.[8]

Kelsall similarly argued that ritual may be more important to reconciliation than truth, suggesting that one can bypass the truth-telling step. Kelsall observed that, while the public testimony at the TRC was delivered unemotionally to a seemingly indifferent audience, the ceremonies of repentance and forgiveness after the district hearings struck a deep chord among victims, even when they were unaccompanied by the truth (actual confessions). Seeing evidence of remorse was therefore more important to victims (and hence to the reconciliation process) than hearing the truth.[9]

If Kelsall and Shaw were correct in saying that traditional methods are more appropriate than a "Western-styled" truth and reconciliation commission, what indigenous methods of reconciliation and rituals were available yet underused? Were localized understandings of reconciliation at odds with the public-hearing format relied on by the TRC? Or had local rituals been undertaken at the conclusion of the war, making further efforts unnecessary? This book will explore the issue of how and to what extent truth commissions should take local understandings into account, and will examine the question of whether the teachings of the great religions should trump traditional views, assuming there are variations. Wilson, for example, argued in the South African case that the township residents he interviewed were much more vengeful and eager for retribution than the *ubuntu*-preaching Archbishop Desmond Tutu had imagined. For Wilson, the "religious-redemptive" approach was coercive and clashed with the retributive notions of justice routinely applied in local townships and in chiefs' courts.[10] However, as I have argued elsewhere, while an ideal of restorative justice did dominate under Tutu's tutelage, it was not at odds with Africans' (especially the rural poor's) conceptions of reconciliation.[11]

Along with extracts from interviews with elite religious leaders, this book includes a chapter that highlights the work of scholars who conducted public opinion polls both before and after the war to gauge people's attitudes about reconciliation and justice and in particular to learn their views of the Special Court and the TRC. Of special interest were the ways in which the opinions of religious leaders might have diverged from those of ordinary Sierra Leoneans. Was the notion of reconciliation—and the need for confession and forgiveness, in particular—at odds with local understandings but nevertheless thrust on a vengeance-seeking population by the elites? Or are religion and tradition mainly complementary, in Africa generally and in Sierra Leone in particular? Do religion and tradition work in tandem toward restorative justice, whereas law privileges retributive justice?

Luc Huyse and Mark Salter, in their wonderful book of case studies of African traditional justice experiments, argued that there is a continuum ranging between the opposite poles of "legal retaliation" and "ritual reconciliation."[12] They offered a host of reasons why African postconflict countries may prefer the latter approach: it is informal, ritualistic, and communal as opposed to trials, which are formal, rational, and individualistic. Individual trials, though often promoted by the international community, may destabilize a fragile peace and also fail to get at the broad sweep of events, since their aim is to emphasize individual guilt and not societal patterns of atrocity. Erin Daly and Jeremy Sarkin argued that while trials focus more on perpetrators and their intent, restorative justice mechanisms such as truth commissions focus more on victims and their feelings.[13] Such restorative approaches might do more to promote healing, restore relationships, and reintegrate communities than a trial can ever hope to accomplish.

Archbishop Tutu, it will be recalled, promoted the notion of *ubuntu* as a traditional concept on which South Africans—and all Africans, in his view—could draw. In *No Future without Forgiveness*, he wrote of the "healing of breaches, the redressing of imbalances, the restoration of broken relationships. This kind of justice seeks to rehabilitate the victim and perpetrator, who should be given the opportunity to be reintegrated into the community he or she has injured by his or her offense."[14] Tutu has been joined by a host of scholars who agree that restorative justice approaches are more fruitful than retributive ones, especially in times of transition.[15]

My own study of traditional conflict resolution methods employed in Sierra Leone found enormous similarities between the precepts of religion—to confess and to be forgiven—and cultural understandings that likewise are based on (vocal) acknowledgment, apology, and forgiveness. I am therefore not persuaded by Kelsall's and Shaw's argument that the culture of secrecy, summed up in the Krio expression *Tok af, lef af* (talk half, leave half), makes verbal acknowledgment unimportant to Sierra Leoneans.

Finally, given the wide array of recommendations made by the TRC (and mostly ignored by the government), what do religious leaders see as their roles relative to reforms and reparations? Does a prophetic ministry exist, or has the mantle moved on to other civil society organizations? In other words, does religion remain relevant as the country rebuilds, reconciles, and repairs the damage from the past?

CHAPTER 1

ROLE OF THE INTER-RELIGIOUS COUNCIL

THE UNCIVIL WAR

The Sierra Leone civil war officially began on March 23, 1991, when a band of rebels calling themselves the Revolutionary United Front (RUF), led by a former corporal named Foday Sankoh and backed by Charles Taylor, invaded the country from neighboring Liberia and ignited a conflict that was to last a decade and wreak untold havoc on its population.[1] The RUF asserted that theirs was a just revolution that sought to end the corrupt rule of the All Peoples Congress (APC) that had ruled Sierra Leone since 1968 (and as a single-party state since 1978) and to establish a more equitable society.[2] In fact, however, the RUF simply capitalized on the "people's suffering to pose as liberators,"[3] and their fight quickly devolved into the indiscriminate killing of the very civilians they claimed to be liberating.[4]

In April 1992, a year after the initial incursion, twenty-six-year-old captain Valentine Strasser seized power from the APC. His justification for the coup was that his National Provisional Ruling Council

(NPRC) would foster democracy, end corruption, set the economy on a sound basis, and defeat the RUF—something the APC had been unable or unwilling to do.[5] After their initial enthusiasm, the people of Sierra Leone became disillusioned as they saw the NPRC seemed to be just as uninterested in ending the war and the profit-taking opportunities the war afforded them as the APC had been. The NPRC presided over an escalation of army abuses against civilians, and increased government involvement in illegal diamond mining, while failing to suppress the RUF—even though the army swelled to ten thousand troops within three years.[6] In fact, elements within the military appeared to be covertly collaborating with the RUF, leading to the phenomenon called *sobels* (soldiers by day, rebels by night), whereby soldiers took off their military uniforms at night to loot and to provide weapons, ammunition, and intelligence to RUF forces.[7]

The NPRC regime attempted to enlist the help of traditional hunters, the *Kamajors*, some of whom had formed the Civil Defense Forces (CDF) at the start of the war to assist in fighting the rebels. The military's collusion with the rebels made that cooperation short lived, and the *Kamajors* soon chose to fight alone. Seeking protection from abuses by both the government and the rebels, people increasingly turned to the *Kamajors* for protection.[8] The *Kamajors*, who formed the CDF, constrained somewhat the ability of soldiers and rebels to harass citizens and illegally mine diamonds, but they themselves targeted civilians suspected of assisting those factions. When the regular army lost all credibility as a disciplined, professional fighting force, the NPRC government hired a South African–based private security firm, Executive Outcomes, to repel the rebels. With just two hundred highly trained and well-equipped mercenaries fighting alongside the CDF, Executive Outcomes was able to rout the RUF from Freetown, secure the Kono diamond mines, and retake the bauxite and rutile mines in the Southern Province.[9]

Under both international and local pressure for "elections before peace"—fueled by the assumption that "peace before elections" would simply play into the hands of those elements who wanted to prolong the war[10]—the NPRC agreed to hold elections, insisting the *P* had stood for "provisional" all along, and it had pledged to return the country over to civilian rule within four years of taking power.[11] In the run-up to the election, both the rebels and government soldiers committed many atrocities, including amputations of the hands and arms of at least fifty-two people.[12] The RUF intended these acts as warnings to people not to vote, after the statement of Sierra Leone Peoples Party (SLPP) candidate Ahmad Tejan Kabbah that "The future is in your hands."[13] In spite of these terrorizing acts, the election was held in February 1996 and was followed by a runoff in March that brought Kabbah to the presidency with 60% of the vote and ushered in civilian control after four years of military rule.[14]

Nevertheless, sporadic fighting continued in the hinterland, compelling the president to negotiate a peace accord with the RUF at Abidjan, Ivory Coast, in November 1996. Kabbah agreed to pardon the RUF, demobilize the rebels, register the RUF as a political party, and expel Executive Outcomes from the country. With the mercenaries out of the way, and the army pruned by Kabbah to just seven thousand soldiers, however, the RUF was emboldened to ignore the ceasefire and refuse to demobilize. This forced Kabbah, who was suspicious of the loyalty and capability of the national army, to rely increasingly on the CDF.

Kabbah had been in office just fourteen months on May 25, 1997, when he was faced with a coup, this time by a group of Sierra Leone Army noncommissioned officers calling themselves the Armed Forces Revolutionary Council (AFRC). They forced Kabbah's government to flee to neighboring Guinea. The AFRC then freed and armed six hundred prisoners from Pademba Road Prison, among whom was former corporal Johnny Paul Koroma, who was being held on treason charges, and whom they immediately set up as chairman. Inviting the RUF to rule jointly with the AFRC, Koroma appointed RUF leader Foday Sankoh as his deputy chair. Sankoh was unable to accept as he was by then in detention in Nigeria, but he gave his blessing to the new regime and urged his men to come out of the bush and join the new government.

The coup ushered in a period of wanton looting dubbed "Operation Pay Yourself," in which thousands of people were raped, killed, or mutilated by AFRC/RUF forces. Public buildings, churches, and mosques were razed. CDF fighters retaliated against AFRC/RUF forces and their supporters and, in the words of one witness at the TRC, "became worse oppressors than the RUF rebels."[15] The Economic Community of West African States Monitoring Group (ECOMOG), a peacekeeping force led by Nigeria, intervened and was able to take control of Freetown, allowing Kabbah to return from exile in Guinea in March 1998.

The war continued nonetheless. Freetown was sacked on January 6, 1999, in the most intensive and concentrated period of human rights abuses committed during the war. In just two weeks, some ten thousand people were killed (including cabinet members, journalists, and lawyers, who were specifically targeted),[16] two thousand women were raped, countless businesses were looted, and some five thousand homes were destroyed.[17] Abductions reached their highest level during this period because AFRC/RUF fighters sought "numerical bulk," so that they might use bodies as human shields.[18] Fighting alongside the CDF, ECOMOG was able to push back the AFRC/RUF forces,[19] but in so doing they indiscriminately killed anyone suspected of being an AFRC/RUF sympathizer.[20] Nigeria, which was under its own domestic pressure to pull out its troops, and other international partners, including the United States, pressured Kabbah to open a dialogue with the RUF.

On July 7, 1999, another peace accord was signed, this one in Lome, Togo. The Lome Peace Accord guaranteed complete immunity from prosecution to Sankoh and the RUF fighters, and offered Sankoh a place in government as head of the new Mineral Resources Commission with the rank of vice president (later on, Johnny Paul Koroma of the AFRC was offered the position of minister of the Commission for the Consolidation of Peace by President Kabbah). Sankoh apologized "for any inconvenience my revolution may have caused."[21]

The new peace was short lived. In early May 2000, RUF rebels captured and held hostage 550 UN peacekeepers who had been part of the United Nations Mission in Sierra Leone (UNAMSIL) to oversee the disarmament and demobilization of combatants authorized under the Lome Accord. Thousands of demonstrators marched to

Sankoh's Freetown home to oppose the RUF abductions and to insist that Sankoh adhere to the Accord's stipulation to disarm. When they broke through the UNAMSIL barricade, Sankoh's bodyguards shot into the crowd and killed at least ten civilians. In response, armed CDF and West Side Boys (a splinter group of the AFRC), who were among the demonstrators fired into the compound. Sankoh was able to escape, but several young children within the compound were gunned down in cold blood by *Kamajors*, West Side Boys, and government forces responding to Johnny Paul Koroma's call earlier in the week for a "Peace Task Force" to remove all RUF leaders.[22] Sankoh was arrested and removed from his government position. With the Lome Accord now discredited and in tatters, Britain sent its own troops under its own command to restore order to Freetown. The final Accord was signed in Abuja, Nigeria, later that year, and President Kabbah declared the war officially over on January 18, 2002. The final toll: some seventy-five thousand civilians killed, two million people displaced, and twenty thousand civilians mutilated.[23]

FAITH-BASED MEDIATION

The civil war provided the impetus for a new activism on the part of religious leaders, who were instrumental in brokering the Peace Accord between the government and rebel forces. During Siaka Stevens's rule (1968–85)—considered one of the most corrupt regimes in Africa and characterized popularly as a "seventeen year plague of locusts"[24]—religious leaders were mainly silent. According to Moses Khanu, the former general secretary of the Baptist Convention, one-time director of the IRC, and later a commissioner on the Human Rights Commission, "The religious leaders were either afraid to talk and condemn the evil that was plaguing the nation or they were part and parcel of the system. . . . It was like every leader forgot their God given religious responsibilities."[25] Khanu explained that those who did speak out were threatened with imprisonment, house arrest, and political marginalization. For reasons of survival and recognition, many religious leaders chose to keep silent.

The TRC report concurred with Khanu's assessment: "It is indeed regrettable that faith institutions seem to have found common cause with the governments of the day and therefore took no stand on the issues that were tearing the country apart between 1961 and 1991. Faith institutions were content to be feted and revered by the respective Governments." They did not use their access "to engage in dialogue with the rulers and try to have them change their oppressive politics."[26] Only once, the TRC report noted, did the religious community publicly criticize the government—when Anglican bishop Keillie of Bo District was assaulted in 1993 by an officer of the NPRC regime: "Up to 1991 therefore, faith institutions in Sierra Leone buried their heads in the sand and intoned that everything was fine in the country, admonishing the faithful through their sermons to be loyal to the constituted authority."[27]

The war was a turning point in the life of the faith community in Sierra Leone. Religious groups had played an increasingly important role in education, sanitation, socioeconomic, and cultural affairs during the corrupt rule of Stevens and his successor, Joseph Momoh, stepping into the breach to provide services that had been neglected by what had increasingly become a "shadow state."[28] With the advent of the war, ordinary Muslims and Christians began to urge their leaders to move beyond their roles as social services providers and to act affirmatively to end the violence.[29] Religious leaders realized, according to the IRC's first secretary general, Alimamy Koroma, that they needed "to tackle the war itself, not just the casualties of war."[30] The inspiration for the IRC was not only an awakening religious commitment to social justice and calls from its members to be more proactive in the peace process but also the example of the IRC of Liberia (formerly the Interfaith Mediation Committee), which was outspoken about human rights abuses committed during the Liberian civil war.[31]

PRECEDENTS FOR RELIGIOUS PEACEBUILDING

There were other precedents, in addition to neighboring Liberia, for faith-based peacemaking on the continent. One early example was the mediation of the Quakers during the Nigerian civil war, which began in 1967. Quakers were invited by the Organization of African Unity to convene a meeting of low-level officials from both sides to search for possible areas of agreement. By acting as go-betweens, passing messages between head of state Yakubu Gowon and the Biafran leader Emeka Ojukwu, the Quakers, over time, helped both sides "re-perceive" each other, to recognize their enemies as "God in every one."[32] Through their efforts, Biafran insurgents and government officials were persuaded to convene a national peace conference that ended the thirty-month civil war. Commenting on the Quakers' success, Cynthia Sampson explains, "The Quaker team was the sole third party that won the complete trust of both parties to the conflict, and they sustained that trust for the duration of the war."[33] As pacifists, they were viewed as having no personal agenda or hidden interests, other than the promotion of peace.

Religious leaders were also in the forefront of promoting peace between the government of Sudan and the Southern Sudan Liberation Movement. Facilitated by a three-man team representing the All Africa Conference of Churches' (AACC) and the World Council of Church's departments of International Affairs and Refugees, a peace settlement was signed in 1972. That settlement was abrogated in 1983, when the government imposed sharia law throughout the country, including in the non-Muslim south, but a final end to the civil war was mediated in 2005 by President George W. Bush's special envoy for Peace in Sudan, Senator John Danforth. The authors of *God's Century: Resurgent Religion and Global Politics* attribute Danforth's success to his having been an Episcopal priest before he became a politician, which garnered him respect from both Muslim leaders in the north and Christian leaders in the south as a "man of God." The authors also credit Danforth for successfully engaging the Sudanese Inter-Religious Council, a forum of Christian and Muslim leaders, to work out disputes in their communities.[34]

Perhaps the most celebrated case of faith-based mediation was conducted in Mozambique by a Catholic lay community. After its independence from Portugal in 1975, Mozambique's Frelimo (Mozambique Liberation Front) government became embroiled in a long civil war with the opposition movement, Renamo (Mozambique National Resistance). The Catholic lay community Sant'Egidio, headquartered in Rome, initiated contacts in the country throughout the 1980s. During that decade, Sant'Egidio representatives became personally familiar with leaders of both sides by developing a "network of friendships."[35] Drawing on Sant'Egidio's reputation for impartiality, they were able to negotiate the release of missionaries taken captive by Renamo, thereby laying a foundation of trust with the insurgents that proved crucial in later peace talks. Sant'Egidio also partnered with the Mozambican Christian Council, made up of seventeen Protestant denominations, to hold talks with Renamo in Nairobi in 1989. Ten rounds of talks were held between 1990 and 1992, culminating in the signing of the General Peace Accord on October 4, 1992, which ended the seventeen-year civil war. At the signing ceremony, alongside Frelimo president, Joaquim Chissano; Renamo leader, Afonso Dhlakama; and other heads of state and foreign dignitaries were two Sant'Egidio representatives—founder Andrea Riccardi and parish priest Mateo Zuppi—as well as Mozambican Archbishop Jaime Goncalves and Italian MP Mario Raffaeli.[36]

South Africa provides yet another example of successful mediation by religious leaders, but in this case the mediation was not to end a civil war but rather to facilitate the transfer of power from the white minority regime to the majority. Beginning in 1978, the South African Council of Churches, headed by Anglican Desmond Tutu and subsequently led by the former Dutch Reformed churchman Beyers Naude and Pentecostal leader Frank Chikane, became the center of political activity, advocating for the end of apartheid and white minority rule. In 1984, when the National Party regime established a Tricameral Parliament giving voting rights to coloreds and Indians, hitherto excluded groups, in separate chambers, but not to Africans, religious leaders like Desmond Tutu and Allan Boesak, leader of the Dutch Reformed Mission Church, became patrons of the United Democratic Front, an umbrella group of several hundred organizations that rose up to oppose it. It advocated for the franchise for all South Africans in a single chamber. When the United Democratic Front was banned four years later, the South African Council of Churches became the only legal institution left standing, and, by virtue of that fact, became the major body pushing for change.

After the publication in 1985 of the Kairos Document, a critique of apartheid penned mainly by black theologians impatient with the pace of change and perceived moderation of the churches, the World Council of Churches sponsored conferences in Harare in 1986 and in Lusaka in 1987, which brought together leading South African churchmen and members of the exiled liberation movements. In 1990, 230 church leaders (both black and white), representing 95% of South African churches, congregated in the town of Rustenburg to look ahead ecumenically to the postapartheid era and, for white pastors, to confess the sin of apartheid. After Rustenburg, church leaders continued to play a mediating role, joining with business leaders to facilitate the establishment of the National Peace Accord. The Accord was a code of conduct between the political parties and their followers that also authorized local peace committees throughout the country to monitor the ensuing violence threatening the transition to democracy and to intervene when necessary, thus containing the violence sufficiently to make elections possible in 1994.[37]

While not all cases of faith-based mediation are successful, the cases above demonstrate there can be advantages to this approach. The sheer numbers of people who adhere to a faith offer religious leaders a special platform. Out of a world population of seven billion people, more than five billion identify themselves as members of religious communities. Of the three billion poorest people in the world, many of whom live in zones of conflict, 90% are members of religious communities.

Moreover, a vast infrastructure accompanies those numbers. In Africa alone, there are some nine hundred thousand congregations, reaching from the smallest village to capital cities.[38] Religious communities also have international linkages and are able to partner for resources through a vast worldwide network. The cases mentioned above owed their success, including essential material donations, in part to the support of outside bodies such as the World Council of

Churches, the All Africa Conference, and Sant'Egidio. However, as those cases also demonstrated, international mediation is doomed without credible partners on the ground, which local religious institutions can sometimes provide, who have access to elite government leaders (and opposition forces).[39]

The quality of religious leadership is important. Religious leaders are effective peacemakers to the degree they are seen as unbiased, honest brokers who are independent from the government. (This explains perhaps why the Catholic Church in Rwanda, historically co-opted by the government, had little input in the Arusha Peace Accord of 1993, or later in leading postgenocide reconciliation activities.)

A final tool in faith-based peacebuilding are religious ideas and values elucidated in the holy texts. Reconciliation is a dominant theme in all the great religions and is a powerful motivator in bringing warring sides who share these faith commitments to the peace table. Empathy and compassion, in particular, are key elements in religious life that religious peacemakers bring to the table and are important for helping warring parties to recognize the dignity in their opponents as they seek to rehumanize the other.[40]

The ubiquity of religious groups, led by respected leaders who have both access to elites in government and bonds to transnational bodies, armed with sacred texts that promote peace and reconciliation, make faith-based peacemaking a potentially powerful force in conflict areas. That was the message from William Vendley, secretary general of the World Conference of Religions for Peace (WCRP), which partnered with Sierra Leonean religious leaders in 1997. Established in 1970, the WCRP is a United Nations–affiliated NGO with over seventy national chapters, four regional bodies, and women and youth networks. The WCRP, also known as Religions for Peace, asserts that religious communities are uniquely placed to educate their communities about the root causes of conflict; to serve as advocates for the prevention of conflict locally, regionally, and globally; to play a central role in mediation and negotiation among armed groups; and to lead their communities in the reconciliation and healing required to transform armed conflict into lasting peace.[41]

FOUNDING OF THE IRC OF SIERRA LEONE

In late 1996, Mariatu Mahdi, president of the Federation of Muslim Women's Associations in Sierra Leone, met with WCRP officials in New York City to learn more about their work. The WCRP's vision resonated with Mahdi, who on her return to Sierra Leone raised with her coreligionists the idea of setting up a coalition of Islamic and Christian leaders who could speak with a common voice to the issues of the day. A one-day conference on "The Role of the Religious Community in Reconciliation, Reconstruction, and Development" held on April 1, 1997, was attended by over two hundred delegates. Two conference statements were generated, "Shared Moral Concerns" and "Shared Values and Common Purpose," which were signed by three representatives from the Muslim and Christian faith communities: Sheik Ahmad Tejan Sillah on behalf of the Muslims, the Reverend Moses Khanu on behalf of the Protestants, and Archbishop Joseph Ganda on behalf of the Catholics. The statements established the IRC of Sierra Leone as a national chapter of the WCRP.[42]

The Council's first secretary general, Alimamy Koroma, served simultaneously as the general secretary of the Council of Churches in Sierra Leone, an umbrella group of eighteen Protestant denominations. Joining the IRC, along with the member churches of the Council of Churches, were the Roman Catholic Church,[43] the Pentecostal Churches Council, and the Evangelical Fellowship for Sierra Leone. Founding Muslim member organizations included the Supreme Islamic Council, the Sierra Leone Muslim Congress, Federation of Muslim Women's Associations of Sierra Leone, United Council of Imams, Muslim Brotherhood Islamic Mission, and Sierra Leone Islamic Missionary Union. The IRC made its headquarters in Freetown in the western area but also established regional councils, in Makeni in the north, Bo in the south, and Kenema in the east, all of which had one Muslim and one Christian serving on their executive committees.

The goals of the IRC were for religious communities to share their respective traditions, principles, and values in order to build a more peaceful and just society; to discern areas of convergence in their religious traditions; and to implement collaborative action programs based on their shared values. They believed that by acting collectively they could be more effective than a single body acting alone. Their subsequent success according to former US ambassador Joseph Melrose is attributable to the fact that churches and mosques are located in virtually every village, town, and city of Sierra Leone, which provided the IRC with "the best network of any group in the country."[44] Moreover, in a country where other kinds of division—ethnic, regional, and urban/rural—have been politically manipulated, the history of religious toleration and cooperation among Christians and Muslims in Sierra Leone has been a model. Interfaith marriages remain common, for example; Sierra Leoneans are quick to point to the example of the marriage between former president Ahmad Tejan Kabbah, a Muslim, and his late wife, Patricia, a Roman Catholic. Christians and Muslims celebrate important occasions together, beginning social functions, religious festivals, and state functions with both Christian and Muslim prayers.[45] Not surprisingly, Cynthia Sampson finds, in countries where religion is not a divisive issue, as it is in Nigeria or Sudan between a Muslim north and a Christian south, religiously motivated peacebuilding has had its greatest impact.[46]

To these factors must be added the fact that religious leaders were and remain among the least-tainted, uncorrupted leaders in the country and were, therefore, widely respected, even by the rebels. According to Alimamy Koroma, "People may not appear too religious but they respect religion and religious leaders."[47] The message of faith communities on peace and reconciliation has been a vital resource in a land weary of conflict and desperate for hope and meaning after years of seemingly senseless killing. Religious communities share transcendent values and have profound insights into tragedy and suffering. Spiritualities can provide believers enormous courage and strength in the midst of tragedy and wickedness, provide a ground for hope when all seems hopeless, and open up the possibility to forgive the unforgivable.[48] Lastly, it is possible that the rebels, many of whom were fellow believers, were more willing to listen to religious leaders than to government officials whom they did not trust.

THE IRC AND THE AFRC COUP

The IRC had been in existence for less than four months when the AFRC overthrew the democratically elected government of Ahmad Tejan Kabbah on Trinity Sunday, July 25, 1997. It wasted no time, however, in condemning the coup in interviews with the BBC and Voice of America.[49] Over the months, the IRC pursued dialogue with the junta leaders and listened to their complaints while also condemning in no uncertain terms both their illegal takeover of government and the human rights abuses they had committed. It warned the coup leaders of the resolve of civil society to continue its campaign of civil disobedience and supported the efforts of the various civil society groups such as students, trade unionists, market women, and teachers. It informed the junta of the international community's intention to isolate them and issued statements urging them to step down.[50] Its unyielding stance resulted in the arrest of IRC secretary general, Alimamy Koroma,[51] on August 17, the day of a planned inter-religious worship service at the National Stadium in Freetown, and the banning of the event.[52]

After the signing of the Conakry Peace Accord in October 1997, the IRC met with AFRC leader Johnny Paul Koroma the following month to congratulate him for his positive contribution to peace in signing the peace plan, to urge him to follow through on those commitments, to register the IRC's own pledge to implement the peace plan, and to offer him the IRC's assistance.[53] Shortly afterward, the IRC sent a seven-person delegation to Conakry to brief the exiled president about the IRC's activities in Sierra Leone. In Conakry, the delegates also met with Peter Penfold, the British high commissioner; the European Union delegate to Sierra Leone, M. Perez Poros; the UN special envoy, Francis G. Okelo; and the Vatican delegate, Archbishop Antonio Linhobello.[54] The IRC returned and once again urged Johnny Paul Koroma to comply with the Conakry Peace Plan for the good of the country, but to no avail. Despite its failure in getting the AFRC to step down, which ultimately required military action, Turay believes that the IRC's "high visibility and engagement with the junta prevented greater abuses against civilians."[55] In any event, it received high marks among the population for speaking out and staying in the country, when most other institutions had collapsed and their leaders had fled.[56]

On February 12, 1998, ECOMOG forces ejected the military/rebel junta regime, and President Kabbah was officially restored to power on March 15, 1998. The service was held at the National Stadium, with the spiritual part of the program conducted by the IRC. Anglican bishop Julius Lynch of the Diocese of Freetown was selected to welcome the president home,[57] and the president in his remarks paid special tribute to the IRC for its stance against the junta and its contribution toward peace.[58] In celebration and gratitude to God for the return of democracy, the IRC conducted nationwide Thanksgiving services.[59]

THE SACKING OF FREETOWN: IRC RESPONSE

Hearing news that the forces of the disbanded Sierra Leone Army and RUF planned to launch an attack on Freetown, the IRC held a number of meetings with ECOMOG, the UN Observer Mission in Sierra Leone team, and the special envoy, Francis Okelo. On January 3, 1999, the IRC met with President Kabbah to warn him of the imminent invasion of Freetown. As had been predicted, on January 6 the combined forces invaded the capital, which not only fell on Epiphany but was also during Ramadan. (The rebels often chose days of religious significance to attack.) As they had done during the coup of 1997, they emptied Pademba Road Prison. For nearly three weeks Freetown was under fire, during which time seven thousand people were killed, tens of thousands were injured, women and girls were raped, children were abducted, and homes were destroyed. More than seventy places of worship were razed,[60] and Holy Trinity Church, an Anglican church dating back to 1877, was totally destroyed. Killings took place in churches and mosques that were serving as refuges for civilians. The rebels attacked the Church of the Brotherhood of the Cross and Star in Wellington, where they gunned down twelve people. The worst massacre was at the Rogbalen Mosque in Kissy, where sixty-six people who had taken shelter there were murdered.[61]

Members of religious groups were targeted for abduction and murder.[62] The Catholic archbishop of Freetown, Joseph Henry Ganda, was abducted, along with six nuns from the Sisters of Charity and four Xaverian fathers.[63] One of the nuns, who could not keep up—they were made to move constantly around the city on foot—was shot on the spot. Ganda was tortured by the rebels until he was eventually saved by ECOMOG forces.[64] (Pham attributes Ganda's targeting to the fact that he was an ethnic Mende with close personal ties to his fellow tribesman President Kabbah.[65]) The rebels were finally halted by ECOMOG and the CDF at St. Anthony's Catholic Church.[66] This led to the church's acquiring an almost mystical status, according to Penfold.[67]

TARGETING RELIGIOUS PERSONNEL

While the rebels' attacks during the war often seemed indiscriminate—grandmothers, nursing mothers, young children—victims also were selected in a way to turn upside down traditional views of power and powerlessness. Authority figures such as clerics, government figures, and chiefs were prime targets of RUF atrocities.[68] Sheik Abu Bakarr Conteh, one of the founding members of the IRC, explained that (like Archbishop Ganda) he was targeted during the sacking of Freetown because he was a person of note in society. He was well known for his position within the IRC and as a regular preacher in his mosque.

During the attack, more than two hundred people took shelter in Conteh's home, which, as the only cement building in the neighborhood, seemed the safest haven from rebel and ECOMOG mortar attacks. He remembers, "The rebels kept coming around, asking 'Where is the sheik?' My good neighbors said, 'No, we have no sheik here.'" Fearing the rebels would return, his neighbors dressed him in a woman's long robe and veil and disguised him to look like one of the suckling mothers with his three-month old daughter tied on his back. "Having been robed, I was in that condition for forty-five hours before tensions subsided, and I returned to my normal garb."[69]

For the Methodist bishop Joseph Humper, those days in January 1999 were harrowing. He recalls his daughter running into his room on the early morning of January 6, shouting, "Daddy, the rebels have invaded Freetown!" Watching from the window, they could see hundreds of women and children hurrying to escape the fighting. After sending the children to a safe place, he hid in his home alone for two weeks. From his hiding place, he witnessed the rebels vandalizing his home and carrying away all his possessions. At some point, his hiding place was discovered, and he was told by the rebels they had already taken the archbishop and he was second on their hit list. The bishop managed to slip away, taking cover at different houses. Eventually, the rebels discovered him, forced him to undress, took his money and his Episcopal ring, and left. Moving about the city constantly for fear of being discovered, Humper made his way toward the mosque near the city center for refuge. Once there he was told the rebels were looking for him, so he left and was eventually rescued by ECOMOG soldiers, who disguised him and moved him to the west end of the city until conditions improved.[70] He later heard that soon after he had left the mosque, rebels entered and murdered several people who had taken refuge there.[71]

J. O. P. Lynch, the Anglican bishop of Freetown, also had a frightening experience with the rebels during the January invasion. Three young rebels came to his home at the Anglican manse, pointed a gun at him, and said, "Pappy, I need fuel." Lynch thought they meant petrol. "I had immobilized my vehicles, so I said 'I don't have fuel; the vehicles are not working.' The rebel replied, 'I'm not talking about fuel. I'm talking about money.'" The bishop pulled three 5,000 leone bills from his pocket and gave them to the rebel, who took two and then, to the bishop's amazement, gave one back to him! "They said, 'Pappy, go back. You are free.'" Lynch went down to the docks, where two rebels with guns stopped him. "I introduced myself as the bishop of Freetown. I showed my identity and photograph taken when I was confirmed in the provinces. I was introduced to the commander. I told him a little bit about myself. I said we are peacemakers.

We have been praying for lasting peace. We are not very happy with the way things are going—the stealing and nepotism [in government] but that's no reason to react this way to that kind of situation. As we were talking, there was loud music and noise making. The commander shouted, 'Keep quiet. I am talking to the bishop of Freetown!' They listened to him. I saw he was really a commander. He asked if I knew who I was talking to. I said no. He said he was Commander Blood. He said he liked me. He said I should go back."[72]

Clerics were targeted because they were symbols of authority, because they supported the SLPP government, or simply because they were relatively affluent (and thus had something to loot). The RUF's stance toward religion was ambivalent, to say the least. Sankoh claimed to have been inspired by visions from God, and he identified himself sometimes as a Christian and at other times as a Muslim.[73] "Footpaths to Democracy," which was written to explain the RUF's platform and ideology, states that the RUF is religiously oriented, and both Christian and Muslim prayers are offered regularly.[74] Richards, an early apologist for an ideological motivation for the RUF, confirmed the presence of both a church and a mosque in every RUF camp, and rebels were required to pray daily under threat of punishment.[75] (Ironically, praying was often a prelude to attacking villages.)[76] In addition to destroying villages, rebels also committed egregious abuses on religious leaders and institutions. They forced Muslims to enter mosques with their shoes on and to drink alcohol; they urinated on the walls of mosques; they defiled and burnt down churches; they stole communion vessels; and they raped girls and women who had taken refuge in places of worship.[77]

Though they were often targeted, religious leaders were at times actually protected by the rebels because they connected on a personal level with the rebels in a nonjudgmental, loving way. For these young men, who seemed to be striking out in a frenzy to overcome the sense of shame they felt as marginalized members of society, the clerics' willingness to see them as worthy of dignity in the eyes of God/Allah made a deep impression and remains an important asset in faith-based mediation.[78] One UN worker perceptively stated, "In a way, what young people want, including rebels, is to be loved."[79] This insight was not lost on religious leaders, who rightly saw they had a unique role to play since they are in the business of extending God's love.

ECOMOG forces repelled the attack. In the aftermath, the IRC held a series of sensitization programs; released press releases domestically and abroad; held consultations with parliamentarians and traditional leaders;[80] and, with the encouragement of UN special envoy Okelo, met with both President Kabbah and the detained RUF leader Sankoh, acting as consultants and go-betweens for both sides. Okelo explained, "The IRC enjoys a unique position within the society, they have the respect and confidence of the people, so it was important to work closely with them right from the beginning of the peace process."[81]

In February meetings with the president, the IRC commended Kabbah for his radio address in which he made another offer of peace through dialogue. The IRC requested the president's permission for the IRC to meet with Sankoh, who was being held in detention by the government. In a communique published on February 25, the IRC highlighted the efforts it had made and urged the government "to talk less and listen much more." It urged the government to give the people an opportunity to hear the positions of the RUF and its allies.[82] But, according to Khanu, the other civil society organizations held the view that the rebels were a "bunch of bandits," and the government should not waste its time talking to them but just "flush them" (referring to the military option).[83]

With Kabbah's approval, a cross section of the IRC met with Sankoh at the military headquarters at Cockarel, where he was being detained, on March 1, 1999. They briefed him on their earlier meetings with the president, with the chiefs, and with civil society groups, and they acknowledged him as one of the key players in the peace process. According to Khanu, Sankoh said he "had been longing to meet with religious leaders and also stressed his trust and confidence in them."[84] He indicated he needed to consult with his colleagues before decisions could be made, recommended a joint cease-fire, and implied that he would be willing to release abducted children to the religious leaders as a show of good faith.[85] Sankoh expressed sympathy for the victims of atrocities, but he would not apologize since it was a "revolution he was leading," and because his court appeal was pending, he did not want to admit responsibility.[86]

Later that month, accompanied by Vija Jetley, the commander general of the UN Observer Mission in Sierra Leone, the IRC had the opportunity to meet with the rebels in the bush. Alimamy Koroma, the IRC's secretary general, who led the delegation, reported, "When we got to the last point of ECOMOG jurisdiction zone near Newton, the ECOMOG officer said to us, this is the last point of our protection, any step beyond this point is at your own risk."[87] From there the delegation traveled by foot through dangerous territory, the heart of RUF activity. As the delegation advanced, they could see the rebels waving white flags as symbols of peace. Additionally, the rebels had tied white pieces of cloth on the arms and heads of thirty-two children, lined them up in single file, and released them to the IRC delegation "as a token to show commitment to continue working with the Inter-Religious Council."[88] One of the IRC delegates, Saimihafu Kassim, explained how she communicated on a personal level: "I talked to the rebels as a mother." She recalled that some of the rebels asked her to pray for them.[89]

After arriving at the rebel base, the delegation was taken farther into the bush for consultations that lasted more than two hours. During the discussions, Sankoh was asked to authorize the release of more abducted children and child soldiers as a sign of his commitment to peace. Before he agreed, Sankoh asked that the IRC provide medicines, food, and other humanitarian assistance to the rebels. The IRC arranged for the delivery of food, blanket, clothes, and sanitary kits, a move that was unpopular in some quarters but one that Alimamy Koroma believes "helped to consolidate real confidence."[90]

From that point forward, a constant line of communication was opened between the Council office and the disbanded soldiers in the bush through radio and letters. Subsequently, the IRC brokered a radio conversation between Sankoh and his field commanders, which resulted in the release of twenty-one additional abducted children.[91] Alimamy Koroma later commented, "We followed like sheep for the slaughter not knowing what will befall us, yet we went by faith and the mission was successful."[92]

In April, a national consultative conference brought together political leaders and civil society representatives, including religious and traditional leaders, who proposed terms for a peace accord broadly based on the provisions in the unimplemented Abidjan Accord of 1996, which would accept limited power sharing, offer amnesty, and establish a truth and reconciliation commission. The conference conclusions were said to reflect a consensus, but a number of participants from the human rights community complained privately about the amnesty provision, with respect to which they had been "bullied into acquiescing in an outcome insisted upon by the government and its international supporters."[93] This reflects the divisions that existed between the purists, who rejected impunity for gross human rights violations, and the pragmatists (which included the IRC), who were willing to compromise for peace.

In mid-April, delegates of the IRC traveled to Liberia to meet with RUF officials, including its spokesman, Omrey Golley, and senior military adviser, Ibrahim Bah.[94] Their decision to meet in Liberia and their appeal to Charles Taylor to help bring peace were controversial to many Sierra Leoneans since Taylor had backed the rebels. But the IRC favored dialogue and was able to convince the government to include Taylor in the peace talks.[95]

THE ROAD TO LOME: IRC CONTRIBUTION

At the invitation of the Economic Community of West African States chairman and Togo president, Gnassingbe Eyadema, and at the request of the RUF, the IRC attended RUF's preliminary meetings, which were held in Lome in May 1999, before the formal peace talks. With a wry grin, Khanu joked that the IRC was promised one airline ticket but brought seventeen leaders, including Alimamy Koroma, who served as the spokesperson for the group.[96] Represented by a fifteen-person team, including representatives from the WCRP and Norwegian Church Aid, the IRC presented a statement in which it appealed to the RUF to abide by any agreement that was ultimately reached. According to Khanu, the RUF expressed great appreciation for the efforts of the IRC.[97]

The formal talks began on June 27, 1999, and again the government and rebels both asked the IRC to play a role as a neutral facilitator between the parties. The IRC delegates, reduced to just ten, found themselves acting as "go-betweens" at times of impasse to convince both sides to return to the bargaining table.[98] UN special representative Okelo recalls that the RUF had such drastic demands that "I needed to use the IRC members constantly in dealing with the RUF and the government."[99] According to then-US ambassador to Sierra Leone, Joseph Melrose, "When things looked bad in the negotiations, they kept the dialogue going."[100] At difficult points in the process—for instance, on the contentious issues of power sharing and the withdrawal of ECOMOG—"the Council members resorted to preaching and praying to sway resistant hard liners."[101]

The Accord was signed on July 7, 1999. At the closing ceremonies, the IRC was recognized as the "kick starter" of the peace process in Sierra Leone and was thanked by both sides. Because of its significant contribution in brokering the Peace Accord, the IRC was given a place in the Council of Elders and Religious Leaders that was to be established to mediate disputes of interpretation of the Peace Accord (but that was never set up because the Accord collapsed).

Not everyone was pleased with the outcome at Lome. Some civil society leaders who had attended the peace talks returned home, complaining that too much had been given to the rebels—not only in terms of appointments (Foday Sankoh was made chairman of the Commission for the Management of Strategic Resources, a position equivalent to vice president, while Johnny Paul Koroma was selected by the president to be chairman of the Commission for the Consolidation of Peace)—but also in terms of the blanket immunity granted to rebels for any and all atrocities committed during the war.[102] "I don't see the problem," reflected Okelo. "Really, human-rights people can be so sanctimonious sometimes. . . . If we did not agree to this amnesty, there would have been no peace. . . . We had no choice."[103] (Despite Okelo's personal view on amnesty, the United Nations instructed him to pen a caveat that the United Nations did not recognize amnesty for genocide, crimes against humanity, war crimes, or other serious violations of international humanitarian law.)

The difficult job of selling the Accord to the general public then began in earnest. On returning to Freetown, the IRC distributed thousands of copies of the Peace Accord for civil society groups to study, and went around the country explaining the Lome Accord to their constituents.[104] From their pulpits, religious leaders advocated for peace and reconciliation. Penfold noted that in all churches and mosques, no family had escaped personal tragedy enacted on them by the rebels. Some of the faithful in the mosques could not hold out both hands for the fatwa, while some congregants in churches were attempting to make the sign of the cross without a hand.[105] Through the work of the IRC, the difficult message of the need for forgiveness was heard widely in churches and mosques across the country. Alimamy Koroma explained at the time, "We have begun sensitizing our various communities on the need to accept the peace and to work together again as one nation. This will mean some aspect of forgiveness and reconciliation, but it will not be easy because our communities have been deeply hurt."[106]

Koroma recognizes that the approach of the IRC has not been accepted by everyone: "Perhaps as religious leaders, we are too bold for our civil society activists, in terms of our method, we are too compassionate, we are too endearing, or we are too tolerant with ex-combatants. . . . We tried to let [other activists] understand that our leaders, our style of work cannot be the same as others."[107] In a nutshell, the IRC had prioritized peace and reconciliation over punishment and justice.

After the signing of the Accord, the IRC leaders sought to welcome Sankoh back to Freetown and to thank him for his commitment to the peace process, but they were rebuffed. After keeping them waiting for an hour, Sankoh burst out of his office and lambasted the religious leaders, calling them "hypocrites." One leader said, "I was not only shocked but nearly shed tears, and we all refused to accept any drink from his servers. We left his house thoroughly embarrassed and humiliated."[108] On the other hand, their visit to Johnny Paul Koroma was positive. One leader said, "He warmly welcomed us and took time to express his apology for what has happened and took time to explain his ordeal with the RUF."[109]

LOME FALLS APART

The situation continued to deteriorate throughout the rest of 1999 and into 2000. On May 5, 2000, RUF forces abducted UN peacekeepers in Makeni, seven of whom were killed. Meanwhile, Johnny Paul Koroma, in his capacity as chairman for the Commission for the Consolidation of Peace, addressed followers at the National Stadium in an incendiary manner, urging them to bring peace by eliminating the RUF leadership.

In a demonstration at Sankoh's home on May 8, demonstrators were shot by Sankoh's bodyguards who feared the UN forces were unable to control the crowd, which included *Kamajors* and those sent by Johnny Paul Koroma as the "Peace Task Force" to kill RUF leaders. Sankoh escaped, after which the attorney general reassessed the situation, and President Kabbah requested the United Nations to set up a special court to prosecute Sankoh and Koroma. Sankoh was later charged by the Special Court for Sierra Leone for war crimes and crimes against humanity, but he died of a stroke in 2003 while he was in custody. (Koroma, who fled to Liberia, was officially pronounced dead.) With Sankoh out of the way, the disarmament and demobilization process began, under the auspices of UNAMSIL. On January 18, 2002, with the symbolic burning of three thousand weapons at the Lungi International Airport, President Kabbah was finally able to declare, "Di wor don!" (the war is over).

CHAPTER 2

THE SIERRA LEONE TRUTH AND RECONCILIATION COMMISSION

SETTING UP THE TRC

With the support of the IRC, the government in the Lome Peace Accord agreed to pardon not only RUF leader Foday Sankoh but also other combatants from all sides of the conflict—the RUF, the Sierra Leone Army, the AFRC, and the Civil Defense Forces (CDF)—"in respect of anything done by them in pursuit of their objectives as members of those organizations, since March 1991, up to the time of the signing of the present Agreement."[1] Amnesty was granted in order to get the RUF rebels to lay down their arms, and it was viewed by the government as the price that had to be paid for peace.

As mentioned in the previous chapter, amnesty was controversial and not unanimously hailed throughout the country. It was created because the government considered it unlikely it would win the war[2] and because of the urgent need for peace, whatever the cost.[3] However, the UN representative at the last minute attached a written addendum to his signature stating that the United Nations did not recognize amnesty for those who had committed genocide, crimes against humanity, war crimes, or other serious violations of international humanitarian law.[4]

Also contained in the Lome Accord—to placate those who were angry about the amnesty deal—was the establishment of a truth and reconciliation commission to begin within ninety days of the signing. The TRC was mandated "to address impunity, break the cycle of violence, provide a forum for both the victims and the perpetrators of human rights violations to tell their story, and to get a clear picture of the past in order to facilitate genuine healing and reconciliation."[5]

President Kabbah had contemplated holding such a truth and reconciliation commission when his government was in exile in Guinea after the AFRC coup. On October 20, 1997, he addressed a conference in London organized by the British government, in which he refuted the idea of treating the junta as war criminals. He explained, "I have instead been giving some thought to the establishment of a Truth and Reconciliation Commission following the example of South Africa. The merit of adopting this latter course can be easily discerned. The people of Sierra Leone need to know and hear from the perpetrators of the atrocities. This is an idea I intend to pursue so that genuine and lasting reconciliation can take place on the return of my government."[6]

The Accord was signed at a time when establishing truth and reconciliation commissions to address human rights violations from an abusive past was in vogue. By the time of the Lome Accord, eighteen truth commissions had been established worldwide, including six in Africa: Uganda (1974), Zimbabwe (1985), Uganda (1986–95), Chad (1991–92), South Africa (1995–2002), and Nigeria (1999–2002). Seven additional commissions continent-wide took place contemporaneously with Sierra Leone's or shortly thereafter: Ghana (2002–04), Morocco (2004–06), Democratic Republic of Congo (2004–06), Liberia (2006–09), Mauritius (2009–11), Togo (2009–12), and Kenya

(2009–12).[7] In offering amnesty to all perpetrators, Sierra Leone drew heavily from the South African example as Kabbah had signaled it would, although theirs was a blanket amnesty that was not conditional, as South Africa's had been, on the acknowledgment by perpetrators of individual guilt.

The abduction of a contingent of UN peacekeepers deployed to monitor the cease-fire caused the Accord to collapse in May 2000. President Kabbah then turned to the United Nations for help in establishing a war crimes tribunal to try Sankoh and the other rebel leaders. Why this change of heart? Penfold believes Kabbah was "persuaded" by the United States, an important donor, to make the request.[8] It is widely believed among Sierra Leone intellectuals that US support for a special court was to demonstrate the viability of an alternative to the International Criminal Court, which the United States had opposed, for handling war crimes and crimes against humanity. Suspicions abounded that the Special Court for Sierra Leone was an instrument of US policy, and the people of Sierra Leone were mere "guinea pigs."[9] From a domestic point of view, with the RUF now soundly defeated, prosecution was an option that had not been available in 1999.

The Special Court for Sierra Leone was authorized on August 14, 2000, by UN Resolution 1315 to prosecute crimes against humanity, war crimes, and other serious violations of international humanitarian law (including, for the first time in an international tribunal, child conscription). It was charged with prosecuting persons "who bear the greatest responsibility" for these crimes.[10] Formally established on January 16, 2002, it began in March 2003 to indict leaders from three major wartime groups: the RUF, AFRC, and CDF (but none from the Sierra Leone Army or ECOMOG forces). Of the thirteen suspects indicted, four have died: RUF leader, Foday Sankoh; warlord Sam Bockerie (allegedly murdered by Charles Taylor, who feared he would testify against him); AFRC leader, Johnny Paul Koroma, who was presumed to be dead; and CDF leader, Samuel Hinga Norman (former deputy defense minister and until his arrest internal affairs minister), who died during the prosecution of his case. Of the nine remaining defendants, all have been convicted and sentenced, including Charles Taylor, who was tried in the Hague for security reasons.[11]

The TRC proceeded even after the Peace Accord fell apart and the war crimes tribunal was established, albeit belatedly—three years rather than three months after the signing of the Accord because of the continued fighting. Not surprisingly, given their role in helping to broker the Peace Accord, the IRC members also took on major responsibilities within the TRC. Bishop Joseph Humper, serving at the time as the IRC president, was chosen to be the chairman of the TRC. Several clerics, including Usman Fornah, also played important roles in training statement takers, organizing the district hearings, and arranging the weekly reconciliation events after the hearings.

Other than that offered by the IRC, institutional support for the TRC is difficult to ascertain and quantify. Civil society leaders who had fled to Conakry had begun discussing the possibility of a truth commission as early as January 1999.[12] The government human rights commission, the National Commission for Democracy and Human Rights, also had begun exploring the prospect of a truth commission. The Human Rights Committee, an umbrella group of NGOs, expressed concerns about using the Abidjan Accord as a basis for Lome since the earlier accord had given blanket amnesty to combatants. It envisaged instead a "Truth, Justice, and Reconciliation Commission" that could recommend prosecutions for some of the worst offenders.[13]

Nevertheless, over two hundred representatives from civil society at the Consultative Conference held in April 1999 endorsed a blanket amnesty clause—arguing that since the RUF would not otherwise sign the accord, they had no choice—while opposing power sharing in government.[14] In June 1999, the National Commission for Democracy and Human Rights and the National Forum for Human Rights signed a manifesto, in which they affirmed that a truth and reconciliation commission should be established. That August, the TRC Working Group was formed under the auspices of the National Forum for Human Rights that would involve civil society and make sure that their concerns were addressed. In November 2000, coinciding with the passage of the TRC Act in Parliament, and again in June

2001, the National Forum for Human Rights held conferences on the TRC with assistance from UNAMSIL. Soon thereafter, the National Forum for Human Rights mounted a sensitization campaign to inform paramount chiefs, and other traditional rulers about the TRC, and to encourage them to allow statement taking and to protect witnesses.[15] IRC secretary general Alimamy Koroma later reflected that, while the IRC was the main voice promoting amnesty, "we brought the others on board."[16] Hayner agreed there was strong support early on among local civil society groups,[17] but Rosalind Shaw maintained that popular support for the TRC was always limited to a small group of Freetown NGOs.[18]

The TRC set up shop in July 2002, with the swearing in of its seven commissioners: Bishop Joseph Humper, Laura Marcus-Jones, John Kamara, Sylvanus Torto, Ajaaratou Satang Jow, William Schabas, and Yasmin Louise Sooka.[19] In addition to selecting the three international commissioners, the UN Office of the High Commissioner of Human Rights (OHCHR) was responsible for raising money. However, the TRC was forced to "realign" its work when the OHCHR proved unable to raise the full amount of $9.9 million.[20] Less than half of the amount (just $4.7 million) pledged actually came through.[21]

The OHCHR blamed its inability to raise funds from the international community on the TRC's reputation for poor management. A review by the UN Development Program (UNDP) in July 2002 found that one third of the TRC's staff was "unqualified for their positions or redundant" and that hiring was "politically driven."[22] The OHCHR and UNDP rewrote the job descriptions and readvertised the positions, and they did not consider Executive Secretary Yasmin Jusu-Sheriff for the permanent secretariat, replacing her instead with Franklyn Kargbo in February 2003.[23] The TRC for its part blamed the international community for not providing enough assistance and for losing interest once the Special Court began.[24] The International Conflict Group reported, "Money is not diverted *per se* away from the TRC and to the Special Court, but as one Western diplomat told ICG, the Special Court, although established well after the TRC, is far ahead in approaching donors and requesting funding."[25] Without doubt there was competition for funding with the Special Court when it was established in January 2002, and the TRC was very much the "poor relation."

The selection of commissioners[26] was also controversial because the four national commissioners—Humper, Torto, Marcus-Jones, and Kamara—were perceived as being pro-SLPP (the ruling party at the time).[27] This was not perceived as an insurmountable obstacle to the process, since they were joined by three international commissioners, who presumably would be politically neutral.[28] While all the national commissioners appreciated the contributions of the international commissioners,[29] there were criticisms from both within and outside the TRC. One criticism had to do with the fact that the act of setting up the TRC required that all commissioners be full time, but with the exception of Jow, they were only in the country on a part-time basis, which limited their usefulness. Another complaint lodged by Jusu-Sheriff, the former executive secretary (of the preliminary phase), who had been fired, was that some of the international commissioners were not very empathetic: "They were too aware of their own status, especially the Gambian commissioner [Jow]."[30] Jusu-Sheriff also faulted Schabas who, while on a sensitization tour in the outlying regions, was given the paramount chief's own bed to sleep on. Schabas complained that "it wasn't fit for human habitation," while the chief and his family slept on the floor.[31]

Despite the large number of Sierra Leoneans hired to staff the TRC,[32] Africans were paid less than the foreign staff according to Jusu-Sheriff. In general, there was concern that expats were too much in control of the process.[33] Given that the OHCHR, which was part of the UN system, had written the statute establishing the TRC, and controlled 95% of its budget, perhaps this should not be surprising. The primarily foreign-staffed UNDP and UNAMSIL served as in-country implementers for the Geneva-based OHCHR.[34] Jusu-Sheriff claimed that President Kabbah's response to her complaints about international control was, "It's their money."[35] She also believes that Humper was "too servile" to the internationals and fearful to "rock the boat."[36]

There was also the feeling that the government was not solidly behind the TRC (confirmed when five serving ministers and leaders of government institutions, including the attorney general and chairman of the SLPP, had to be subpoenaed to testify rather than coming willingly).[37] The government's puny contribution of just $97,000 plus the donation of a building for the secretariat also suggested that it did not consider the TRC a top priority. According to Schabas, this small contribution "seems to indicate an indifference to its mission, despite grand statements to the contrary."[38] He adds that the lack of substantial financial commitment no doubt hurt the sense of local ownership.[39]

In December 2002, the TRC began collecting statements from citizens of all wartime affiliations, and in April 2003, it commenced public hearings. By August 2003, it had taken 7,706 statements, including ones from Sierra Leoneans living in Guinea, Gambia, and Nigeria, and had received an additional 1,500 statements from a local NGO.[40] From April through August, 350 witnesses testified publicly in ninety hearings in each of the twelve provincial districts as well as in Freetown. The TRC held hearings for one week in each of the district headquarter towns (and two weeks in Freetown) but was unable, for lack of both time and funding, to get into the smaller villages.[41]

In each district, one day was set aside for closed hearings for all child witnesses (on the basis of UNICEF recommendations that children not be allowed to testify publicly), for sexually abused women who chose to testify in this way, and for perpetrators who requested anonymity. In addition to the general witness hearings, there were thematic hearings on topics such as good governance, the role of civil society, management of mineral resources, and corruption. Institutional hearings on the roles of the media, military, and police (among others) were also held, as were event hearings on important episodes such as the 1992 and 1997 coups, the 1999 invasion of Freetown, and the May 2000 taking of UN peacekeepers as hostages. The TRC drafted a 1,830-page report that was printed in November 2004, some fourteen months after the conclusion of the hearings, but not publicly released until August 2005. In addition, a children's version was published by UNICEF and a secondary school edition was published by Forum of Conscience.

Sierra Leone is the first postconflict country to set up both a truth commission and a war crimes tribunal at the same time[42]—albeit by accident rather than design—and provides a fascinating case of both justice and reconciliation at work simultaneously. Although TRC chairman Bishop Humper had described the two institutions as "going to the promised land but by different roads,"[43] these two bodies actually had very different objectives: the Special Court emphasized justice through prosecution of perpetrators, whereas the TRC prioritized reconciliation through a process of truth-telling, apology, and forgiveness. Put another way, the Special Court pursued *retributive* justice by targeting perpetrators for punishment, while the TRC, in focusing on both victims and perpetrators for healing, promoted *restorative* justice.[44] Describing the different objectives, former registrar of the Special Court Robin Vincent explained that there would be punishment for the few masterminds and forgiveness for the many foot soldiers.[45]

In addition to promoting healing for victims, the TRC was mandated with creating an impartial record of violations of human rights committed between 1991 and 1999, addressing the conflict's root causes, and making recommendations to the government to prevent future conflicts. In many ways it resembled the South African Truth and Reconciliation Commission (SATRC), which had been set up a decade earlier to deal with apartheid-era crimes.[46] Like the SATRC, which was chaired by former Anglican archbishop Desmond Tutu, this truth commission too was headed by a religious leader, Joseph Humper, bishop of the United Methodist Church and then president of the IRC.[47] Like the SATRC, it instinctively turned to religious notions of confession and redemption that resonate in a very religious society. Predictably, religious leaders were in the forefront of efforts to promote it.

Immediately after the Lome Accord was signed, the IRC began working for reconciliation, disarmament, and reintegration of former combatants. In biweekly "experience-sharing" sessions, the Council provided a forum for combatants to ask for forgiveness and for victims to express their grief about the harm that had been done to them. As Usman Fornah, a Wesleyan minister with the IRC, explained, "We are always preaching the ministry of reconciliation. No matter what those guys may have done, there is room on the side of the Lord to forgive them and to bring them back on the road they are supposed to be on."[48] These "experience-sharing" sessions under the auspices of the IRC became the prototype for the hearings that would later take place at the TRC. The hearings were also structured to resemble those of the SATRC, which had pioneered the concept of victim hearings alongside institutional and thematic hearings.

RESTORATIVE POWER OF TRUTH-TELLING?

Perhaps it should come as no surprise that religious leaders favor reconciliatory approaches. Archbishop Desmond Tutu had preached the virtues of restorative justice over retributive justice as a justification for the SATRC's approach.[49] In a provocative study of religion and transitional justice instruments, Toft, Philpott, and Shah argue that there is a strong link between religious involvement during transitions and reconciliatory instruments (amnesties, reparations, apologies, and truth commissions). In the nineteen post-transition countries they analyzed, those in which religious actors played influential roles opted mostly for truth commissions over trials.[50]

Whereas most analysts of transitional justice point to the power of the outgoing regime (whether the end of conflict is a result of a negotiated accord or victory on the battlefield) as an explanation for whether restorative or retributive justice measures will be initiated,[51] Philpott maintains that "the preferences, not just the power, of negotiators, matter."[52] Religious actors that are independent from the state and espouse a theology of reconciliation will in most cases recommend restorative instruments like truth commissions over trials, argues Philpott.

The TRC's aim was "to work to help restore the human dignity of victims and promote reconciliation by providing an opportunity for victims to give an account of the violations . . . suffered and for perpetrators to relate their experiences, and by creating a climate which fosters constructive interchange between victims and perpetrators."[53] Public hearings were held under banners, exhorting, "Truth hurts but War hurts more" and "Truth today, peaceful Sierra Leone tomorrow." Witnesses were encouraged to tell the truth as the first step on the road to recovery. On the issues of apology and forgiveness, TRC chair Humper stated, "We will not expect you [victims] to forget, but we will expect you to forgive. And the message to the perpetrator will be that by our own cultural standard [there is] a duty to express remorse, to confess, and to accept forgiveness because forgiveness cannot come on a silver platter."[54]

Yet Humper also made clear at the hearings that there was no legal mandate to apologize or to forgive. Victims were never asked directly to forgive perpetrators by commissioners,[55] who perhaps had learned a lesson from criticisms lodged against the SATRC that Bishop Tutu, by his forceful personality, had put undue pressure on victims to forgive.[56] Rather than asking victims if they wanted to *forgive* perpetrators, commissioners in Sierra Leone asked them if they wanted to *reconcile*—a less coercive question implying that forgiveness was not a one-sided but a two-sided process that required something from the offender. The final report explains, "Accountability requires that the perpetrator acknowledge the harm done to the victims and takes [*sic*] action to repair that harm. Acknowledging harm may lead to an apology offered by the perpetrator. . . . While the victim may voluntarily choose to forgive, the Commission is of the opinion that forgiveness by a victim is not a necessary element in this process and cannot be forced. The Commission also notes that an admission of remorse by the perpetrator cannot be forced. Remorse, while desirable, is not necessary for reconciliation to obtain."[57] At the early hearings, seemingly to prove the point that an apology would not be coerced, RUF rebels were cautiously questioned and they expressed no remorse. Three weeks into the hearings, according to Stovel, Humper implored them to confess and apologize, usually unsuccessfully.[58]

The value of including the voices of both perpetrators and victims is the assumption that doing so may create mutual understanding as conflicting parties hear each other's grievances and experiences of suffering. Building empathy may deter acts of vengeance and stop the cycles of violence and counterviolence that could arise from the past.[59] Then attorney general Solomon Berewa explained, "Far from being fault-finding and punitive, it is to serve as the most legitimate and credible forum for victims to reclaim their human worth, and a channel for the perpetrators of atrocities to expiate their guilt, and chasten their consciences. The process has been likened to a national catharsis, involving truth-telling, respectful listening and above all, compensation for victims in deserving cases."[60]

One supposed benefit of truth commissions is that they put victims center stage, giving them a safe space to be heard as they relate their stories unhampered by hostile cross examination. Two important categories of victims were amputees and women. When the commissioners visited the Aberdeen Amputee Camp in August 2002 to garner this important constituency's support for the TRC, the amputees threatened to boycott the hearings unless their demands were first met. They presented a seven-point document addressing their needs, which included shelter, 200,000 leones per month for life, free education for their children, provision of medical facilities, and a reintegration allowance. The commissioners accepted the document without making promises, but they urged the amputees to come forward with their stories so that the record of the conflict would be complete.[61] According to Jusu Jaka, a leading spokesman for the amputees, former SATRC co-chairman Alex Boraine ultimately convinced them to testify in order to preserve their rights to reparation.[62] Likewise, President Kabbah assured the amputees that their needs would be a high priority with his government. The amputees dropped their boycott, and the first person to testify at the hearings was amputee Tamba Finnoh.[63]

Women, too, were encouraged to testify before the Commission. While they had the option of testifying in closed hearings about sexual abuse, many women insisted on telling their stories publicly as part of the regular hearings[64] despite the cultural taboo against speaking about rape and the fact that the TRC encouraged them to testify privately. In nearly all districts, 35% to 45% of those testifying were women.[65]

But Shaw notes that, in most of the public hearings, audiences were smaller than expected.[66] How can empathy and acceptance of victims flourish without the community there to hear? She claims that the numbers only rose dramatically when former combatants rather than victims spoke.[67] Kelsall confirms that at the hearings he attended, the crowds seemed almost indifferent to the horrifying but unemotionally recounted testimonies of the victims.[68] The public's indifference to the victims—if this indeed is the correct interpretation of its reaction—could lead one to question the healing efficacy of sharing one's story. Acknowledgment of one's suffering by the community may be essential, but Beth Dougherty disagrees that the public was indifferent to victims' suffering. She says the public hearings were well attended except in Freetown, and since media coverage in the capital was widespread, this was not seen as a sign of disinterest.[69]

In addition to victims, perpetrators were expected to share their perspectives on the war. Perpetrator participation was considered important in terms of accountability because even with the Special Court, the numbers prosecuted were very few. Many perpetrators had been wary about returning to their communities out of fear of rejection and retribution for their prior deeds, the knowledge of which may have preceded their homecoming. For them, the TRC would provide a way to confess what they had done in order to ease their eventual acceptance back home. Their numbers, some 72,500,[70] make their reintegration vital if reconciliation is to take place.

An important subcategory of perpetrators is perpetrator-victims. Of the former combatants, 70%, including many children, claimed they were conscripted, making them both victims and perpetrators. Especially in the case of women combatants, many of whom were forcibly conscripted and sexually abused, the line between perpetrator and victim is blurred.

Using a UNICEF-developed format, the TRC held special hearings for juvenile offenders, borrowing from the South African example.[71] Half of all RUF combatants were between eight and fourteen years old, and a significant number of youths also fought in the CDF, in a war that has aptly been described as a "case of organized mass delinquency."[72] In fact, more children testified as perpetrators in these closed hearings than adults. The assumption was that acknowledging their crimes before the TRC, which was the only forum available to them, since there were no prosecutions of children in the Special Court, would help facilitate their own healing and acceptance back into their communities.[73] In addition, the thematic hearing on children drew a packed house, which may have been an indication that people were able to empathize with children who committed atrocities under duress.[74]

Since the Special Court was mandated to prosecute "those who bear the greatest responsibility," and because funding shortages limited the number of indicted to just thirteen individuals,[75] the vast majority of perpetrators were exempted from prosecution and instead were invited to share their stories before the TRC. With no mechanism to compel testimony, and no incentive in the form of amnesty to testify (once the Accord reached in Lome had been breached and considered null and void),[76] people wondered whether perpetrators would come forward to confess. Although *some* perpetrators did come forward to testify, the suspicion among the population that the Special Court would use perpetrator testimony to make indictments was never fully allayed, despite Special Court prosecutor David Crane's numerous announcements that the two bodies were separate and independent and despite his many pledges not to use perpetrator testimony to build a criminal case.[77] Confusion about the mandates of two institutions working at the same time no doubt contributed to the fact that only 1% of narratives collected by the TRC were from perpetrators.[78] Contrary to the expectations of the commissioners, even fewer numbers of perpetrators actually apologized or asked for forgiveness from their victims.[79]

Shaw observes, "No commander in . . . any of the hearings I attended acknowledged any personal responsibility for child abductions, rape, amputations, and other violations, leading to considerable probing and heated exchanges when the Commissioners questioned them."[80] She also notes that rank and file former combatants, who felt it was not their place to speak, left that role to their commanders. In particular, few soldiers from the progovernment CDF testified, believing they were blameless because they were defending the country against the RUF/AFRC forces. Those who did testify denied committing any crimes. It is unfortunate that the Special Court would not allow CDF leader Samuel Hinga Norman to testify before the TRC as he had requested (discussed below). His testimony would have added to the historical record about the war, and he might have apologized for the human rights violations committed by his forces, thereby setting an example for his followers to confess as well.[81] While the TRC's final report found that the majority of abuses (60.5%) were committed by the RUF/AFRC, the CDF was also guilty of violations, especially late in the war.[82]

Perpetrator testimony is vital, not only because of the combatants' unique knowledge of the conflict, including who fought and why (necessary data to contribute to the historical record), but also because of their need to expiate their guilt. The latter reason may be the more important since, unlike in countries where the state supported hidden violence (the "disappeareds" for instance in Argentina), violence in Sierra Leone was very public. Cutting off a hand was meant to be visible, a reminder from the rebels that the government was unable to protect them; the hand symbolically represented the hand that had voted for the government that could not protect them.[83]

Apart from the public hearings, the TRC was able to facilitate victim-offender mediation in some cases in which the victims welcomed it. Since a majority of the victims and perpetrators who submitted statements said they wanted to meet the person who had harmed them, or whom they had harmed, this was especially important.[84] Each week, assisted by religious and traditional leaders, a reconciliation ceremony was held where perpetrators and victims could come together. According to Moses Khanu, one of the IRC's original founders, those witnesses who wanted to participate in the reconciliation ceremony would receive counseling from religious leaders in advance, and often these sessions resulted in a perpetrator's willingness to confess. On other occasions, a perpetrator would ask to be forgiven by the community, even if he had not committed crimes in that district.[85] According to Tim Kelsall, these events, which included a special cleansing ceremony for those who acknowledged their crimes, represented the perpetrators' symbolic reintegration back into the community, and seemed to resonate profoundly with the crowds, much more so than the hearings.[86]

At the close of the TRC, a final reconciliation service was held in Freetown. A procession marched to the National Stadium, which became the setting for speeches and apologies. From there, the people crossed over Congo Cross Bridge, appropriately renamed the Peace Bridge. However, unlike the APC leader of the opposition, Ernest Bai Koroma, the president did not apologize to the nation, either at the National Stadium or on the final day of hearings, where he was encouraged to make a public apology. Instead, President Kabbah offered only this: "Now, I think what you are asking me to do is this: to apologise to people for wrongdoing. Of what use is that?"[87] The president was faulted by the commissioners in their final report for missing an opportunity to set a positive example. This was all the more regrettable since prior to the start of the TRC, on the occasion of the thirty-ninth anniversary of Sierra Leone's independence, the president, like President Mandela in South Africa, had urged the people to forgive their enemies to bring about reconciliation and peace.[88]

TENSIONS WITH THE SPECIAL COURT

In addition to inadequate funding, one of the main impediments to the TRC's success was the existence of the Special Court operating at the same time. Although William Schabas, one of the three international commissioners, had termed the relationship between the TRC and Special Court "synergistic,"[89] the TRC report was not as positive in its characterization. No less than sixty-eight pages are devoted to the uneasy relationship between the two transitional bodies.

There can be no doubt that Sierra Leoneans were confused about the different mandates of the two institutions. Schabas minimizes the importance of this misunderstanding when he writes, "But is this really a problem? Most law students would be challenged to explain the difference between the European Court of Justice and the European Court of Human Rights, so is it reasonable to expect a sophisticated grasp of the distinctions between post-conflict transitional justice institutions from ordinary people in a country with a high illiteracy rate? The fact is, if average Sierra Leoneans now understand that there are two institutions working towards accountability for the atrocities and victimization that they suffered, this is mission accomplished."[90]

Schabas also discounts the significance of the lack of amnesty and the possibility of the sharing of information with the Special Court as impediments to perpetrator testimony before the TRC: "Willingness or unwillingness to testify seems to have more to do with the mysteries of the human soul than it does with issues of amnesty, use immunity and compulsion to testify."[91] He cites as an example the tendency of some defendants in the United States to blurt out confessions despite having been read their Miranda rights warning them that what they say can be used against them in court. He also points out that most perpetrators in South Africa, despite their receiving guarantees of immunity from prosecution within the Promotion of National Unity and Reconciliation Act, still refused to confess before the SATRC.[92]

In contrast to this view are the comments of PRIDE, a local NGO that worked closely with former combatants, on the importance of a credible assurance that the TRC would not share information with the Special Court: "From our daily interactions, we know that many are willing to participate with the TRC so long as they can be guaranteed that this will not send them to the Special Court as a defendant or a witness against their commanders."[93] There were in fact real fears from perpetrators that if they testified before the TRC, they would risk indictment before the Special Court, or at the very least would receive subpoenas to testify against former commanders, an equally unwelcome prospect. Despite announcements from the Special Court and TRC that they would not share information, this was not a foregone conclusion in people's minds.

The relationship between the TRC and the Special Court may have begun with "respect and deference," according to the TRC Report,[94] but it faltered over the right of detainees at the Special Court to testify before the TRC. Because the names of the indicted had arisen in many witnesses' testimonies before the TRC, the TRC sought to engage the defendants in information gathering and public testimony, but it was informed by Special Court registrar Robin Vincent that the defendants did not wish to speak with the Commission while their trials were pending.[95] A few months later, however, CDF leader Samuel Hinga Norman wrote the TRC indicating a change of heart: "I was arrested, charged and detained on the 10th March 2003, thinking that by now, 25 August 2003, my trial would have started long ago; but I thought wrongly. Since there is no news about the start of my trial and there are signs that the TRC may soon close its sittings, I would prefer to be heard by the people of Sierra Leone and also be recorded for posterity."[96] The two RUF defendants, Augustine Bao and Issa Sessay, decided they too would like to testify in the TRC public hearings.

In October the TRC applied for permission to grant Norman a public hearing. The case went before the presiding judge of the trial chamber, who rejected the TRC's request. His decision was made in part on the basis of a narrow interpretation of "perpetrator" in the TRC Act, which for the judge was limited to those offenders who were "willing to confess their guilt." This did not apply to the indictees who had pled "not guilty." The TRC was dumbfounded by this reading of the act; most perpetrators who had testified before the TRC had in fact *not* admitted to any wrongdoing! Nevertheless, the TRC felt it was valuable to hear their stories to gain a better understanding about the causes of the war. According to the TRC report, Judge Thompson's decision "heralded a significant turning point in the public appraisal of the relationship between the two institutions."[97]

The TRC appealed the decision to Geoffrey Robertson, president of the Special Court. He denied permission for Norman to testify in public, but he did allow for Norman to send a statement to the TRC in writing or for the TRC to apply for a confidential meeting with Norman. The TRC found this unpalatable for two reasons: First, there was no longer time to submit questions before the conclusion of its term in December 2003, and second, any interaction between the TRC and Special Court indictees had to come under the procedures of the Practice Direction, which had been hastily established in September with no input whatsoever from the TRC staff or commissioners. This required that the TRC apply for permission to interview detainees. In considering the request, the Court would insist on seeing the questions to be asked, which had to be approved by a Special Court judge; that the interview be supervised by a Court officer, who could intervene and stop the interview; that the interview be recorded; and that the transcript be handed over to the prosecutor for use at trial. The Revised Practice Direction was later amended, so that the record of the interview would not automatically be sent to the prosecutor but would instead be sent to the registrar, who would make it available to any party in the proceedings by order of the presiding judge. Even "confidential" information could not be guaranteed use immunity; the prosecutor could apply to the Court for an order that the confidential information be disclosed in the interest of justice. The TRC Act directed that all testimony given to the TRC could be given confidentially, and the TRC believed that should include testimony from detainees as well. Because the TRC did not want to jeopardize the rights of the accused to a fair trial, it decided not to interview Norman without the assurance of confidentiality.

In a press release in December, the TRC stated, "Hinga Norman has been denied his freedom of expression and his statutory right to appear before the TRC to tell his story. The people of Sierra Leone have been denied the opportunity of hearing from Hinga Norman in an open and transparent manner."[98] Even worse than the legal argument, with which the TRC vehemently disagreed, was Robertson's choice of words when he said that a public hearing of an indictee "paraded" before a bishop would be a "spectacle."[99] To the commissioners, this connoted a lack of respect for the significance of the TRC as an equal transitional justice partner. TRC executive secretary Jusu-Sheriff later confided that while she had been initially supportive of the work of the Special Court and the notion of not allowing "impunity to reign," she "will never forgive it for spoiling the TRC!"[100]

THE SPECIAL COURT: ALIEN AND ALIENATING

The Court appeared indifferent to the views of the TRC staff, although on the surface the relationship was "superficially good"—at least until the dispute over Norman's testifying before the TRC.[101]

The Court also seemed oblivious to public opinion. While a great deal of time and money was spent on community outreach—the Special Court took particular pride in its efforts at training lay magistrates, setting up Accountability Now clubs in schools, holding over seven thousand outreach sessions, and providing video summaries of case highlights—communication was all one way. That is, the Court was concerned with explaining its functions and human rights/international law, rather than getting input from the population. When Crane was asked, for instance, whether the Court had done any polling on popular perceptions of the Court's work, he responded dismissively, "We're not in the popularity business."[102] This lack of solicitation of feedback was to be expected perhaps, since from the beginning there was "no broad based consultation to set it up."[103]

In the early days, the Court brought most of its staff, including even gardeners, cooks, and guards, from outside the country, according to Alfred Carew, the executive secretary of the National Forum for Human Rights.[104] This did not sit well in a country with staggering unemployment, and it smacked of a sense of superiority. The impression was that no Sierra Leonean was qualified to work at the Special Court. It was perceived as an *international* court, with top positions going to expatriates, and only a handful of professional Sierra Leoneans were in major posts. In time, 60% of the staff were eventually hired from within the country,[105] but these were usually in the lowest level positions. In addition, the salaries paid to judges and other court officials were "exorbitant compared to salaries outside," according to Peter Penfold, who notes that a security guard was paid more than the Sierra Leone chief of police![106] When the Court appointed a twenty-six-year-old American, newly minted attorney as a "domestic advisor," rather than choosing from seasoned attorneys in Sierra Leone, this was viewed as a lack of respect to the local bar.[107] Only after the conclusion of the major trials of the RUF, AFRC, and CDF, and the resignation of the third chief prosecutor—an American— was a Sierra Leonean jurist selected. Joseph Fitzgerald Kamara was chosen as the acting chief prosecutor pending the choice of a permanent prosecutor.[108] But Kamara was demoted to deputy prosecutor in February 2010, when Brenda Hollis (another American) was selected by the UN secretary general as the chief prosecutor.[109] At the Hague, moreover, the Special Court employed just one Sierra Leonean lawyer, Mohamed Bangura, on the prosecution team that tried Charles Taylor, leading Courtenay Griffiths, Taylor's defense attorney, to lament, "I think that's a crying shame. I think that's an absolute disgrace."[110]

Whatever local criticisms were waged against the TRC, they paled in comparison to those against the Special Court. For one thing, the number of Sierra Leoneans hired by the TRC was far higher than those hired for the Special Court,[111] even if most of the top positions were also held by foreigners. (This may have had as much to do with the TRC's having a smaller budget to hire expensive expatriate labor than with its having more respect for local talent.) Mohamed Suma, director of the Sierra Leone Court Monitoring Project,[112] and the Court's first outreach director, admitted that the Special Court was more difficult "to sell" among the people than the TRC. It became even more difficult, he says, with the indictment in March 2003 of Norman, who was viewed by most people as a hero and certainly not as one of those who bore "the most responsibility" for wartime atrocities.[113]

Penfold agreed that the indictment of Norman was a terrible mistake. The TRC found the CDF had committed just 6% of the wartime atrocities—far fewer than the RUF, which was responsible for more than 60%.[114] In Penfold's view, once the major combatants—Foday Sankoh, Johnny Paul Koroma, and Sam Bockerie—had died, leaving only Norman, who of the major players clearly did not bear "the most responsibility," the Court ought to have disbanded. He wrote, "I see no further purpose for this expensive and divisive piece of judicial machinery"; rather, the other defendants should have been turned over to the local courts, "which are perfectly capable of trying them."[115] Gberie agreed: "My idea of the Special Court is more exalted than trying common criminals, thieves, murderers.... These people are not significant enough to justify a trial of this magnitude."[116]

Tim Kelsall also argued that there was a disconnect between international law and local understandings, especially in the case against Norman. He contended that, because of the nature of neopatrimonial rule in Africa, the notion of a bureaucratic formal chain of command, by which Norman should be held responsible for the actions of his subordinates, made little sense to Sierra Leoneans. The Court likewise seemed incapable of dealing with the defense's arguments based on magic. The defense argument was that CDF leaders were not responsible for wanton acts committed by their followers, since these followers knew if they violated the strict code of conduct (against rape and looting), they would no longer be protected from bullets as their initiation rites had guaranteed. Likewise, indicting Norman for the conscription of child soldiers made little sense to Sierra Leoneans given that the army had previously enlisted boys as young as sixteen and this practice wasn't illegal (or more importantly against local understandings of right and wrong) at the time of the war. And, finally, abducting women as bush wives, which was portrayed by the Court as a violation of the individual woman's right, was more likely to be seen by traditionalists as an affront mainly to the woman's family, which according to cultural norms had the right to make the decisions about their daughter's marriage.[117]

Another practice that hurt the reputation of the Court was the payment of monies to prosecution witnesses. There was already resentment because defendants were living in relative luxury under international standards of detention—three meals a day, 24-hour electricity, air conditioning, and exercise facilities—in a country that often ranked close to last place in the UN Development Program's Human Development Index, and where 70% of the population lived on less than $2 a day. Suspicions were rampant that the fees paid by the prosecution to witnesses may have encouraged them to "massage the truth" to fit the prosecution's theory.[118] Some witnesses had received 1 million, 1.5 million, and 2 million leones—as much as five times the nation's average annual income per capita.[119] Tim Kelsall wrote, "The result was that a few figureheads were imprisoned for crimes over which they had little control while lower-level commanders, who were often the direct perpetrators of atrocities, walked free, their pockets bulging with payments from the court."[120] Lastly, the price tag of "international justice" was a topic widely debated in opinion pieces in the daily newspapers. Including the prosecution of Charles Taylor, the Court spent $300 million.[121]

After resigning from the Special Court to become the US ambassador at large for war crimes, the chief prosecutor, Stephen Rapp,[122] in a revealing interview in *Time International*, admitted, "The concern all of us had was that we were conducting justice in a comfortable courtroom with long trials and well-paid attorneys. Prisoners had single cells, and they had committed the worst crimes. A mile away in the local prison there were simply no resources. Cases can't go forward, witnesses are lost, and people stay in detention for many years at a stretch. [If I were] to do it over, I would try to develop a court within the national system. That would be my preference. Maybe not a court that costs $30 million a year like the Special Court, but an appropriate court."[123]

CHAPTER 3

WOMEN AND TRANSITIONAL JUSTICE

How were women's expectations for justice and reconciliation met through the two transitional justice mechanisms: the Special Court for Sierra Leone and the TRC? While both institutions made notable attempts to include gender-specific crimes as an important component of their work, the all-important third ingredient in the "toolkit" of transitional justice—reparations and reforms—remained underutilized, and would have had a more positive impact on women's lives than the two institutions. This chapter highlights some of the achievements of the Special Court and the TRC that were arguably superior to earlier transitional justice institutions such as the International Criminal Tribunal for Rwanda (ICTR) and the SATRC in addressing women's needs. But it concludes that unless social, political, and economic improvements that empower women are made, women will remain vulnerable to sexual and other human rights abuses, not only in times of war, but in peace time as well.

WOMEN DURING THE CIVIL WAR

The civil war in Sierra Leone was marked by barbarous attacks, including killings, amputations, and sexual violence, on civilians. Human Rights Watch estimates that between 215,000 and 257,000 women were victims of sexual assault during the conflict,[1] while Physicians for Human Rights concludes that in one out of eight households, someone had been subjected to sexual violence.[2]

Women of all ages, from young girls to grandmothers, were raped, both individually and by gangs, often in front of their families. Some women were forced not only to have sex in front of family members but also with family members. Many pregnant women had their wombs ripped open and their fetuses speared by assailants, who took bets on the sex of the unborn child.[3] Rebels took women as "wives" and branded the name of their group on the women's breasts. Perhaps 60% of girls involved with fighting forces were taken as spouses.[4] If progovernment forces found these marked women, they killed them, accusing them of aiding the enemy. Virgins, or those perceived to be virgins, were preferred,[5] which explains the young ages of many of the victims. The TRC's final report indicates 25% of rape victims (when age was documented) were thirteen years of age or younger and 50% of sex slaves were fifteen or younger when they were abducted.[6] Because of the high value placed on virginity in Sierra Leone culture, these women were undesirable as marriage partners, which meant the postconflict impact on women, families, and communities was enormous.[7] Every side of the conflict perpetrated human rights violations against women—not just the RUF, AFRC, Sierra Leone Army, and CDF, but also peacekeeping forces with UNAMSIL and ECOMOG.[8]

PROSECUTING GENDER CRIMES AT THE SPECIAL COURT

Unlike its predecessor, the ICTR,[9] which had to be persuaded by international women's groups to include rape in its indictments,[10] the Special Court for Sierra Leone indicted suspects for gender crimes not as an afterthought or an add-on but as a central part of its work.[11] In the statute, the crimes that could be prosecuted included "rape, sexual slavery, enforced prostitution, forced pregnancy and any other form of sexual violence," when conducted as part of a widespread attack against civilians.[12] When the Special Court's first prosecutor, David Crane, handed down his first indictments on March 7, 2003, four of the five specifically included crimes of sexual violence. This marked the first time that an international tribunal had addressed the prosecution of rape as a major war crime in and of itself in a situation not marked by genocide.[13]

The seriousness with which the Court viewed sex crimes was indicated by the number of investigators assigned to sexual assault violations (two women, or 20% of the investigation team, compared to fewer than 2% of the ICTR's investigators who dealt with these crimes).[14] One attorney was specifically dedicated to prosecuting the sexual violence crimes, and four out of eleven judges (two in the trial chambers and two in the appeals chambers) were women. Perhaps learning from the poor record of the ICTR when it began its work,[15] the Statute of the Special Court specified that due consideration be given to the appointment of prosecutors and investigators experienced in gender-related crimes.[16] The Women's Task Force on the Role of Women in the TRC and Special Court, an umbrella group of women's groups, civil society groups, and international and local NGOs, also advocated for gender balance among the staff.[17]

The Special Court indicted leaders on all sides of the conflict. This evenhandedness may be perceived as an advantage over its predecessor the ICTR, which prosecuted Hutu accused of genocidal crimes against Tutsi, but not Tutsi who were involved in revenge killings (and rapes), in the aftermath of the genocide.[18] However, like the ICTR, the Special Court went only after leaders with overall command responsibility and not after the foot soldiers or the actual rapists.

In addition to rape, other forms of gender violence were prosecuted. Crane added the charge "forced marriage" under "other inhumane acts" in the legal category of crimes against humanity, arguing that what happened to the women was more than just rape, since they were held for long periods and forced to clean, cook, and porter for their "husbands." The indictments against the six RUF and AFRC defendants included forced marriage.[19] However, the Court found the AFRC defendants guilty of rape but not sexual slavery or forced marriage.[20] It was only in February 2009, with the rulings against the RUF defendants, that the crime of forced marriage in addition to rape was successfully prosecuted. In a press release heralding the verdict, lead prosecutor Stephen Rapp said, "The Court today for the first time in world history convicted each of these individuals of 'forced marriage' as a separate 'crime against humanity.' In doing so, it recognizes the very deep and long lasting suffering inflicted upon women through conscription as 'bush wives' during the Sierra Leone conflict."[21] He told journalists after the verdict that the decision "will become a precedent for other cases in the International Criminal Court and possibly act as a deterrent in future conflicts."[22]

Unfortunately, the Court would not allow charges of forced marriage, sexual slavery, enforced prostitution, or rape to be lodged against the CDF defendants.[23] It ruled that the prosecutor had waited too long to amend the original indictments of the three CDF defendants to include these acts.[24] Therefore, women who testified against the CDF defendants were not permitted to speak about the "principal manner in which they were victimized during the Sierra Leonean conflict."[25]

The Court's decision to privilege expediency and the rights of the accused over the needs of the female victims in the CDF cases points to the limited ability of jurisprudence to deal adequately with sexual violations.[26] Unfortunately, the CDF's victims interpreted the Court's refusal to hear testimony of a sexual nature to mean that the Court either thought rape was unimportant or thought they were lying.[27]

This missed opportunity to allow victims of sex crimes committed by the CDF to testify is especially regrettable in that one of the alleged advantages of this hybrid court over the ad-hoc tribunal for Rwanda was that, by including both foreign and domestic jurists within the country where the violations took place and prosecuting both domestic[28] and international crimes, the Special Court would make international law locally relevant and, in particular, could raise awareness about the seriousness of gender crimes within Sierra Leone.

The raising of awareness was considered a potentially important contribution since Sierra Leone was not advanced in terms of legal protections for women against sexual violence. At the time, for instance, rape, unlike most serious crimes, was usually prosecuted under customary law rather than general law. Only the rape of a virgin was considered serious (in Krio "to virginate"),[29] whereas the rape of a married woman or nonvirgin was considered a contradiction in terms, and thus not a crime at all.[30] Furthermore, it was only illegal to have sex with a girl under fourteen if she were not a prostitute or someone of "known immoral character." Thus, the diffusion of legal knowledge, it was believed, could help the country internalize international human rights norms, such as the rights of women not to be sexually violated.[31] Successfully prosecuting the AFRC and RUF for sexual crimes may have had some effect on people's attitudes about rape during peacetime, but the failure to prosecute the CDF for these crimes might lead the population to assume rape is condoned if it's committed by the "good guys" (a popular view of the CDF).

One advantage of having the Court conduct its work in Sierra Leone was doing so made it easier for female witnesses to testify and to see justice being done. "In this respect," writes Eaton, "the impact of the SCSL's rulings may be felt more widely by the victims than has been the case with the [previous] ICTs' [International Criminal Tribunal for the former Yugoslavia and ICTR] decisions."[32] As was the case with the ICTR, the prosecution limited the number of witnesses with the expectation that having just a few strong witnesses would speed up the trial. As in all court cases, witnesses were sometimes subjected to adversarial cross examination and were not allowed free rein to tell their stories in their own ways. On the way that courts curtail women's testimony, Mertus writes, "Law does not permit a single witness to tell . . . her own coherent narrative, it chops the stories into digestible parts, selects a handful of these parts, and sorts and refines them to create a new narrative—the legal anti-narrative."[33]

But despite the adversarial setting, witnesses were generally treated with respect and dignity, and psychological counselors were provided for witnesses to help them get through difficult testimony.[34] Witnesses often felt a sense of release and closure by providing testimony—except those who felt angry and hurt because they were denied the chance to testify about sexual violations during the CDF trials[35]—and judges sometimes stopped defense lawyers' hostile questioning of female witnesses. Most witnesses were provided security at a safe house in Freetown once their identities were revealed to the defense, with victims of gender-based crimes having their own safe houses away from other witnesses. Human Rights Watch reported that the female witnesses they spoke with applauded the work of the Special Court, saying "They stand up for women there."[36]

ACKNOWLEDGING VIOLATIONS AGAINST WOMEN AT THE TRC

While very few women actually testified before the Special Court about sexual abuses, many more were able to speak in front of the TRC. Of the 7,706 statements submitted to the TRC, 2,728 came from women. In nearly all districts, 35–45% of those testifying in the hearings were women, many of whom included stories of sexual violations.[37] A study conducted in 2002 on war-related sexual violence found that the majority of women surveyed who had suffered from sexual violence did not believe their perpetrators should be punished. The most common reason given was "in the spirit of reconciliation" (68%), which suggests that the TRC may have been the better forum for women to voice how they had suffered.[38]

Like the Special Court, the TRC also focused on sexual abuses committed against women during the war. The Lome Accord had directed that, since "women have been particularly victimized during the war, special attention shall be accorded to their needs and potentials in formulating and implementing national rehabilitation, reconstruction and development programmes, to enable them to play a central role in the moral, social and physical reconstruction of Sierra Leone."[39] The Sierra Leone TRC Act followed up on the notion of targeting women by ordering that the Commission "take into account the interests of victims and witnesses when inviting them to give statements . . . and to also implement special procedures to address the needs of such particular victims as . . . those who have suffered sexual abuses."[40]

Duggan and Abusharaf attribute attention to women's needs to pressure from national and international women's groups.[41] Whereas earlier transitional justice institutions, such as the ICTR and the SATRC, included gender concerns only after they had begun their work, and in response to pressure from women's organizations,[42] consideration of women's needs and women's particular types of violations was no mere afterthought but was central to the workings of the TRC from the outset. Even before the TRC was established, the Women's Task Force had lobbied the government demanding gender balance among the staff of the TRC. Three out of the seven commissioners selected were women, no doubt in deference to the task force's recommendations. Two of them—Commissioner Ajaaratou Jow of Gambia and Commissioner Yasmin Sooka from South Africa—had extensive experience dealing with gender crimes.[43] And there were two female statement-takers in all the districts, so that women could tell intimate details to another woman.[44]

Taking a page from the South African playbook,[45] women were encouraged to testify at special women's hearings held over three days in May 2003. These hearings were dedicated to looking at the specific ways in which women were targeted. Women walked to the YMCA building where the hearings were held, carrying signs that read "Justice for Women" and "No Violence against Women."[46] They were permitted to testify behind a screen with their identities hidden, in camera, or publicly if they so chose. The sessions were opened by the Ministry of Social Welfare, Gender, and Children's Affairs, and women from the Family Support Units were sent by the national police to observe. Although male commissioners attended, only female commissioners questioned these witnesses.[47] In addition to the testimony from individuals, a number of women's groups provided submissions and oral testimony.

Nowrojee reports that women's groups spoke positively about the special hearings, and rape victims "appeared to have few complaints about their experience testifying."[48] Indicative of women's voices being heard and of the crime of sexual violence being taken seriously is the fact that the hearings on gender had the largest attendance of any of the hearings.[49] Audiences heard vivid testimony about torture, rape, sexual abuse, sexual slavery, trafficking, enslavement, abductions, amputations, forced pregnancies, forced labor, and detention, which were later highlighted in the final report.

In each district as well, one day was set apart for closed hearings, not only for children (who were not permitted to testify in public hearings), but also for women who had been sexually abused, to testify before only female commissioners and staff. However, many women chose to tell their stories publicly as part of the regular hearings, and not in the closed hearings, despite the cultural stigma about rape.[50] In fact, rape victims were among the very first to come forward to testify in the open hearings, which counters the view that people don't want to speak about gender crimes.[51]

However, victims of sexual violence at the hands of the CDF were not acknowledged by the perpetrators. Although the CDF committed fewer offenses than the other armed groups, they too were involved in gross human rights abuses, including rape, especially late in the war.[52] And while the overall percentage of human rights abuses committed by the CDF was just 6% of the total, the percentage of all sexual violations by the CDF was twice as high (12%).[53]

The Special Court refused to let Norman testify publicly before the TRC, arguing that he had a right not to incriminate himself. This was especially unfortunate since the Court would not allow the prosecutor to add rape (and other acts of sexual violence) to the CDF defendants' indictments, saying that their due process rights would be harmed, since the original indictments did not include sexual abuses. Thus, for victims of sexual violence at the hands of the CDF, there was no acknowledgment—either through the Special Court or the TRC. There was also no acknowledgment from UNAMSIL or ECO-MOG forces, who raped women but neither participated in the TRC hearings nor were indicted by the Special Court.[54]

The TRC's final report established that 36% of all victims who gave statements were women, and it identified war widows, aged women, girl mothers, victims of displacement, and female ex-combatants as particularly vulnerable groups.[55] Many "war brides" stayed with their "husbands" because of intimidation, lack of viable options, and fear of rejection from their communities.[56] Others were abandoned by their husbands, and the children from those unions, "bush children," or *rebel pikin dem*, were not likely to be welcomed back to the mother's community, not only because family lines are patrilineal, but also because women who were with the rebels for a long time were blamed for not escaping. It was hoped that the attention paid to these crimes by the TRC would provide their communities with the understanding and compassion to accept these women and their progeny.

Not all women's voices were heard. Women who had fought for the rebel RUF, even if they had been abducted and had fought under duress, did not testify, either before the TRC or before the Special Court, out of fear they might be prosecuted.[57] Although women made up 10–40% of the fighting forces on all sides (with the highest proportion among the rebels), women fighters have experienced more stigmatization and difficulty in returning home than their male counterparts.[58] They have also tried to keep their combatant status hidden.[59] For instance, Carlson and Mazurana discovered that one-third of the 48,000 child soldiers were girls, but most girls pretended to be "refugees" rather than ex-combatants, because of social taboos, and therefore did not testify about their actual experiences. Likewise, the shame associated with being a "wife" of a rebel soldier, and the stigma associated with rape, kept some women from testifying.[60]

Still other women and girls, according to Rosalind Shaw, decided either not to give public statements or gave statements that withheld information they thought would be damaging to families of ex-combatants in order to protect them.[61] This probably had more to do with their uncertainty as to whether their testimony would be turned over to the Special Court, their fear of retaliation from former combatants, and their shame over being defiled than with any cultural aversion to verbal discourse of memories in favor of social forgetting, as Shaw maintains.[62]

Jamesina King, of the Human Rights Commission, believes that female victims hesitated to testify because they "did not fully understand the TRC's objectives, and, second, they did not think the commission would meet their immediate needs of medical assistance, microcredit schemes, and shelter programs." Once the commissioners explained the TRC's objectives and the possibility of reparations, "women were more willing to talk about the violations perpetrated against them and their families."[63]

THE LEGACIES OF THE TRC AND SPECIAL COURT

The two institutions' focus on gender-based violence may have helped to raise consciousness about gender violence as a human rights issue, but the impact of the Special Court will be limited. The force of law alone will not end violence against women; at most, it may provide "symbolic value in condemning the acts, demonstrating intolerance or moral repugnance for acts committed."[64] That a handful of wartime leaders were charged and convicted of rape for the acts of their followers will not resonate among those followers unless steps are taken to make rape a serious crime domestically.[65]

While some might see the passage of the 2007 gender bills (discussed below) as evidence of the impact of the Court's work on gender-based crimes, Lotta Teale disagrees, arguing that the Domestic Violence Act, which made marital rape a crime, and the Child Rights Act, which criminalized forced marriage, were passed *before* the Court's rulings on these issues.[66] She claims the Court's impact on this legislation was nil, although speeches given by Special Court judge Renate Winter at the time the legislation was passed may have given the impression that the Court had been involved in the passage of the acts.[67] Likewise, Jamesina King believes the passage of the gender bills is not a legacy of the Court but rather shows "the importance of strong women leaders."[68]

While the TRC's offering a forum for women to tell their stories of sexual violations may have begun the psychological healing process that reconciled them with their memories, and engendered sympathy in their communities, this process had its limitations. While women who testified may have been "reconciled" with their memories, it is hard to believe they were reconciled with their assailants, as few perpetrators acknowledged responsibility for gender-based violence against women. If contrition is necessary for reconciliation, little was forthcoming. However, the process is ongoing; Fambul Tok (see chapter 6) is eliciting heartfelt admissions and apologies at the village level that include in some cases acts of rape.

Whatever compassion was engendered for victims must be translated into concrete programs that empower women socially, economically, and politically. This is exactly what the TRC recommended in its final report, *Witness to Truth: Report of the Sierra Leone Truth & Reconciliation Commission.*[69]

The report called on communities to accept survivors of sexual violence.[70] It advised the Ministry of Social Welfare, Gender, and Children's Affairs to establish a directory of donors and service providers for women.[71] It recommended that the government provide free physical and mental health care for life to certain categories of victims, including victims of sexual violence.[72] It also urged the government to provide monthly pensions not only to amputees and other war wounded but to victims of sexual abuse as well.[73] By categorizing victims of sexual violence as a prioritized category eligible for reparations, the TRC's report elevated rape as a serious human rights violation.

The TRC also advocated for reforms in the legal, judicial, and police systems to make it easier for women to report cases of sexual and domestic violence. In particular, it mandated that laws linking the prosecution of sexual offenses to the moral character of the complainant be repealed—an imperative recommendation.[74] It advised the government to campaign against the customary practice, whereby a victim of rape is obliged to marry the rapist.[75] It urged the government to enact specific legislation to address domestic violence, help facilitate the prosecution of offenders, and empower women to access protective orders.[76]

Pointing to the structural inequality of women, the TRC report called for the repeal of all statutory and customary laws, including marriage, inheritance, divorce, and property ownership laws, that discriminate against women. This would require the repeal of certain sections of the Constitution that exempt areas of family life from protection against discrimination. The TRC also called for the codification of customary law, with special emphasis on the rights of women, and harmonization of customary law and common law to comply with international standards.[77] Furthermore, it called on the government to ensure women's and girls' access to education and skills training. It recommended that the government work toward providing free and compulsory education to girls up to senior secondary school. An imperative recommendation was to stop expelling girls who become pregnant.[78]

To end the marginalization of women in political and social life, the TRC suggested that legislation be passed requiring that 30% of all candidates be women and that the government aim for 50/50 gender parity within ten years. It urged the government to work toward having women hold at least 30% of cabinet posts.[79]

Since the TRC's enabling legislation mandated that the government (albeit "within its means"[80]) enact the TRC's recommendations, there was initial optimism that the government would begin implementing the much-needed reforms.[81] The government responded in a White Paper (discussed in chapter 7) eight months after the TRC submitted its report by acknowledging the enormity of women's suffering during the war and expressing its sympathy to female victims "who have in one way or the other been subjected to these indignities [torture, rape, sexual abuse, sexual slavery, trafficking, enslavement, abduction, amputation, forced pregnancy, forced labor and detentions]."[82] However, the White Paper made no commitment to improve women's status, and very little progress has actually been made since the war ended in 2002. According to King, "In the post-conflict period, the Government of Sierra Leone . . . [has] yet to convince the public that they are willing to effectively address the issues affecting women and seriously take into account the abuses women suffered and continue to experience."[83]

Even a reform as simple (and costless) as gender parity in politics has proved to be problematic. The government said it would "continue to encourage greater participation of women in politics and public affairs" but made no explicit commitment to the 30% quota for female candidates or eventual 50/50 parity goals.[84] The SLPP government gave no details about what specifically it was doing to encourage greater political participation of women, except to mention that it had appointed some female judges and some women to head government offices.[85] In fielding candidates for the first post-TRC elections in 2007, none of the three major parties came close to meeting the TRC-mandated gender benchmarks: 15.2% for SLPP, 9.8% for APC, and 8.9% for PMDC.[86] Of 121 parliamentarians, only 16 (13.2%) in the 2007 election were female.[87] Additionally, according to the Human Rights Commission of Sierra Leone, women's representation in government at all levels stood at just 13%; in the following year, just 7% of senior civil servants were women.[88] In parliamentary elections in 2012, just 11% of the candidates were women, and only 16 won their races, making the percentage of women in Parliament slightly less than 13%.[89] In total disregard of the TRC's recommendation, the Constitutional Review Committee tasked with reviewing the 1991 Constitution for revision had not included in its 2009 Constitutional Review Draft Report the 30% quota for women.[90]

In the area of education reconstruction, which the World Bank heralded as a "remarkable recovery,"[91] there are still gender imbalances. While there is parity between boys and girls at the primary level, 48% of boys attend secondary school, compared with 42% of girls.[92] (Girls who are pregnant are still expelled from school despite the TRC's recommendations.) According to local NGO 50/50 founder, Nematta Eshun-Baiden, most families do not send their girls to school: "Our people believe that a woman cannot be educated more than the men . . . this is serious barrier we are facing in our struggle for empowerment," she said.[93] UNICEF statistics for 2013 confirm her observation; the male literacy rate stands at 57% compared with 35% for women.[94]

Rallying behind the TRC's gender recommendations, on International Women's Day on March 8, 2007, various groups including the Women's Forum marched to the National Stadium with banners demanding that then president Kabbah enact the three gender bills (on domestic violence, intestate succession, and customary marriage and divorce), noting that since independence the "laws remain exactly the same."[95] On June 14, 2007, the three gender bills were passed[96] and widely hailed as positive steps toward gender equality; they banned marriage before the age of eighteen, required that marriage be consensual and registered with the government, allowed women to acquire property in their own names (and not be required to pay back dowries if the marriage ended), provided for inheritances to pass to the wife and children rather than to revert to the parents and brothers (bringing an end to the practice whereby women were forced to marry their husband's brother), and introduced the new offense of domestic violence.[97] The domestic violence bill defined domestic violence to include sexual abuse and provided mechanisms to address punishment of domestic violence through criminal law, and to protect women through civil law.

However, according to one analyst, "Since enactment, little has been done in the process of implementing the key provisions of the Act."[98] High rates of gender-based violence and domestic violence continue to be reported.[99] In the year the gender bills were passed, there was not a single conviction in Freetown courts for sexual violations.[100] Nor were there any convictions arising from the 927 sexual abuse cases reported in 2009.[101]

In 2012, an even tougher law was passed. The Sexual Offenses Act[102] criminalized all nonconsensual sex (including spousal rape) and made eighteen the age of consent for sexual intercourse, mandating steeper sentences (5-to-15 years for rape compared to just 2 years under the Domestic Violence Act of 2007). Despite these changes, in the first eight months of 2013, more than 6,500 instances of gender-based violence were reported, with only 399 convictions.[103] The Ebola crisis of 2014–15 also contributed to soaring numbers of sexual assaults because young girls who were sent out to work when adult breadwinners became sick or died turned to "transactional sex"—selling their bodies for necessities to support their families.[104]

Having the laws on the books is a positive first step and is no doubt attributable in some measure to lobbying by women's groups, who consciously mobilized around the TRC's recommendations.[105] But taking advantage of those laws is another thing. For instance, despite the passage of the Registration of Customary Marriage Act, one of the three gender bills passed in 2007, which requires that all marriages be registered, very few customary marriages have been registered because doing so requires that rural women, those most likely to be in informal marriages, travel great distances to the district capital.[106] Having access to the formal justice system remains a challenge for most women.

DISTRIBUTIVE JUSTICE FOR WOMEN

During the civil war in Sierra Leone, women experienced serious human rights violations that centered on their sexuality. King asks, "Did the fact that women endured such a low status in sociopolitical life in the country even before the conflict make them easy targets?"[107] Women in postconflict Sierra Leone continue to feel the effects of violence as they confront a myriad of problems, including stigmatization, poor health, AIDS infection,[108] and lack of physical security. Incidents of rape and domestic violence often skyrocket in postconflict societies,[109] and Sierra Leone is no exception. Rape has actually "been on the increase since the end of the civil war," according to Amie Tejan-Kellah, program officer for the Rainbow Center.[110] In Sierra Leone, where cultural beliefs in male supremacy and dominance are widespread, women continue to suffer gender-based human rights violations.

In stressing gender violations as an important component of its transitional justice work, Sierra Leone has made an important contribution. The Special Court and the TRC upheld the norms of justice and reconciliation, respectively. But repairing the damage done to victims in an effort to make them whole is crucial. One often thinks of restorative justice as returning the situation to the status quo ante, but in Sierra Leone, where women held such a low status before the war, much more is required. Since the prewar status quo marginalized women severely, a return to those cultural norms is hardly a desirable goal. The Nairobi Declaration on Women's and Girls' Rights to Reparation asserts that reparation entails helping girls and women to rebuild their lives by restoring their dignity and sense of self, not as they were prior to war, but in a way that *transforms* the sociocultural injustice and structural inequalities that predate the conflict.[111]

Implementing the recommendations in the TRC report would go a long way toward transforming gender inequities. In the absence of gender equality, violence against women pervades peacetime and will likely erupt on a massive scale should intrastate conflicts reignite. Nordstrom wisely notes, "What people tolerate in peace shapes what they will tolerate in war."[112] Thus, reparations for past injustices and reform for women's current unequal status are necessary components of the ongoing transitional justice agenda.

Unfortunately, reparations and reforms remain the stepchildren in the transitional justice family, and they are at a disadvantage in the competition for funding for justice and reconciliation instruments.[113] Even where truth commissions have made recommendations for governments to provide reparations and institute reforms, these are often ignored. The failure to compensate victims is regrettable, since compensation can directly alleviate suffering in tangible ways.

A recent study on postwar experiences of women in northern Sierra Leone suggests that women who returned with some financial resource (either through a DDR grant or skills training) were much more likely to be accepted back into their communities—despite the stigmas of having been raped or having fought with the rebels—rather than to be ostracized like the many women who returned with no monies, and who were regarded as financial burdens on their families and communities.[114] The material aspect of transitional justice, what might be called distributive justice, should not be minimized. Given the choice between acknowledgment of human rights violations, whether through prosecution or truth commission, and compensation, Zeigler and Gunderson consider the latter to be the more ethical choice: "Compensating the injured must take precedence over assigning responsibility."[115]

Acknowledging a preference for reparations, one survivor of sexual violence explained, "All things being equal, I don't mind prosecutions, but we have other priorities."[116] Unfortunately, only about three thousand female victims of sexual violence have received any kind of compensation—a payment of 300,000 leones (about $75) in 2009 and another disbursement of 940,125 leones ($225) in 2011, followed by small distributions in both 2012 and 2013. These disbursements fell far short of the recommendations for lifetime monthly pensions.[117] Some of the eleven thousand who registered as "war widows" may have been sexually violated women who wished to avoid the stigma of rape.[118] Mohamed Suma, then director of the Centre for Accountability and the Rule of Law,[119] surmises that the registration process for the War Victims Trust Fund he witnessed in Waterloo, if practiced elsewhere, may have discouraged sexually victimized women from applying. All victims, with the exception of those who had been raped, were registered in the open; those who had been raped were asked to come to a special room in private. While the intention was good, the effect was to signal their status, which was uncomfortable for many women.[120]

Women's groups that had pushed for both a gender-sensitive court and a truth commission will continue to pressure the government of Sierra Leone for economic justice (and the political reforms that would require), to empower women and make them whole.

CHAPTER 4

POPULAR VIEWS OF THE TRC AND THE SPECIAL COURT

Various polls, interviews, and focus groups probing public opinion toward the Special Court and TRC were conducted between 2001 and 2012. Conducting polls in postconflict countries can be hazardous. For instance, respondents may say what they think the interviewer wants to hear and give "correct" answers in the hope of receiving tangible benefits. Making policy recommendations based on a "snapshot" of opinions held on a particular date can also be dangerous. Nevertheless, polls can serve as a general barometer of public sentiment. For my purpose, they are significant in helping us understand whether religious leaders' views were at odds or consistent with those of the population at large.

EX-COMBATANT PERSPECTIVES: MAY 2001

One of the first surveys assessing fighters' opinions about the TRC was included in a report written by local NGO Manifesto 99, which

TABLE 1. Preferred method of reconciliation

	Fighting group				
Method	RUF (%)	CDF (%)	AFRC (%)	SLA (%)	Totals (%)
Nothing	5.5	2.4	16.7	10.9	4.8
Beg for forgiveness	87.6	96.5	75.0	87.0	90.5
Don't know/ not sure	6.8	1.2	8.3	2.1	4.7
Totals	100.0	100.0	100.0	100.0	100

Source: Manifesto 99, "Traditional Methods," 56–57.

was commissioned by the United Nations High Commissioner for Human Rights to investigate the potential of using traditional conflict resolution methods in the upcoming TRC process (an idea that was ultimately rejected).[1] Some 1,500 individuals were interviewed from the Western Area, Port Loko, Kenema, Koinadugu, and Moyamba, which were the districts that were readily accessible to researchers at the time of the polling in May 2001. This survey took place before either the TRC or the Special Court was officially established.[2]

A majority of the fighters (58.6%) were unaware of the amnesty provision in the Lome Accord, but when it was explained to them, a large percentage (63.4%) quite naturally supported it.[3] Only a small percentage (22.2%) of fighters claimed knowledge of the TRC.[4] Once it had been explained to them, however, 71.3% of respondents expressed willingness to face the TRC; the CDF registered the highest percentage at 84.4%, perhaps because the respondents felt no shame for what they had done to defend the nation.[5] On the question of whether fighters were willing to talk about their actions during the war, 72.6% expressed their willingness to do so. When asked to choose between begging for forgiveness or doing nothing, 90.5% chose the former method (see table 1).[6]

Of the respondents, 88.6% expected to be forgiven by the victims. A majority (56.6%) expressed regret for the roles they played, but a sizable minority (40.6%) expressed no regrets. The largest percentages of "no regrets" came from the Sierra Leone Army (88.9%) and the CDF (65.4%), who felt they had fought for a just cause. On the other hand, the overwhelming majority (74.3%) of RUF respondents regretted their wartime actions.[7]

EX-COMBATANT PERSPECTIVES: MAY–JUNE 2002

The following year, local NGO Post-conflict Reintegration Initiatives for Development and Empowerment (PRIDE) asked 176 former combatants from Freetown, Bo, Kailahun, and Makeni a series of questions about the Special Court, which had been formally established in January of that year, and the TRC, in order to gauge their understanding of the two institutions and the relative support for each. Polling revealed high levels of support for both institutions but lower levels of understanding about the institutions and their different mandates.[8]

In response to the low level of understanding, PRIDE held workshops to explain the two institutions and then redid the poll.[9] After the workshops, support for the TRC rose from 53% to 85%[10] and support for the Special Court rose from 59% to 75% (46). After the workshops, 74% said the TRC was important for their reintegration (46), 84% believed the TRC would bring reconciliation (45), and 60% said they would give statements to the TRC (45). A solid majority said they would testify before the TRC, even if information was widely shared with the Special Court; although they preferred that information not be shared, they would testify either way (7). One man explained, "[The TRC] will give us a chance to explain why we fought" (12). Far more wariness was expressed about testifying before the Special Court, however. Just 24% of ex-combatants expressed willingness to testify before they took the sensitization workshops, 43% said they would testify against their comrades after the workshops, and 40% said they would not testify (50).

TABLE 2. Do you think you've done anything wrong?

Before workshop	Total respondents (#)	Positive responses (%)	RUF (#)	Positive RUF responses (%)	CDF (#)	Positive CDF responses (%)
Yes	27	17	15	16	9	17
No	118	75	69	75	39	75
Don't know	13	8	8	9	4	8
Left blank	18	100	14	100	4	100
Totals	176		106		56	

After workshop	Total respondents (#)	Positive responses (%)	RUF (#)	Positive RUF responses (%)	CDF (#)	Positive CDF responses (%)
Yes	25	15	16	17	5	9
No	129	78	74	77	46	84
Don't know	11	7	6	6	4	7
Left blank	11	100	10	100	1	100
Totals	176		106		56	

Source: PRIDE, *Ex-combatant Views,* 52.
Note: Positive responses are calculated by subtracting blanks. Ex-combatants were instructed to leave sections blank under certain conditions preworkshop. Postworkshop, blanks indicated that ex-combatants did not understand the questions.

Startlingly, only 17% of former combatants responding to the PRIDE poll felt they had done anything wrong. After the workshops, that number actually dropped to 15% (see table 2), perhaps because 72% of ex-RUF (as opposed to 9% of ex-CDF) said they were forcibly recruited (70% of whom were children or teens). They may not, therefore, have felt responsible for their actions because they considered themselves to have been victims, but this was still a lower percentage than had expressed regret a year earlier in the Manifesto 99 poll (8).

However, during the focus groups, RUF ex-combatants tended to express regret, while CDF fighters continued to justify their actions. Of those few who felt they had done something wrong, 96% wanted to ask for forgiveness (52). Comments from former fighters included, "The truth will help families and victims to forgive us" and "It will let our families accept us in good faith" (12).

While 77% believed war victims should receive reparations, only 3% felt that those reparations ought to be paid by the ex-combatants. An additional 7% believed they should contribute to reparations along with the government and international community (51). One combatant expressed the view that compensation "would soften the aggrieved heart for forgiveness" (14).

EX-COMBATANT PERSPECTIVES: JUNE–AUGUST 2003

In summer 2003, just a few months after the Court handed down its first indictments, another study of former fighters was conducted by Professors Macartan Humphreys and Jeremy Weinstein in partnership with PRIDE. This poll, which solicited the views of 1,043 former combatants, centered on their perceptions of their wartime activities; their experiences with disarmament, demobilization, and reintegration programs; and their experiences with reintegration generally. It did not specifically ask about fighters' positions on the TRC or Special Court. The data are relevant, however, in light of possible motivations combatants had for wanting to testify before the TRC. The study revealed that 66% of RUF soldiers had not returned home, perhaps because they feared they would not be welcome, whereas close to 75% of CDF had returned to their original communities.[11] Some 16% of RUF combatants said they had experienced "some" or "big" problems with their families.[12] Many AFRC and RUF combatants also experienced problems in their new communities.[13] Abductees especially had trouble returning to their home communities, perhaps because, as Humphreys and Weinstein suggest, they were forced to commit atrocities there.[14]

OVERVIEW

The desire to testify expressed by large numbers of ex-combatants in the Manifesto 99 and PRIDE polls is striking, yet fewer than 1% of statements collected by the TRC came from perpetrators. What accounts for this discrepancy? I would argue that there are two explanations. First, there was the controversial indictment of Samuel Hinga Norman, the popular CDF leader, whom much of the country considered to be a national hero for fighting to reinstall the democratically elected president. Handed down just as the TRC began its hearings, the indictment had a bewildering and chilling effect on all fighters, especially the CDF fighters, and clearly affected people's decisions to testify. Even Peter Penfold, the former British high commissioner for Sierra Leone, found it appalling that Norman was indicted. In an interview, he said, "In the eyes of most Sierra Leoneans, and me, he is a hero. That he should now find himself indicted for 'war crimes' is an outrage and an injustice. What message does Sam Norman's indictment send to others who are prepared to fight for the cause of peace and democracy?"[15]

After the indictment, the Special Court decided it would not allow Norman to testify publicly before the TRC as he wished. Even though the prosecutor had said on numerous occasions that evidence before the TRC would not be used by the Special Court, he filed a motion to stop Norman from giving testimony, which the Court upheld in order to protect Norman's due process rights not to incriminate himself. How would his testimony have incriminated him, unless Crane used the testimony as evidence in the Court? When pushed, Crane admitted that, of course, had Norman testified before the TRC, he would have used his testimony against him![16] Had Norman testified, it is possible that his followers would have followed his example and chosen to come before the TRC themselves, as the early polls indicated they wanted to speak.

A second explanation for the low participation level, despite an initial enthusiasm to testify, lies in the perceived relationship between the TRC and Special Court, and the fear that information would be shared (despite proclamations by the prosecutor to the contrary), giving perpetrators the impression that they would not be safe from the clutches of the Special Court if they went to the TRC. Rumors circulated that there was a secret passage connecting the TRC and the Special Court, which were located on the same street in Freetown. The hiring of former TRC employees by the Special Court also fueled speculations. Finally, combatants were dubious about promises they would not be indicted themselves, or, nearly as unappealing, called to testify against former commanders. During focus groups, it became clear that the rank-and-file soldiers felt they could not testify against their former commanders because they were financially dependent on them.

In short, having transitional justice institutions operating simultaneously kept perpetrators away from the TRC. This was expressed in PRIDE's focus groups: "The fact that the Truth and Reconciliation Commission and the Special Court will be operating almost simultaneously will discourage fellow ex-combatants from participating. Even if they [are] truly independent from each other, we will not participate." And "I don't trust either institution (the TRC or the SC) as long as they will be working simultaneously."[17] When the Special Court made public its first indictments, the TRC had just begun its public hearings, "an unfortunate coincidence of timing," writes Arzt.[18] According to Rosalind Shaw, ex-combatants went into hiding during the TRC hearings, even at times driving TRC staff away.[19] Shaw, however, believes this reticence can be attributed to culturally based resistance to truth-telling, a conclusion I do not believe the evidence supports.

The combatants' numbers—approximately seventy-five thousand[20]—made them potentially important actors in the reconciliation process. As the PRIDE report states, their unique knowledge of the conflict—how it was fought and why people joined—was vital to producing an accurate historical record, which was part of the TRC's mandate.[21] Without reconciliation, many ex-combatants were afraid to return to their communities for fear of being rejected by their own people, whom they had harmed, as suggested from the data in

Humphrey and Weinstein's report. Their interest in testifying before the TRC was in part to facilitate their return to their communities.[22] Their participation was also seen as vital for victims' healing. As the PRIDE report asks, "How can a victim reconcile with an individual perpetrator if there is no perpetrator participation in the process?"[23]

POPULAR PERSPECTIVES: MAY 2001

In addition to polling combatants, Manifesto 99 held focus groups of the population at large to assess their support for, and willingness to participate in, the TRC. Participants from the fourteen major ethnic groups were questioned about whether they would publicly share their stories of victimization during the war, whether they would name individual perpetrators, and whether they would be willing to forgive their perpetrators. Willingness to participate was impressive—ranging from a high of 100% among the Loko to a low of 65% (still a sizeable majority) among the Koranko. However, even though the participants' willingness to speak about their own victimization was high, the participants' willingness to actually name perpetrators was relatively low. For instance, while 75% of the Creoles were willing to speak about offenses committed against them, only 35% were willing to name perpetrators. The reason they gave for their reluctance was fear of being attacked by the perpetrators or by their friends or relatives.[24]

The percentage of victims who were willing to forgive perpetrators was over 90% for eight of fourteen ethnic groups. Among the Fullah and Soso, 65% were willing to forgive those who had harmed them during the war. Over 60% of the Kissi expressed willingness to forgive the perpetrators, adding that they expected them to first ask for forgiveness.[25] Of the Sherbro, 67% (10% of whom said forgiveness was contingent on their first receiving an apology) said they would forgive the perpetrators. The percentage for Creoles was 62%. The Koranko, who had the lowest percentage of victims who were willing to testify, also had the lowest percentage (just 12.5%) of victims who expressed willingness to forgive.[26]

POPULAR PERSPECTIVES:
NOVEMBER 2002–JANUARY 2003

Another population poll to gauge perceptions of the TRC and the Special Court was undertaken in the provinces (November 2002) and in Freetown (January 2003) by another local NGO, the Campaign for Good Governance. (At this point, the Court had begun hiring staff but had handed down no indictments, and the TRC had embarked on statement-taking throughout the country.) Of the 1,280 people polled, 62% said the Special Court was necessary and 59% expressed the belief it would serve as a deterrent against future conflicts.[27] Support for the TRC was also high, with 65% saying the TRC was necessary and 60% saying it would benefit all Sierra Leoneans.[28] Respondents appeared realistic in their expectations about what the TRC could deliver. In answer to the question, "Do you think the TRC will help make up for what was lost during the war by victims," only 19% said yes.[29]

Two findings stand out in this study. When asked whether the TRC should be decentralized or located in Freetown, 83% said it should be decentralized.[30] On the question of which institution should have received the most funding, 45% said the TRC compared to 28% who favored the Special Court (see table 3).[31]

In retrospect, had the TRC been able to decentralize more of its activities, especially its follow-up activities, and had it received more funding, it might have had more success, and its legacy might have

TABLE 3. Which should have received more funding: TRC or Special Court?

Organization	No. (%)
TRC	500 (45)
Special Court	316 (28)
Equal Funding	171 (15)
Unsure	133 (12)

Source: Campaign for Good Governance, Opinion Poll Report, 14.

been greater. The TRC spent just $5 million. The Special Court, meanwhile, is estimated to have spent between $250 million and $300 million trying the nine defendants in Freetown[32] and Charles Taylor in the Hague.[33]

ELITE VIEWS AFTER THE TRC: APRIL–AUGUST 2005

In early 2006, the Sierra Leone Truth and Reconciliation Working Group (formerly, the Sierra Leone TRC Working Group), another local NGO, published its report from interviews it had conducted between April and August 2005, after the TRC had completed its work and submitted its final report to the government. Almost without exception, the respondents decried the decision to hold the Special Court at the same time as the TRC. Few felt that the timing was "coincidental," believing instead that the Special Court had been subject to political manipulation. An anonymous government official even asserted that, although the government had requested the Special Court (when the Lome Accord fell apart), it was a "forced request."[34] He may have been referring to the widespread belief that the US government coerced President Kabbah into requesting an international tribunal in order to prove that the International Criminal Court, to which the US is not a signatory, is unnecessary to prosecute war crimes.

The arrival of the Special Court on the scene, it was believed, "effectively relegated the TRC to 'second class status,'" and donors "increasingly deserted the TRC."[35] Regarding the TRC's inability to raise funds, most respondents criticized the Office of the High Commissioner for Human Rights for failing to raise sufficient funds internationally for its operation, being slow to release funds, and trying to micromanage the process.[36]

The majority of those interviewed believed the TRC should have come first, while a minority felt the Special Court should have preceded the TRC.[37] A few respondents wondered in retrospect whether, once the Special Court had been requested, the government should have amended the TRC legislation to offer an amnesty procedure (like the South African TRC), which could have offered immunity to perpetrators who were not indicted by the Special Court. Not only would amnesty have persuaded more perpetrators to acknowledge their guilt, it would have addressed the feeling among many victims that these (lower-level) perpetrators had entirely escaped justice (9). Unisa Sesay of the National Commission for Social Action shared the following: "I supported the Special Court in principle but in practice it was not necessary. I would have preferred the South African model—truth for amnesty" (27).

Interestingly, international respondents in the main felt that the problems associated with holding a truth commission and a court simultaneously were not insurmountable. While they believed the relationship was poorly handled, they did not feel it would necessarily be a bad arrangement for other countries.[38] Former Special Court prosecutor David Crane asserted, "Sequencing would have been a disaster for the Special Court" (26). He instead blames the TRC for its own failures: "I was the TRC's biggest supporter but it undermined itself, it drifted. It had an inferiority complex" (11). Smitten with Sierra Leone's experience, Crane claims to have persuaded Luis Moreno Ocampo, the International Criminal Court's chief prosecutor, to follow its example of holding simultaneous transitional justice institutions in other countries (10).

Most international and local interviewees agreed that the TRC had fallen short of what had been hoped for in terms of local participation and ownership.[39] Reasons cited, in addition to the lack of funding, were an inability to use local NGOs effectively, and the failure to employ traditional conflict resolution methods (12). International and national respondents alike expressed disappointment with the performance of the UN Office of the High Commissioner of Human Rights, which had never before operated a truth commission (5). Some Sierra Leoneans felt that local ownership had effectively been ceded to international experts: "This was supposed to be our baby," one interviewee lamented (12). There was considerable local resentment against international groups, like the International Center for Transitional Justice and the International Human Rights Law Group, for being too connected to the UN System (14). One respondent, the former executive secretary of the TRC, referred to it as an "incestuous relationship" (15). Nevertheless, interviewees felt that, however flawed, the TRC "started the process" of reconciliation. Others felt the TRC's final report would be a great "advocacy tool" (20).

POPULAR VIEWS AFTER THE TRC: JULY–AUGUST 2005

Around the same time that the Sierra Leone Truth and Reconciliation Working Group was conducting its polling of elites, student researcher Edward Sawyer was polling average citizens in three of Sierra Leone's fourteen districts (Freetown in the west, Tonkolili in the north, and Kenema in the east) about their perceptions of the two institutions. (Around this time, the TRC officially submitted its final report to the government, and the Special Court was in the midst of the hearings against the RUF, AFRC, and CDF.) Like the Campaign for Good Governance researchers, Sawyer found wide support for both institutions; a majority found them "quite successful" or "very successful." Respondents felt that the Special Court had been marginally more successful than the TRC. However, there was less understanding about what the two institutions actually did. Respondents had only a slightly better understanding of the Court than of the TRC. Most respondents perceived few contradictions between the two institutions, but again this was based on low knowledge about the institutions. Some 75% believed that the TRC was "very important" or "quite important" to the consolidation of peace in Sierra Leone, while the number was 70% for the Special Court.[40] Sawyer's conclusions dispute Shaw's notions that support for the TRC came exclusively from a small group of Freetown-based NGOs, and not from the population at large.[41]

The difference in the responses between men and women is stark. More men considered the TRC and Special Court to be successful.[42] A greater percentage of men than women also believed the two institutions were important to peace.[43] More significantly, men were more likely to understand the differences between the TRC and Special Court. This was problematic for both institutions, but more so for the TRC, which had considered women—257,000 of whom had been subjected to sexual abuse during the war[44]—fundamental constituents for successful reconciliation. However, it appears that this vulnerable group, which was specifically targeted by the TRC, was nevertheless more removed from the work of the institution in terms of understanding and perception of success.

Another interesting finding was the support from youth. Of all demographic groups, youth were the most knowledgeable about both institutions, held the most positive views about their success, and felt that both institutions helped consolidate peace. Given that the crisis among alienated, frustrated, and excluded youth was one cause of the war,[45] the knowledge and support of this group was critical. However, among the more educated youth, the percentage who held positive opinions about the success of the Special Court was the lowest among all groups, while support for the TRC was higher; 8% said the Court was "very successful" compared with 21% who considered the TRC a success.[46]

Sawyer also looked at religious understanding and support for the Special Court and TRC. Christians had a better understanding of the two institutions—especially the TRC—than did Muslims.[47] Christians also perceived the two, especially the Special Court, to be more successful. The difference in opinion about the importance of the TRC to peace was slight, with 76% of Christians saying it was "very important" or "quite important" compared with 74% of Muslims. But differences of opinion were greater regarding the importance of the Special Court in promoting peace: 78% of Christians, compared with 67% of Muslims, rated the Special Court as "very important" or "quite important" for peace.[48]

POPULAR VIEWS FROM FREETOWN:
JANUARY–FEBRUARY 2006

In early 2006, Amadu Sesay conducted field interviews in Freetown to assess opinions about the TRC. His research had the advantage of coming later in the transitional justice process, well after the TRC had concluded. (It was limited, however, by its restriction to Freetown,[49] and its small polling sample of only around 200 respondents.) At this time, 93.8% of respondents were aware of the TRC, more so than in earlier polls, as might be expected. However, it is unclear whether he probed respondents, as Sawyer did, to assess if the respondents' awareness of the TRC correlated with an actual understanding of its mandate (and its difference from the Special Court), or if the respondents had simply heard about it.[50]

Sesay found that 30.1% of respondents had expected the TRC to unite victims and perpetrators, 26.8% had expected the TRC to bring lasting peace, and 20.3% had expected it to determine the cause of the war. For Sesay, the small percentage who expected the TRC to discover the causes of the war is surprising, since conventional wisdom suggests that uncovering the truth is one of the prerequisites for reconciliation in postconflict societies. (But the nature of the civil war—during which atrocities were committed in public to inspire fear—meant that most people had a pretty good idea of what had happened; the respondents' low expectations for the TRC's ability to uncover the causes are not that surprising in my view.) The percentage of respondents who felt their expectations had been only partially met was 58.2%.[51]

On the appropriateness of the TRC's methods, 56.8% of the respondents believed they were satisfactory, while 35.2% felt they were not.[52] Among elites—Sesay divided his group into elites, the public, traditional leaders, and religious leaders—63.6% believed that the methods were not satisfactory because the perpetrators had not been made to apologize to the victims. But 76.0% of traditional leaders believed that the methods used had been appropriate (36). This result is perhaps surprising since traditional leaders had been expected to play a major role in the process, yet traditional methods of conflict resolution had not been employed. Asked specifically whether they were aware of local methods for promoting truth and reconciliation, 64.8% of respondents overall believed that there were no local methods. Of elites, 66.7%, and of traditional leaders, 59.1%, believed that local methods would have been more successful, whereas 62% of the public and 61.5% of religious leaders believed that local methods would not have been as successful as the methods used by the TRC. (In focus groups, however, most respondents stated that, had local methods been adopted, they would have been more successful.) Cleansing ceremonies were cited in focus groups as an appropriate strategy (44). While respondents believed the TRC's methods were appropriate, they also believed that local methods would have been more successful.

Of the total sample, 43.8% felt that people had cooperated with the TRC. Reasons given for any lack of cooperation had to do with the short amount of time the TRC spent in each locality, the fact that hearings were only in the district towns, and ambivalence surrounding its role with respect to the Special Court. The last was a constant theme among all the polls. The existence of the Special Court was the main reason cited for the lack of cooperation, and also for the failure of respondents to tell the entire truth.[53] (Only 46.1% of the total sample believed that the truth had been told during the hearings, while 61.5% of religious leaders held that view [39].)

On the question of whether the TRC facilitated reconciliation, 54.3% overall believed that it had. Elite opinion was more critical than public opinion: of the elites, 65.8% believed it had not facilitated reconciliation, while of the public, 72.7% believed it had.[54] A question related to whether the TRC had facilitated reconciliation was whether the respondent could be reconciled with the perpetrators: of elites, 100%, and of the public, 82.3%, said they could be reconciled with the perpetrators (42). Perhaps the conclusion to be drawn is that reconciliation is a process that was ongoing apart from, or in addition to, the TRC. People had decided in their own ways to move on, regardless of whether or not the TRC had accomplished anything.

On forgiveness, 100% of elites and traditional leaders, 80.8% of religious leaders, and 87.1% of the public said they could forgive the perpetrators for wartime atrocities.[55] What is surprising is that religious leaders were no more able to forgive than the population at large and were less able to forgive than elites. This rebuts the view that religious leaders have a monopoly on forgiveness, or that religious leaders coerce their followers to forgive. (A critique against Archbishop Tutu in South Africa was that he put undue pressure on victims during hearings to go against their natural inclinations and forgive their perpetrators, but there was no evidence of this in an analysis of the public hearings.[56]) A majority (58.5%) of all respondents believed the TRC had healed the wounds from the war.[57]

BBC WORLD SERVICE TRUST/SEARCH FOR COMMON GROUND POLL: JUNE–JULY 2007

In the summer of 2007, five years after the official end of the war, the BBC World Service Trust/Search for Common Ground conducted an extensive study, canvassing 1,717 individuals in nine districts (Bombali, Port Loko, Kono, Kailahun, Kenema, Bo, Pujahun, Western Area–urban, and Western Area–rural).[58] They were asked about their perceptions of justice and reconciliation and about their support of the TRC and Special Court.[59] Some 96% of these respondents were aware of the Special Court, but only 7% of those said they knew "a lot" about it.[60] Of those who were aware of the Court, 68% felt positively about its performance. The percentage for Kailahun, a site where there was major wartime destruction, was only 14% (20). Some 88% of those polled believed those involved in wrongdoing should be prosecuted. Of these, 87% felt that commanders should be tried, while just 29% believed lower-ranking combatants should be prosecuted (17).

Just over three-quarters of those polled felt the Special Court could bring about justice, and just under three-quarters believed the Court would deter future crimes. The more highly educated were more likely to express the latter opinion (20–21). On the question of whether the right people had been indicted, 43% believed that "mostly" the right people were on trial, 28% stated that "completely" the right persons were on trial, and 30% believed that "some" of the wrong people were prosecuted (21).

Views were mixed about the national courts in the BBC World Service Trust/Search for Common Ground study. Just as many respondents (50%) would refer grievances to community leaders as would take their cases to the state courts. The percentage who expressed confidence that the state courts could bring about justice for wartime crimes was 64%; trust was lowest in Freetown (40%) and highest in Kailahun (90%) (26).

Awareness of the TRC (89%) was somewhat lower than that of the Special Court (22). This was probably because the Special Court hearings were very much in the public's mind since the AFRC verdicts and sentencing had taken place in June and July, which coincided with the time frame of the polling. (The TRC had concluded its hearings four years earlier.) Of those who were aware of the TRC, only 23% knew of its recommendations,[61] just 14% of whom believed the government was "very successful" at implementing the recommendations.[62] With respect to the TRC's four goals—contributing to reconciliation, to justice, and to truth and creating an accurate account of the atrocities—73% believed it was "good to excellent" at contributing to reconciliation, 57% thought it was "good to excellent" at contributing to justice (only 6% believed this in Kailahun), 68% believed it was "good to excellent" at contributing to truth, and 66% considered it "good to excellent" at creating an accurate account.[63]

Two-thirds of respondents were aware of reparations to victims. When asked what kind of reparations should be made, 80% of respondents said housing, 66% said food, 48% said education, 47% said skills/training, and 37% said physical/mental care. When asked to whom reparations should be made, 30% said to individuals; 25% said to communities; and 45% said to both. There was variation among districts on this question: 98% in Kailahun preferred that reparations be given to both individuals and communities, but only 19% in Kono—also an area hard hit by the war—preferred that reparations go to both.[64]

How did the BBC World Service Trust/Search for Common Ground respondents define justice and reconciliation? Strikingly, 66% associated "justice" with "trust." Only 7% associated it with "punishment," and even fewer (5%) associated it with "trials" (see table 4).[65]

This cautions us, I believe, to take with a grain of salt those polls that indicate strong support for punitive justice because the word *justice* in Africa in general, and in Sierra Leone in particular, may have a different meaning than in the West. It connotes not retributive but

TABLE 4. What is the definition of justice?

Definition	Respondents (%)
Trust	66
Giving someone their rights	24
Doing things the right way	24
Fair treatment	14
Forgiveness	11
Punishment	7
Trials	5

Source: BBC World Service Trust and Search for Common Ground, "Building a Better Tomorrow," 18.

rather restorative justice, which seeks to rebuild relationships and bring people who have harmed together with those who were harmed. Also surprising were the respondents' characterizations of "reconciliation," which 57% defined as "togetherness/unity," 39% as "forgiveness/let bygone be bygones," 31% as "forget about the past," and 6% as "justice"; just 2% identified reconciliation with "compensation."[66]

FORMER COMBATANT AND NONCOMBATANT PERCEPTIONS: AUGUST–SEPTEMBER 2007

At the same time the BBC/Search for Common Ground study took place, student researcher Johanna Boersch-Supan interviewed seventy-one community members, former RUF combatants, and opinion leaders (including the heads of NGOs, members of the clergy, traditional leaders, members of the security forces, and the leaders of youth organizations). Interviewing people individually and through focus groups, she targeted respondents in Central Freetown, Calaba Town, and Mayemi Village in the west; Makeni and Magburaka in the north; and Kenema and Tongo Field in the south. (Because of security concerns leading up the elections in 2007, she was unable to conduct interviews in Kailahun district in the east, where most of the former RUF rebels now reside, as she had planned; she admits she is, therefore, missing data on the perspectives of those who were most directly and for the longest time affected by the war.[67])

Boersch-Supan did not ask the respondents for their views specifically on the Special Court or the TRC; her questions were more broadly oriented around their perceptions of reconciliation, justice, forgiveness, and reintegration. While the majority of respondents indicated that combatants and community members were living together in peaceful coexistence,[68] Boersch-Supan discovered this was only superficially the case—a pragmatic, rather than emotional decision.[69] In probing her informants, she found that most were dissatisfied with the lack of apologies from ex-combatants and with the paucity of events bringing perpetrators and victims together to forge reconciliation.[70] Her interviews showed that victims wanted to hear apologies or see displays of remorse. They also wanted combatants to be held accountable.[71] (Her findings contradict Shaw's thesis that verbal apology is unnecessary, and all that is needed is evidence of changed behavior, a "cool heart."[72]) Boersch-Supan notes that many respondents had expected apologies and displays of remorse, but none of the respondents who had been combatants demonstrated either. Instead, they hid behind the rationalization that they had been victims themselves. The inability of the TRC to elicit apologies from perpetrators was viewed by some as a failure of the institution.[73]

Boersch-Supan also discovered that in addition to apologies, punishment of perpetrators was foremost in the minds of the respondents. This was especially the case among those, particularly women, who had experienced extreme violence during the war.[74] (Another study, however, had indicated that women did not want perpetrators to be punished.[75]) Her informants disagreed about whether enough perpetrators had been prosecuted (representative perpetrators, that is, those "most responsible") or whether lower-level commanders should have been prosecuted as well.[76] Amputees, in particular, felt that more perpetrators should have been prosecuted. Boersch-Supan quotes one amputee, who said, "You know, Charles Taylor did not cut off my arm," implying that the actual perpetrators should have been on trial (59).

Boersch-Supan's research indicated that reintegration is not complete. Former combatants suffer from discrimination—"a form of subtle punishment" (71)—and are the objects of gossip and labeling (66). This accounts for the decision by many former combatants, especially women, who are more stigmatized for being fighters than for being bush wives, to move to places like the larger towns or mining fields where they were unknown and to lie about their pasts (68–69). Finally, she gleaned from her interviews that reintegration will only be successful when the economic needs of people are met. This is true for perpetrators as well as victims.

Respondents also linked the provision of material resources with the ability to rebuild lives and hence the willingness to forgive. Boersch-Supan found those most affected by the war, and women in general, were the most vociferous in calling for economic assistance and linking it to reconciliation (72). She quotes one respondent who said, "Asking for forgiveness is not enough, we need to be provided with opportunities, with changes, then we can totally forgive them" (73). Many expressed a desire for compensation over sending perpetrators to prison. Likewise, former rebels saw their economic sufficiency through employment as beneficial to the whole community and expressed the view their contribution to development would engender trust and acceptance from the community. One said, "If people know you are busy and are contributing, they will see that you are different" (75). This conclusion about the importance of economic well-being to reconciliation is borne out by the testimony from victims at the TRC hearings. In most cases, when asked what they would like from the TRC, respondents said economic assistance. Only 2% of respondents asked for justice.[77]

POPULAR OPINION IN MAKENI: DECEMBER 2008–MARCH 2009

Other studies as well as anecdotal evidence suggest that compensation was perceived as a vital ingredient and as a necessary precursor to reconciliation. Gearoid Millar's survey in the northern city of Makeni, undertaken between December 2008 and March 2009, found that whether or not one had access to the benefits of the postwar peace determined one's opinion about the TRC's success. (Millar did not probe attitudes about the Special Court.) The educated-elite minority largely endorsed the view that the TRC promoted healing and reconciliation, while the majority of local residents (the uneducated, non–English-speaking nonelites) held overwhelmingly negative attitudes. Millar found that the Christian-Muslim, male-female, elder-youth, Temne-Mende divisions were not analytically useful, since the *only* characteristic associated with differing views of the TRC turned out to be elite versus nonelite status: the educated, English-speaking minority versus the non–English-speaking majority, most of whom were less educated.[78]

Millar discovered that the nonelite respondents had believed that the TRC would provide money in exchange for their telling their stories before the TRC. After all, he notes, "A UN project, run by white people from America and Europe, provides resources, not talk."[79] They were disappointed, then, when the TRC did not provide healthcare, housing, education, or financial assistance.[80] Whereas nonelites lamented the TRC's inability to transform their lives, the elites, many of whom were employed by the TRC or one of the development organizations working in the area at the time, had received the necessary resources to rebuild their lives and thus had a positive view of the TRC's contribution.[81]

POST-TAYLOR SENTENCING POLL: JUNE–JULY 2012

The Special Court for Sierra Leone commissioned the international NGO No Peace Without Justice to conduct a nationwide study, which was to be carried out immediately after the conviction and sentencing of Charles Taylor, on perceptions of the effectiveness of the Court.[82] Brenda Hollis, the last prosecutor of the Special Court, has heralded the Court's accomplishments, in part on the basis of this poll.[83]

In its report on the poll results, which reflected the views of 1,502 Sierra Leoneans in the twelve provincial districts plus the Western area, No Peace Without Justice conceded there were problems with the study. Because of the rush to do the polling immediately after the sentencing of Charles Taylor,[84] the time available for the survey and analysis was "squeezed into a shorter period."[85] Working against a self-imposed publication date, the surveyors had less time for interviewing, analyzing data, and drafting the report. The authors of the report also admitted that, because the sentencing occurred as the rainy season in Sierra Leone was commencing, making it impossible to move easily around the country, they were able to conduct fewer interviews than they had anticipated.[86] They also lacked sufficient time to conduct interim samplings of surveys to work out the kinks and retrain enumerators when glitches were discovered. Nor was there time to hold focus groups as planned or to conduct comprehensive data analysis.[87] Still, despite these caveats, they concluded that the survey was not flawed and the overall assessment of the Special Court was "very positive."[88]

Although polling was scheduled to take place immediately after the sentencing of Charles Taylor, ostensibly to take advantage of a "bump" in positive feelings about the Court, there was no discernible uptick in public opinion after 2007, when the BBC had partnered with Search for Common Ground to conduct a similar poll. The percentage of people (92%) who were aware of the Special Court in 2012 was comparable to the percentage (96%) who knew about it in the earlier study.[89] In the No Peace Without Justice poll, 77% of Sierra Leoneans expressed the belief that the Court had accomplished what it set out to achieve, compared with 75% in the BBC study, who felt the Court could bring about justice.[90] In both polls, most people were aware of the Special Court and the TRC, but few participated in either initiative.

On an issue that was very controversial, whether or not an international court or a national court would bring about justice, those surveyed picked national courts over the Special Court as the proper venue (see table 5).[91] But this option was not really possible given the destruction of the justice sector during the war, and the fact that the national penal code did not include crimes against humanity and war crimes. Nevertheless, critics of the Court suggest that the money

TABLE 5. Necessary to achieve justice

Type of court	Respondents (%)
National court system	71.45
Special Court for Sierra Leone	51.52
International Criminal Court	48.42

Source: No Peace Without Justice, "Making Justice Count," 15.

spent on this expensive court could have been better spent on the local justice system, building its capacity to enable it to conduct trials. Prosecutor Hollis agrees that while it is preferable for state courts to try perpetrators of war crimes, this was impossible since the Lome Accord had granted amnesty at the local level.[92]

The preference for the involvement of the national court system may be explained by responses to another query. On the issue of dominance by foreigners, the respondents overwhelmingly believed that there were not enough locals as senior staff members of the Court: only 23% responded affirmatively, confirming the perennial complaint about the lack of local ownership.[93] In the national court system, locals would be in charge.

The survey reveals other interesting findings. To the question, "Is it important to know the truth about war crimes and crimes against humanity committed in Sierra Leone and Liberia?," 97% responded affirmatively.[94] This finding, in my view, demonstrates the desirability of establishing a truth commission or other restorative processes rather than a court, since truth commissions aim to find a broader truth that includes not only what happened but what led up to it and why; trials define truth narrowly as attributing blame for particular acts in order to punish the perpetrators. More importantly, how do Sierra Leoneans see the link between truth and punishment? When asked, for instance, "What does 'justice' mean?," 72.49% of respondents answered "establishing the truth," and only 22% said "punishing those responsible." Again, this confirms the view that truth is superior as a value to punishment.[95] (Recall too that in the BBC/ Search for Common Ground poll, just 7% had defined "justice" as "punishment.")

To the question, "What should be done for victims?," the top response was "receive money" (42.42%); "punish those responsible" was cited by far fewer people (26.21%). This suggests that both restorative justice and distributive justice are higher priorities for Sierra Leoneans than the retributive approach pursued by the Special Court.

Lastly, the poll failed to elicit opinions about the most controversial case the Court prosecuted: Samuel Hinga Norman, who was the popular leader of the CDF during the civil war. Perhaps since he died during his trial, before a verdict was announced, the pollsters felt they could justify the omission (there is no explanation why he was omitted from the report). Views were solicited about the appropriateness of the trials for all other defendants, including Norman's codefendants in the CDF.[96]

SUMMARY OF THE DATA

What can we gather from the various polling data? Levels of support were generally high for both institutions, although there were lower levels of comprehension about the actual differences between the two institutions. Both perpetrators and victims had expressed willingness prior to the TRC to testify, yet few perpetrators actually came forward to confess. Perpetrators had said they wanted to explain what they had done and why and to beg for forgiveness, seeing this as the only means for returning to home communities. Likewise, victims had indicated an interest in meeting with perpetrators and reconciling, although this did not often take place. Forgiveness was ranked high by most people, and people criticized the TRC for not eliciting verbal apologies. Most respondents, when asked, criticized the decision to have both institutions operating at the same time, and some suggested that more localized processes would have been preferable to the TRC's more formal, centralized approach. Some respondents linked reconciliation to meeting the economic needs of victims and valued economic compensation over punitive justice. To many Sierra Leoneans, justice meant establishing the truth more than punishing those responsible.

In the next chapter, I turn to religious leaders' understandings of reconciliation and justice and their opinions about the relative advantages of the TRC and the Special Court. Did their views contradict or reflect the views of the people at large?

CHAPTER 5

PERCEPTIONS OF RELIGIOUS LEADERS

During the summers of 2006 and 2007, I interviewed members of the IRC of Sierra Leone, the interfaith network of Christian and Muslim leaders that had been established as an affiliate chapter of the World Conference of Religions for Peace in 1997.[1] The IRC is made up of members of the Council of Churches in Sierra Leone (an umbrella group of Protestant denominations), the Roman Catholic Church, the Evangelical Fellowship, and the Pentecostal Churches Council. Member Islamic organizations include the Supreme Islamic Council, the Sierra Leone Muslim Congress, the Federation of Muslim Women's Associations of Sierra Leone, the Sierra Leone Muslim Missionaries Union, the Muslim Brotherhood Islamic Mission, and the United Council of Imams. I asked the religious leaders, most of whom were the top persons in their denominations or organizations, a set of questions about their views on the meaning of reconciliation, the differences between Christian and Muslim views of reconciliation, the relative value of the TRC and Special Court, the degree to which perpetrators have come to acknowledge wrongdoing, the value for victims of testifying, and the importance of implementing the recommendations.[2]

RELIGIOUS LEADER AS HEAD

Because of the criticisms lodged against the South African TRC from some quarters that its discourse was overly religious, and it was dominated by the theological commitment of its head, Anglican archbishop Desmond Tutu,[3] I asked my subjects whether or not it was helpful to have a religious leader at the helm of the Sierra Leone TRC. The leaders were nearly unanimous in their view that it was. Catholic bishop George Biguzzi said it was appropriate because religious leaders were the only group that people could trust during the war. According to Usman Fornah, then IRC interim secretary general, "It was very valuable, because what happened in Sierra Leone had spiritual and physical dimensions. You cannot just go with the physical. That is why the DDR [UNAMSIL's Disarmament, Demobilization, and Reintegration] program had trouble. Those working through DDR were working for a living. If they had religious leaders work with them in the DDR, they could have appealed to the spiritual minds of those combatants. Combatants had a high level of respect for religious leaders. Whatever you say, they are willing to listen. It was very appropriate that the Commission was headed by a religious leader."[4]

Even though Christians are a minority in the population, making up just 30% of Sierra Leoneans, the Muslim leaders also supported the choice of Joseph Humper, a Methodist bishop. There was no resentment that a Muslim leader was not selected. They attributed this to the religious tolerance that marks Sierra Leone. Many pointed out that then president Kabbah is a Muslim who was married to a Catholic. Intermarriage is common in Sierra Leone, and Sierra Leoneans celebrate major life events—weddings, funerals, celebrations—in mosques and churches together. One leader, in explaining why the Muslims accepted a Christian as head of the TRC, said that during the war Muslims were going to Christian churches. "Everybody kind of recognized the fact that there is power in the name of Jesus. Everyone went to church to pray."[5]

Some leaders felt Humper was selected as chair because he was head of the IRC at the time of the selection process, and anyone who had been leading the IRC would have been selected. But Mariatu Mahdi, president of the Federation of Muslim Women's Associations of Sierra Leone, and a member of the selection panel for commissioners, denied that it was a requirement that the chair—or any of the commissioners—be a religious leader.[6] Another Muslim religious leader who had been on the selection committee asserted, "The commissioners were chosen in their individual rights, not as religious leaders."[7] However, Henry Samuels of Vine Memorial Baptist Church noted that Humper's ties to the ruling party SLPP made him a less than neutral choice.[8]

A minority opinion was expressed by Abdul Karim Koroma, a leader in the Muslim Brotherhood Islamic Mission, and also an APC stalwart, who thought that appointing a religious man was a mistake: "I would have picked a person of strong character with a legal background. Then he would speak things from the law with the strength of his character and know when to forgive and when not to forgive. A religious man can get carried away!" He remarked how Archbishop Tutu in South Africa would break down and cry, but he could not recall if Humper had cried during the hearings.[9] Overall, however, most leaders felt the choice of a religious leader was a good one given the importance of religion in the country, the high esteem in which religious leaders were held, and the faith community's association with the message of reconciliation that is preached widely in mosques and churches.

RECONCILIATION FROM CHRISTIAN AND MUSLIM PERSPECTIVES

Some Christian leaders believed that their views on reconciliation were different from those of Muslims. Some expressed the view that Muslims believe in retribution rather than forgiveness. One Christian leader said, "It's hard to find a Muslim who forgives. They don't believe in forgiveness. They only believe in an eye for an eye, a tooth for a tooth."[10] Another said, "The Muslims always want to retaliate. And to get them out of that path is not easy."[11] According to Joseph Konteh of the Wesleyan Church, "The Muslim point of view is if you do something to me, I have to retaliate. If you hit me, I have to hit you. But the IRC is modernizing things. Muslims say 'you have to confess' but Christians make more emphasis on forgiveness."[12] Likewise, A. A. Bangura believed that Muslims "very much believe in paying for the crime committed before reconciliation, whereas the Christian may just decide to forgive and reconcile with the person without even forcing the payment for the crime the person has committed." He added, "To a very large extent Muslims would have loved to see those people—all those people involved not just the few arrested and sent to Special Court—actually punished and an example set so that others would not commit the same thing."[13]

Evangelical Lutheran bishop Tom Barnett observed, "Both religions proclaim peace, but in terms of practice Muslims live much more by the Word. Sometimes the practice of forgiveness is difficult because the Word says if you commit adultery, you should be stoned to death. And to be charged faithful you need to live by the word." But he believed that Muslims had accepted the TRC, pointing to the fact "that quite a number of them testified."[14] Anglican bishop J. O. P. Lynch believed that "Muslims might have a more difficult time reconciling after war." He gave as an example an imam who had been responsible for burning down houses. He was captured by his own people and killed. "Christians would never have done that!" he exclaimed.[15]

Some leaders, however, downplayed the differences between the Christian and Muslim views. "Even if there is a difference, it's not much. They do accept forgiveness. It's only extremists that don't," said Samuels.[16] For Methodist cleric Francis Nabieu, the issue of forgiveness was more "in depth in Christianity than in Islam, but it is still there. We have a picture of a loving father. Sometimes in Islam, God tends to be a warrior God."[17]

Abdul Karim Koroma explained the Quran's teaching on forgiveness this way: "The Quran says if out of conviction, not out of weakness, you decide to forgive, Allah will give you blessings in heaven. And even though revenge is possible, you are enjoined to forgive because Allah says, 'I am the one who should punish, not you.'"[18] Notwithstanding the view of many Christians that Muslims insist on punishment, Sheik Fomba Abubakar Swaray agreed that Islam teaches "whoever forgives and reconciles, his reward is with Allah." He agreed that Allah should judge, not humans: "If someone has wronged you, accept that defeat within yourself. To take revenge will not solve the problem. Vengeance is God's. Allow the Almighty to revenge for you. If I say someone burned my house, and so I am going to burn that person's house, the destruction will never end. It is better for me to reconcile and leave the Almighty the most just God to retaliate for me."[19]

Sheik Abu Bakarr Conteh cited the example of the prophet Mohammed, who, although persecuted, humiliated, and forced to migrate from Mecca by the pagans, did not retaliate. "But when victory came, and he reentered Mecca in victory, those who did all those atrocities against his person and against his followers thought he was going to retaliate. And yet he said you are forgiven."[20] Sheik Swaray, like his Christian brother Joseph Konteh, also cited the example of Joseph forgiving his brothers rather than retaliating against them.[21]

Muslim leaders emphasized their religion's commitment to peace and reconciliation. Swaray pointed out that chapter 42 of the Quran is "'Shura,' which means consultation. For him, Islam teaches that, when a situation is difficult, the Quran urges its people "to consult and reconcile."[22] Sheik Conteh argued, "I don't think there's any other civilization that gives more prominence to reconciliation than Islam." He cited the decision about what to do with the seventy captives taken during the Battle of Badr (the first encounter between Muslims and non-Muslims): "There were various schools of thought as to what punishment was to be inflicted on them. It was determined that instead of punishment, each captive should teach ten Muslim children how to read and write."[23]

THE NEED FOR ACKNOWLEDGMENT

Views differed on the importance of acknowledgment, with mainly Muslims saying it was necessary. Some maintained that acknowledgment by perpetrators was a requirement for forgiveness. Sheik Sillah, chief imam of the Freetown Central Mosque, was adamant: "You cannot reconcile with someone who claims his innocence!"[24] Some cited examples of acknowledgment in the public hearings, with one leader saying, "I witnessed the TRC. Some people came out and asked for mercy. Some wept openly." He believed that had the president offered an apology (as the opposition leader did), "others would have followed."[25]

John Meindy of the Church of God of Prophesy Mission did not see how reconciliation was possible if the perpetrators did not apologize: "Somebody comes forward and repents for what he has done. Then you can forgive and reconcile. But if he doesn't come forward, how are you going to reconcile with him?"[26] Abdul Karim Koroma said that for child rebels who were abducted, indoctrinated, and forced to commit atrocities, "We forgive those people because they were acting outside their conscience. But we also believe personal responsibility must be taken, especially people over a certain age." Asked if it is possible to forgive in the absence of acknowledgment, he replied, "I have not seen that in my religion. It may be there [in the Quran], but from what I know I do not see that. My religion preaches justice." He added, "According to my faith, Islam is very forgiving in several ways. It accepts those who prostrate themselves, but those who murder, Islam says they must face justice. I believe in [forgiving] people who are prostrate. But I take great exception to reconciling with people who deliberately went out to murder, to destroy, to loot property of innocent people."[27]

Prince Charles Brainard of the Catholic Bishop's Conference said, "If he has not accepted that he has done anything wrong, I don't see a true sense of reconciliation coming to play. It's a two-way issue: you have to accept your wrong if someone is ready to forgive you. Forgiveness is not reconciliation. I can forgive but we cannot reconcile. If you don't accept your wrong, in as much as I have forgiven you, there will not be that intimacy again."[28]

Others, however, said that their Christian faith required them to forgive even in the absence of an apology. One leader said that acknowledgment "should not be the deciding factor in accepting that individual who has wronged you. All have fallen short of the glory of God. You are liable to do wrong and need forgiveness. That should make you more open to forgive."[29] For the Reverend Reuben Dove, "Even without acknowledgement there should be forgiveness. Christ forgave."[30] F. T. C. Randall noted that "Jesus said, 'Father forgive them, for they know not what they do.' He forgives, so we forgive."[31]

Bishop Joseph Humper told me, "You have to extend the olive branch, whether or not someone apologizes. Some perpetrators are adamant. They will not admit. But you must reconcile in order to live in community without suspicion." Often forgiving was seen as beneficial to the victim. Humper said, "It is a Christian duty to forgive. Without forgiveness, you cannot be at peace with yourself. Without forgiveness, if you continue to hold a grudge, every time you see that person, you cannot have a composed mind to carry out your work."[32] United Brethren in Christ minister Billy Simbo also believed that forgiving helps the victim: "If you don't forgive him, you do more harm to yourself than to the other person, because he'll go on and live his life. But if you forgive him, then you take ownership of that situation. Whether the person confesses or not, it doesn't matter, because you have taken care of that situation."[33]

Konteh pointed to the biblical story of Joseph and his brothers who sold him into slavery: "In their hour of need, sick and without food, he [Joseph] made the move. After which the brothers confessed and said 'I am sorry.' As far as reconciliation is concerned, one has to make the move. And Sierra Leoneans made the move. Let us forget about what happened. Let us embrace our brothers and sisters back into society—which we did." Konteh felt that, according to his culture, there has to be acknowledgment first: "But, from my evangelical point of view, Jesus Christ is our example. We turned against God, and God himself made the move, and even though we were still rebellious, he brought us to himself." He added that it would be very difficult, humanly speaking, to reconcile with someone who would not acknowledge they had done anything wrong.[34]

Fornah said, "I have to let go even before I am asked. So, whether there is remorse, whether there is a request for forgiveness or not, I must be willing from the religious perspective to let go. If the Savior was waiting for people to ask for forgiveness, he would never have forgiven them! That was a perfect example that was set for us. Right on the cross while being beaten, mocked, chastised, without any request from the perpetrators, he was able to say, 'Forgive them, Father, for they do not know what they are doing.'"[35]

Solomon Kampbell agreed that Christians are taught to forgive, citing the scripture where Peter asks Jesus how many times do I forgive someone who has offended me and is told, seventy times seven: "Whether the person that offended you actually acknowledges that he has offended you or not, you as a Christian must take the initiative, but let me hasten to say it's not easy."[36] Aiah Foday-Khabenje explained, "If God can forgive me, I can forgive others. We pray in the Lord's prayer 'God forgive me as I forgive those who offend me.' Considering my own sins against the Creator—and what He has done to forgive those—this is the basis for me to forgive others. I think there is no wrongdoing that probably is more evil than my own evil."[37]

As a Christian, Milton Marah of the Missionary Church of Africa believed that one can forgive without waiting for the person to apologize: "It is difficult though. This is a conflict between the scripture and the human tendency. The human tendency will say 'I've been wronged. I am going to wait. Someone has to come and tell me I'm sorry. Then I will say, yes, I forgive you.'" Marah, who had been injured during the war, said, "If I cannot forgive someone myself, I have no business preaching anymore on forgiveness and reconciliation!"[38] Evangelist M. O. Ekemode of Christ Apostolic Church echoed this view when he said that it is hard to forgive when someone does not acknowledge the harm he did to you: "It takes extraordinary grace for people to be able to do that. It's not impossible, only hard."[39]

One leader ventured that one reason why so few perpetrators come forward to confess is that so many were child soldiers who were "drugged and so cannot remember what they did. Sometimes when the drugs have left you, you are not conscious enough to know you did something bad. They never knew what they were doing until now people are telling them this is what you did, and it's hard for them to accept it."[40] Another explained, "They were not much more than fifteen. So what would they know? Telling them to talk does not mean much to them. At that age, they are too young to understand. Probably those perpetrators grow up, when they've understood the dynamics of the war, they will know what they did before is not correct."[41]

Bishop George Biguzzi said, "I did not see any real repentance [among those perpetrators who testified]. Most went through the motions. To me it was mostly a stance of convenience. I didn't see any real contrition. Some said they were sorry but felt they were victims too. Cutting hands off, or raping, cannot be justified by war. Certain things you can never justify by war. If you've done it, you must realize it's an evil act. 'I'm sorry' doesn't mean anything. But you can change yourself after that." Biguzzi worried about the long-term consequences of not coming to terms with one's actions: "If you don't recognize this particular act is evil, and you are only changing because the situation is changed, tomorrow, given the same situation, you might repeat it. The crucial thing is to tackle the causes. Otherwise, given the circumstances you'll go back to the same thing."[42]

Simbo regarded the small number of perpetrators who acknowledged their deeds to be a real problem: "I think they would have done more for the country and peace process and reconciliation if they had gotten more perpetrators to acknowledge what they did." Instead, "he says in disbelief, "when the election campaign started, the political parties hired these same thugs to be bodyguards! People are saying this is what brought us to where we were before, and now you are making them guards, blessing them!"[43]

Time constraints were identified as one explanation for why there were so few acknowledgments of guilt. Hearings were over in one week in each district. According to Humper, just as people started to understand the process and wanted to come testify, the TRC had to leave: "If we had had two weeks, we could have accomplished more."[44] Fornah, who had been regional TRC coordinator for the North, said,

"I can remember people begging us to put their names on the board [to testify] in Makeni. But they weren't selected because there was a limited number of people the Commission could listen to. But people were very eager to speak out." He believed that even if there is a culture of silence in Sierra Leone, that culture was being broken down.[45]

Even absent public acknowledgment (because of shame, memory loss, or fear of being prosecuted), some leaders noted that perpetrators confessed privately. Bankole Large, of the African Methodist Episcopal Church, reported, "They are afraid to come out. We know it. Some of them are confessing to some of us personally that the war was senseless. Maybe they were forced or brain washed. What they have done is unspeakable. Some of them would not like to go in public and confess. But to us personally, they share their view with us."[46]

Marie Barnett, wife of Tom Barnett, and copastor in the Evangelical Lutheran Church, rejected the need to receive an apology in order to be reconciled, saying, "I don't think it should be mandatory. Rather, judge by action. If you come back to reconcile, I already know what you have done. If you come like Mary Magdalene, you don't have to say anything. She only fell at the feet of Jesus. She didn't say anything. Her action was humility. Jesus already knew. So if you come to me with a contrite heart, and I know that you have wronged me badly, even to have the courage to come back to me and say 'hello,' I think it's contrition enough." She added, "We can reconcile without your speaking. Your actions speak louder than your voice." She pointed out that people who had committed atrocities were back in the villages. "Just going back and starting to rebuild their lives and helping others, I think that speaks volumes." She contrasted this with someone who makes a public confession, someone who says "I'm sorry" but really is not: "You come back and do the same thing!"[47]

HELPFUL TO VICTIMS AND PERPETRATORS?

How helpful was the TRC for perpetrators and victims? Opinion was divided. One Muslim leader expressed the belief that, "If you have something deep down inside, instead of letting it eat you up, the best thing is to tell it. You are released from bondage. You feel a lot better. You no longer feel scared or timid."[48] Dove agreed that speaking out was beneficial: "I think when they talk about it, some who were traumatized may get some kind of healing because people show concern."[49]

Marie Barnett believed it was psychologically healing for victims to tell others what happened to them.[50] Her husband, Tom Barnett, agreed with her that it provided "an enabling environment for people to express themselves and feel that they were cared for." He admitted there was hesitancy at first to come forward, but in time, "people opened up and there was quite a lot of enthusiasm for it. If things had gone on a little longer, more people would have come forward, and its impact would have been greater than it is now."[51] Reluctance to testify before the TRC and the low level of participation, especially among perpetrators, was often said to have had more to do with shortness of time, lack of understanding about the TRC's mandate, and reservations about the TRC's relationship with the Special Court than to a cultural aversion to speaking out.

Abdul Karim Koroma doubted that the hearings were helpful for victims. He explained, "They thought it would help. They saw the South African case, where people came in to wash themselves clean and say 'we're sorry.' But, here very few people admitted [guilt]. I am convinced that nothing was done for the victims. How do you appease someone whose mother was killed right in her presence? Even if that person says, 'I killed this person's mother,' how does that help the victim? Just because you admit it publicly? The victims were not mollified, actually. Personally I don't think the TRC was of much use."[52]

Meindy did believe there were cultural barriers, especially for women, to testify. "Some of them hide because they do not want people to know they were raped. Many were raped outside their communities, and it has remained hidden. So you can be in society without people knowing you went through certain things. No one would run them from society. The problem [of testifying publicly] is the fear that people will be pointing. They will say, 'Look at that woman. She was raped by five men.' Everybody will be laughing at that person. They don't want that to happen."[53]

Marah agreed that it might bring embarrassment to women who had been raped to testify: "Making them open up in public before the people, it sounds like it's happening again when they're talking about it. The mind goes back; psychologically the impact grows more and more and more. After going home, there is depression."[54] But Simbo felt that the TRC had helped those women who had talked about rape to be accepted: "The community has embraced those people, brought them in with the understanding that this is something that happened to all of us. She was raped, this house was burned down, and so forth. The specifics of the victimization may not be the same but the results are the same; it broke the community down."[55]

Pentecostal minister Daniel Desay believed confessing was important to the well-being of the perpetrator: "If you don't confess it, in the long run you will be a mad person."[56] Another leader pointed to the ceremonies at the end of each week of hearings as especially healing for the perpetrators: "At the end of every public hearing, there was a symbolic ceremony of request for forgiveness by the perpetrators, before religious and traditional leaders, whom they prostrated themselves before and begged for forgiveness. We saw people crying and shedding tears, they thought the ceremonies were so sorrowful and solemn."[57] On the other hand, Nabieu dismissed the reconciliation ceremonies as "superficial" and as having little impact.[58]

Foday-Khabenje believed that testifying was more beneficial for the perpetrators than for the victims: "It doesn't help me to tell everybody that my office is burned, except of course if I need help from them. Possibly that is the motivation. And from that point of view, if they don't get help, it's demoralizing. I don't want to come to cry to you and you turn a blind eye."[59]

CULTURAL APPROPRIATENESS

On the question of the cultural appropriateness of the TRC model, some found the TRC unnecessary as people had already been able to move on. For instance, Large expressed the view that "Even without the TRC, we would have put the war behind us and looked toward the future. Individually, Sierra Leoneans had decided to put the war behind them."[60] Another said, "The victims were forgiving even before [the] war ended. Many people said, 'Let's forget about it, we cannot go back and talk about this issue.' As far as the church is concerned, people had already forgiven."[61] Simbo agreed that by the time the TRC began, people had moved on. He observed, "There's no doubt about it that people had made their decision to move on. But it was nice to have that official sanction put on it."[62]

Simbo roundly rejected the notion of a culture of secrecy that made speaking out in a TRC inappropriate: "I am no anthropologist, but whether you're Mende, Temne, or Krio, it's typical in our traditions to talk. You are required to make confession. I think that's very strong in Sierra Leone, and African tradition generally, where chiefs or elders call you in and say 'This is what we've heard. Now what do you have to say?'"[63]

Moses Khanu, a member of the Human Rights Commission and a former IRC director, also emphasized the public nature of traditional conflict resolution:

> For some offenses in the traditional sense, the apology is not between you and the individual. It is a community affair. If somebody steals, you may have stolen from my neighbor, but the crime was also against the community. Therefore there are certain crimes that although I would have gone and apologized to you for because I have offended you, the general forgiveness would come definitely from the community, either from a public kind of confession or some ritual to appease. Depending on the nature of the offense, you might have also gone against the ancestors. There must be some kind of atonement. In some communities, it is at a public meeting where you pay penance for the crime. In some places you perform certain rituals in order to appease the living but also the ancestors because they were equally offended.[64]

But Marah believed that the public aspect of the hearings was not culturally appropriate: "In our culture, to confess publicly, that is difficult. Usually, when someone commits an error in the community, you find someone he can trust to ask the person about the crime. And after that, the message is brought before the entire body, which is told he has admitted a wrong. To bring someone to the public and say 'confess,' that is wrong, culturally speaking."[65]

Others felt the TRC would have been more successful if it had been more decentralized, relying on local traditions and understandings. Tom Barnett said, "If the TRC had been given more time and resources to go down into the communities, this would have undergirded that traditional system and strengthened the hands of traditional leaders to continue this process of reconciliation. Reconciliation would have been facilitated by these traditional leaders. But we could not give time for the TRC to link with that system."[66] Marah believed that the TRC would have been more fruitful if interviewers had been employed who could "mediate, men talking to men, women to women, speaking heart to heart, one on one."[67]

Abdul Babatunde Karim of the Muslim Congress asserted, "The IRC did more on the reconciliation side. The TRC did a lot on the truth side. But on the reconciliation side it was very, very weak. Little to nothing was done."[68] He was referring to the reconciliation activities that were conducted in 2003 and 2004 through the IRC with funds from the UNDP (discussed in chapter 6). Using their members in the various districts, the IRC trained local district coordinators. Meeting with traditional chiefs, the IRC representatives formed committees and local people were asked, "What do you need to facilitate reconciliation?" According to Mabel Mbayo of the IRC, some communities wanted to play football together, to share a meal together with former enemies, or to have mass graves identified.[69]

RELATIVE VALUES OF TRC AND SPECIAL COURT

The religious leaders were divided about the value of the Special Court. Some, such as West African Methodist minister D. M. Speck, endorsed it: "I personally support what it has done. At least people cannot just go free. That will send a signal to the rest of us. That is what is going to happen to you. People will learn to put their tails between their legs and behave properly."[70]

Brainard linked retribution to reconciliation: "When we talk about reconciliation, when we talk about the act of forgiving, there should be what we call retribution, what in the church's language we call penance. In order to really heal, I think there should be retribution, in the sense that to help heal the wounds that have been created, it's very vital also that justice has to prevail. We must allow justice to take its course so that in the future such things would not happen."[71]

Sillah agreed that "The TRC has its own role, but the Special Court has also recognized something: you cannot get peace without trying some people."[72] For Kampbell, the Special Court was important: "Justice is levied upon the ringleaders. It will serve as landmark for the future."[73] Simbo also saw value in the prosecutions: "It's sending notice to other violent people that you will be held accountable for what you do. But," he added, "look at how much money is spent!"[74] Although supportive of the Special Court, Bangura commented on the recently sentenced AFRC defendants that, "These people have been sentenced to fifty years imprisonment. But these people are going to be taken care of with lodging and feeding. But the man who has had his hands and feet cut off, what provisions have been made for [him]?"[75]

A few, however, dismissed the Court entirely. "I wish the war crimes tribunal had not come in," commented Marie Barnett. "I was one of the few MPs [serving from 1996 to 2002] who said we should give the TRC a chance to work." She added, "If some of that money could have been used to educate people, to make them self-reliant, to give them some form of empowerment, I think we would be consolidating the peace."[76] Tom Barnett agreed: "I would have been much more content with leaving things at the TRC level, with no prosecutions, because there are many out there who were equally responsible, many more than the three who have now been convicted. We cannot say with all sincerity they were the most responsible. And the judgment is going to affect not only them as individuals but their families as well. For me the Special Court has raised more questions than answers to our process."[77] Dove also expressed the view that the "TRC was enough."[78]

Others were more supportive, with Large noting, "they are both valuable."[79] The predominant view, however, was that the TRC was the more important institution and would leave a greater legacy. "I cannot emphasize justice over reconciliation," said Fornah. "If I forgive you, I see no reason why I should want punishment for you. I would leave that with the Lord to do. When you come to the secular, the philosophy is 'no peace without justice.' I beg to differ." He continued, "If the causes of the war are not addressed, even if you punish those people, and you continue to have the problems that created the war, there is a possibility of a re-occurrence."[80]

Marah believed sin should not go unpunished, "but in the case of Sierra Leone, with all the atrocities that have been committed, we have to be careful how we make that portion of scripture practical. If we chop all the hands off of those who used their hands to chop off hands, then everyone becomes an amputee." He believed the guilt in the person's heart may be punishment enough.[81]

Humper recognized the value of both institutions, saying, "Reconciliation for the many is essential. Justice for the few is essential." However, he believed that Sierra Leone became a "laboratory" for the international community, which "forsook the many for the few." He criticized the way budgets were slashed for the TRC, while the Special Court was relatively well funded. According to the bishop, when the idea of a truth commission began, international agencies were supportive, but once the Special Court was established, international interest declined.[82]

Simbo noted that the decision to indict Norman was widely condemned because he was seen by many Sierra Leoneans as a national hero, who had fought on the side of the government. This hurt the reputation of the Special Court in people's minds. "Here was a good man who stood up to the rebels," Simbo pointed out. "Wrong is wrong. Kamajors killed people indiscriminately, and they should answer for it. But almost everything I heard said that's ungratefulness, having him tried, when all he did was stand up to the rebels when even the military was running away. I think people would have thought the Special Court was doing a better job if it hadn't gone after Norman."[83]

Foday-Khabenje was especially critical of the fact that Norman was prosecuted but not UNAMSIL or ECOWAS soldiers. "If there was any direct molestation during the war, it was ECOWAS. But there was not one indictment against ECOWAS or UNAMSIL. These people committed atrocities. There's nothing like a clean war." He noted that all the major leaders—Foday Sankoh, Johnny Paul Koroma, and Sam Bockerie—were dead, adding, "I would have been up there [watching] if Sankoh had been convicted!"[84] Simbo felt it was a boost to the reputation of the Court when it got its hands on Charles Taylor. "That's the one point everybody agree[d] on: They want[ed] Charles Taylor prosecuted."[85]

The decision of the Special Court not to allow Norman to speak before the TRC was also criticized. "For me, personally, the TRC is incomplete without the stories of some key people. It would have been good for Hinga Norman to tell his side of the story," opined Nabieu. "He was not allowed. So it's unfinished business."[86]

While most of the religious leaders felt the TRC would have the greater legacy, many added this caveat: *if the recommendations of the TRC are implemented.*[87] A minority view was that the Special Court would have the greater legacy. For Abdul Karim Koroma, the Court "definitely will have the greater impact," but he would have preferred to see more perpetrators prosecuted in local courts rather than in the Special Court: "For me, justice should have been meted out in the local courts. They could have saved a lot of time and money."[88]

CONTEMPORANEOUS INSTITUTIONS

Many saw the difficulties of having a court and truth commission at the same time. Most believed that it explained why only a small number of perpetrators came forward to confess during the TRC hearings (the TRC final report stated that just 1% of testimonies gathered were from perpetrators). As Large pointed out, "If they confess in public, then the Special Court would pick them up. They are afraid to come out."[89] Fornah observed, "When the first prosecutor of the Special Court said 'I will go wherever the evidence leads me,' people feared if they came to the Truth Commission and told what they did, they were afraid that information would go to the Special Court, and be the basis for their arrest and indictment."[90] There was confusion about the meaning of "those who bear the greatest responsibility." Some wondered if they had committed egregious acts, like amputations, might not they be included among "those who bear the greatest responsibility" and be indicted by the Special Court?[91]

"It is my view," said Lynch, "that you cannot have a properly functioning TRC alongside the Special Court. Some of these [perpetrators] would have testified." There was confusion, he believed, since the "Special Court [was] saying one thing and the TRC [was] saying another thing. The Special Court [was] about punishing. The TRC [was] about reconciling."[92] But Bishop Biguzzi was not convinced that more perpetrators would have come forward if the Special Court had not been held at the same time because "I think anybody could testify privately."[93] Desay believed that the fear preventing perpetrators from speaking at the TRC was not because they feared being indicted by the Special Court but because they were afraid of retaliation from the families of the victims. Even if the victim might forgive, "the family behind, the children, may not."[94]

While some leaders, such as Large, believed prosecutions should have gone first, most felt the Special Court should have waited until the TRC process had come to an end. "I'm pretty sure the government and UN could have waited for eighteen months [for the TRC to do its work]," commented Fornah, adding, "I had a good number [of perpetrators] come to me and say, 'Look, Reverend, I regret I did not come to the Truth Commission. Honestly, I was afraid I would be jailed because of the Special Court. I really regret that. I wish I had the opportunity.'"[95] Lynch also believed the TRC should have gone first, then the trials, since "rebel leaders are not difficult to locate."[96] When he first heard about the Special Court, Marah said, "I thought, the timing [was] too early. That is the first thing I said. Because with no doubt it sent shock waves across the minds of people."[97]

COMMISSION'S RECOMMENDATIONS

Very few leaders knew what the actual recommendations of the TRC were. This is attributed to the fact that so few copies of the final report were published—just one thousand according to Humper[98]—but I noticed more awareness of the recommendations in summer 2007 than in 2006. (In July 2007, the IRC held workshops across the country on the topic of the recommendations.) Lynch noted that very few people know about the report's recommendations: "How far have those recommendations been followed? Things are happening, but we are not informed. We still don't know the government's stand on what was recommended."[99]

Many felt the government was doing what it could. Catholic priest Paul Sandi believed that the government "with so many problems is swamped trying to do this and that."[100] Speck expressed an often heard statement: "I want to believe that whatever was done was done in good faith."[101] Conteh opined, "I am sure some effort was done by government to implement these short term recommendations, though not perhaps to the expectation of the Commission or the public."[102] And Sillah echoed, "I'm sure the government is doing something."[103] "To be fair," suggested Foday-Khabenje, "it's not that the government is not doing anything. They have probably done some things but [have] not necessarily said, 'we are doing this because of the recommendations of the TRC.'"[104] Desay insisted the government was helping the amputees: "I believe the government is taking care of them. They have an association. Those who are begging, it is so pathetic. I don't know whether government is responsible for their feeding. That's the main reason for their begging. I believe the government is trying."[105] Almost everyone agreed with Desay that implementing the recommendations would "take time."[106]

Some pointed to limited resources as the major reason for the government's inaction: "When we talk about [helping the] amputees, the money is not there. How can the fund be established if somebody doesn't put something in it? Government will try hard, but I don't think government is really in the [financial] position."[107]

A few, however, were highly critical of the lack of implementation by the government. Bishop Tom Barnett said, "Putting those recommendations through is the crux of the matter. And a lot has yet to be done. A lot of victims feel aggrieved, unattended to. Quite a number of the recommendations of the TRC regarding the victims have yet to be implemented. I have heard quite a few complaints that the perpetrators seem to have a better deal, whereas programs for the victims have not yet been done. That needs to be pursued much more vigorously, attending to the victims."[108] Sillah, for one, disagreed: "I don't believe perpetrators have gotten more than victims. I don't feel they [victims] are left out."[109] But Foday-Khabenje's view was similar to Barnett's: "Mind you, while the TRC was going on, the perpetrators were being compensated with DDR packages, training, and so on, and the victims expected some reparations as well, some benefits. And that is not happening!"[110]

Leaders voiced special concern for the needs of youth, raped women, and amputees. For Pentecostal pastor Tamba Koroma, "The youth area is very important. According to the report, because the youth were left out by previous governments, they were not catered to and because of unemployment—that's why these boys and girls went into the bush to create havoc."[111] Bangura agreed that taking care of the youth is an important recommendation: "Knowing that the youth were involved, one of the recommendations is to engage the young people in meaningful activities, so that in the future they cannot allow themselves to be used."[112] Randall worried about young former combatants: "People don't think about after the war, what happens to these boys? They're young with no skills, and you give them guns. After the war, it still remains in their head. Personally, I am worried about it. You see a lot of street boys not going to school, begging and pickpocketing."[113] Marie Barnett cited women and girls as an especially vulnerable group and argued that compensation should have been paid to women affected by the war and safe homes constructed where women could run from abusive situations.[114]

"One major thing we were looking to see is whether the government was serious about implementation of the War Victims Fund," Fornah remarked. "And since that fund has not been established, when I look at that, I would rate the government at zero in terms of implementing the report."[115] He added that the government points to schools and clinics it has set up, "But for me, I don't see that as an implementation of the Truth and Reconciliation Commission report. Those were projects approved by the World Bank and the African Development Bank for the reconstruction of Sierra Leone after the war."[116] Abdul Karim Koroma concurred: "The government has done nothing. The victims have seen nothing. So they feel it was useless. I am pronouncing the TRC useless! You don't set up a TRC and then not follow up on the recommendations."[117]

ON CORRUPTION

Given that endemic corruption was cited by the TRC as one of the major causes of the war, it is perhaps surprising that the religious leaders did not see this as a major issue for the religious community. Paul Khazili of the National Christian Evangelical Mission said, "The churches are not preaching about corruption. They are preaching about salvation."[118] And Abdul Karim Koroma expressed the same view about the mosques: "The mosques are not against corruption. They are more reticent to speak out than the churches. A lot of the imams are not Western-trained people. A lot of our Muslims are trained in Egypt and Saudi Arabia, where apart from Egypt teachers are not critical of the government. Who will speak out against a state? Those in Christian organizations have been to university, are very critical, and take that to the pulpit. While the Quran does say something about corruption—leaders who betray the trust of the people—the message is watered down here. On Friday people are preaching the same old 'Let God give us the leaders we deserve.'"[119]

Koroma believed that those who were vocal as preachers had been silenced in the past by being given positions on commissions and advisory boards that brought them closer to the political leadership. Speaking of his colleague (and political adversary) Abu Bakarr Conteh's decision to serve on the advisory board of the Anti-Corruption Commission, he insisted, "There's no way he can end corruption; he shouldn't have taken the position."[120] Samuels commented that the Anti-Corruption Commission is "a toothless dog,"[121] and Nabieu agreed that only when it starts to go after people in high places—which it had not, in his opinion—could he say it was really fighting corruption.[122]

Simbo believed that religious leaders were "not taking advantage of the respect and position they're given by speaking out on national issues, like corruption. I think somewhere along the line, what happened is church leaders themselves got corrupted by being close to power, they were given things, and that silenced them." (Nevertheless, he felt it was a good thing for Moses Khanu, a founding member of the IRC, to accept a position on the Human Rights Commission: "I think those are the places we should be.")[123] For Dove, the problem with the Anti-Corruption Commission was that the government, controlling it, interferes with its work. But he felt there was nothing wrong with religious personnel being involved in commissions. "They should be the light, provided they know why they're there."[124]

Conteh considered the source of corruption to be at the level of the family rather than the government: "For me, the problems stem from the home, and then people blame institutions. For a well-refined home that knows the truth, that knows the Creator, that knows what is expected by the Maker, a home that practices accountability, a home that practices transparency, when they go out, however external influences may be strong, it will be difficult for those from that home to be overrun entirely. Transparency, accountability, justice, and honesty are developed in society in the home."[125]

Salia also seemed uncomfortable about the church speaking out against government corruption, noting, "There's corruption in every society." He argued the church has to "start working to clean our own house first before we can get the speck out of the others' eyes."[126] Although recognizing that corruption "was one of the reasons for the war," Kampbell nevertheless felt the church "must try to address this thing more in our own settings and within our target communities. You can't preach what you don't practice."[127] Foday-Khabenje ventured that even if corrupt ministers and officials could be removed and replaced, "It would be the same thing. There are some systemic problems we need to address and change."[128] Large expressed one of the strongest rebukes of religious institutions for not preaching forcefully against corruption: "Churches and mosques should be very active in talking against corruption," he said. "These government officials are either Muslims or Christians, going to church or mosque. We know that. The church should be in the position to tell someone to his face what you are doing is evil. Whether that person is contributing a lot to the church, it is blood money. You are involved in blood diamonds."[129]

SELF-CRITICISM OF THE RELIGIOUS COMMUNITY

Nabieu lamented, "We have yet to see that the recommendations are carried out. I will also say that we on the religious side have failed also. We have done so much in trying to accomplish the [peace] process, but after the process we have not been able to sit down and have a proper reflection on the recommendations we can use to pressure the government. I also believe at this point reconciliation just in words is not enough. These should be accompanied by action, things that would be of benefit to the people. I think government will only do the things [necessary] when there is a pressure group. The pressure group is the religious people."[130] Tamba Koroma believed that the church should speak for the voiceless, and it is better positioned than other actors in civil society to push the government on the recommendations. "They're not doing much, the civil society. They are joining the government. This is bad."[131]

Konteh also was critical of the religious community's role in not pushing the government forcefully enough. The reason for this, he believed, was that many religious leaders, especially those from the evangelical wing, felt that Christians should only pray and forget about politics: "When I was a young boy, we'd hear the Council of Churches making pronouncements against the government. That is not so now."[132]

Marah agreed that it was partly the fault of the religious communities that the government has not moved forward with the recommendations: "What I'm saying is religious leaders could have done something, but some of them are involved with the government. Some might be playing government roles, which is making it difficult." He believed there are divisions within the faith community, which make it incapable of speaking with one voice. He also added that the existence of the Special Court has gotten the government off the hook: "Who is going to set up anything now while the Special Court is going on?"[133]

Fornah believed too that the faith community is not playing a strong advocacy role because they have taken partisan sides. "Most key religious leaders who should have been speaking as prophets of old have taken sides with political parties. So when you want to talk about issues of national importance, when it has to do with a political party they belong to, and it will be negative, they aren't ready to talk." He reasoned that, "The government has used the principle of divide and rule with clerics. Appointed to special commissions, they now think, 'I can't bite the hand that feeds me.' Because of that, they can't be players and referees at the same time!" He concluded, "Unless we take the neutral position and speak like prophets of old, who said, 'Thus sayeth the Lord,' we won't be proactive and contribute to democracy."[134]

Khanu lamented that those who had been courageous enough to talk to the rebels were now silent. He attributed this in part to their being given government appointments "and so they cease coming to IRC, cease even giving us information."[135]

Abdul Karim Koroma was candid: "Our organization [IRC] is not doing anything. We were involved during the war in going into the jungle in efforts to get these rebels out of the bush. We helped to talk to them, and some became converts. When the war ended, everyone said, 'I better protect myself.' We played quite a role in the past, but postconflict we have not been very engaged."[136] Biguzzi also noted that the IRC had lost its focus after the war,[137] while Bangura called for a more prophetic role for the churches: "One thing we have come to realize is that for many years the church has been silent. If the church had acted like a proper church, saying no matter what the consequences, we have to say the truth, we could have done more. But the church has been silent." Bangura attributed this silence to political and regional loyalties. A religious leader from the south or east who is Mende might not speak out against the SLPP, and one from the north, who is Limba or Temne, might not speak out against the APC.[138] Tom Barnett attributed the silence of the churches on public policies to the colonial heritage: "When Christianity was introduced by missionaries, they endeavored to draw a strict line between religion and the secular world. We have cared more about individual salvation and individual morality than in using the church as an agent of transformation in the community. But that is now changing with the IRC. The line is gradually being narrowed. It's still there, but it has narrowed now."[139]

THEOLOGICAL INSIGHTS

These religious leaders—both Christians and Muslims—expressed a belief in the importance of reconciliation and maintained the conviction that their religions had something to contribute to this process. Since reconciliation is a major theme in most religions, this was not surprising. Likewise, their support for the TRC was predictable given that truth and confession as precursors to reconciliation are recurring themes in both Christianity and Islam.[140] Religion scholar Marc Gopin agrees that forgiveness as a means of healing relationships and solving human conflicts is an age-old practice that appears in many religious traditions.[141]

For Christians, forgiveness and reconciliation are interrelated. God was in Christ, reconciling the world to Himself. Christ gave his life to atone for mankind's sins, which were thus forgiven by God. For Christians, then, to forgive is to participate in God's act of forgiveness in Christ. Because we are forgiven by God, God's children are likewise urged to forgive their enemies and welcome sinners back into the family of God. Jesus is the model for Christians, who from the cross urged his Father, "Forgive them for they know not what they do."[142] The biblical injunction—as many of the Christian leaders reminded me—is not to forgive seven times but, as Jesus told Peter, seven times seventy, that is, infinitely.[143] The parable of the unforgiving servant who had been forgiven by his master but himself refused to forgive a fellow servant highlights the importance of this duty.[144]

Islam too values forgiveness. Forgiveness is mentioned in no fewer than twenty-three verses in the Quran and is a prized virtue in Islam, greater even than justice.[145] In more than one hundred verses, God is portrayed as *Ghaffaar*, the All Forgiving.[146] In addition to the focus on divine forgiveness, which is contingent on human repentance, there is also an emphasis on bilateral forgiveness. More than sixty verses speak of *taba*, turning toward someone in penance. Although people have the right to repay evil for evil, and there is no blame for those who cannot forgive, those who forgive and reconcile have the greatest reward from Allah. According to the Prophet, "God fills with peace and faith the heart of one who swallows his anger, even though he is in a position to give vent to it."[147] The Prophet himself serves as the exemplar of forgiveness, as he chose to forgive the Meccans who had sorely persecuted him. He implored Allah, "Forgive them, Lord, for they know not what they do."[148] Mohammed, like Jesus in the Sermon on the Mount, beseeches his followers to first seek forgiveness from the persons they have wronged before turning to God.[149]

While forgiveness is important in Muslim teaching, Christianity's doctrine of forgiveness is more radical.[150] For some (but not all) Christians, forgiveness is required even in the absence of an apology or contrition (this was confirmed in my interviews with Brainard, Barnett, Dove, Humper, Simbo, Konteh, Fornah, Kampbell, and Marah). For other Christians, and for all Muslims, forgiveness requires an acknowledgment from the wrongdoer. Acknowledgment in Islam, according to Mohammed Abu-Nimer, is the first step—a "turn to God," an act of asking forgiveness (*ghufran*)—and requires humbling oneself.[151] John de Gruchy explains that Islam requires genuine sorrow for the sin committed, the resolve not to commit it again, and due reparation for the injustice.[152]

What surprised me is that Christian leaders often stated that Muslims were not very forgiving, asserting that Muslims believed in "an eye for an eye." Christian leaders assumed that Muslims would be more in favor of punishment through a tribunal than forgiveness through a truth and reconciliation commission, but I did not find this to be the case. Although the Christian respondents seemed unaware of Islamic teachings on punishment, believing that a bad act always requires the meting out of an equivalent punishment, that is not the correct view of Islam, argues scholar Daniel Philpott. Of the three categories of crimes—Hudud, Qisas, and T'azir—only Hudud carries a specific punishment for a specific crime (amputation for theft, death by stoning for adultery, and so forth). Qisas, while covering serious crimes like murder and assault, nevertheless permits a surviving relative or victim to choose "remission," whereby the offender pays compensation. Philpott writes, "Forgiveness and mercy, then, are combined with reparation for the victim's family that function as a punishment for the offender, a punishment that he is called to accept through remorse and repentance."[153] T'azir covers less serious crimes that do not carry mandatory sentences and is also restorative, as it seeks mainly to "chastise" the offender in order to rehabilitate him. By repenting of the crime, the offender can reduce or abolish the sentence.[154]

Most respondents of both faiths said each institution had its own purpose, but they were often critical of aspects of the Special Court, including the amount of money spent, the choice of the defendants, the inability of the Court to deal with the causes of the war, and the fact that the Court was held while the TRC was operating. Although the IRC had officially supported both the TRC and the Special Court, and had used its clout to sensitize people to their work, the secretary general in his 2003 report expressed doubts about having two concurrent transitional justice institutions: "It is however of great concern that while many hold the view that the peace is still fragile, the TRC and the Special Court are running concurrently. This has consequence on the peace process."[155]

Not just reconciliation but also justice (*'adl*) is a key concept in Islam, as evidenced by the over two hundred commands against injustice and the no less than one hundred passages urging justice in the Quran.[156] However, justice is interpreted in a broader sense than merely punitive justice or punishment. Khadduri notes that *'adl* in Arabic means "right relationship."[157] Accordingly, retribution tempered with pardon leads to restoration in the Muslim community. Mercy is, therefore, a behavior expected of Muslims, and one of the most frequently cited attributes of Allah.[158] The importance of mercy is highlighted in the Prophet's response to his followers, who urged him to invoke the wrath of God on the Meccans for their persecution of Muslims. He responded, "I have not been sent to curse anyone but to be a source of *rahmah* [compassion and mercy] to all."[159] Mercy comes into play also in Islam's injunction to punish in moderation in order to bring about right relationships. Carol LaHurd points out that Mohammed granted a general amnesty to his former opponents, when he could have executed them.[160]

Sierra Leonean Islamic scholar Saeed G. Kalokoh explains that for the wronged, "The most he can do is to demand equal redress, i.e., a harm equivalent to the harm done to him. . . . But the ideal mode is not to slake his thirst for vengeance, but to follow better ways leading to the reform of the offender or his reconciliation. One can take steps to prevent repetition, by physical or moral means; the best moral means would be to turn hatred into friendship by forgiveness and love."[161] Still, forgiveness does not preclude punishment: "Even when the injured one forgives, the State or Ruler is competent to take such action as is necessary for the preservation of law and order in Society. For crime has a bearing that goes beyond the interests of the person injured: the community is affected."[162]

Christianity too recognizes that God's judgment can be meted out through the arm of the state. Willa Boesak argues that the wrath of the marginalized reflects the wrath of God, and the evildoer should be punished.[163] However, theologian Wolfram Kistner counters that there are two theological approaches to justice and reconciliation, only one of which (Boesak's approach) calls for atonement through the punishment of evildoers in a court of law, which becomes God's rightful avenger. The other approach is to make the decision on whether to punish on the basis of considerations of how healing and reconciliation would best be promoted in the lives of both the victim and offender.[164] The better option may be through a court of law, where the perpetrator would be punished so that he may learn and change, making reconciliation possible.[165] Or it may be that renouncing punishment would be most likely to promote reconciliation between offenders and victims.

In any case, despite there being a place for punishment in both Christianity and Islam, reconciliation is usually prioritized over punitive justice. And both religions conceptualize justice more broadly than strictly as punishment or law and order. In times of political transition, in particular, when a nation is moving away from an era of massive violations of human rights, a restorative approach that focuses on the healing of victims and the restoration of right relationships may be more salient than a punitive approach that targets offenders without tending to the needs of the victims or the community at large.

The call to justice in the Quran is the call to establish a just social order by redressing social injustices in the community and rejecting oppression at both the interpersonal and structural levels.[166] (Islam's early rapid growth is attributed to its commitment to empower the weak.)[167] According to Abu-Nimer, acts of social and economic justice are so important in Islam that they are elevated to the practice of worship.[168] Not only Islam but also Christianity endorse a broad view of justice that is at odds with the narrow legal interpretation of mere punishment. Trials are about individual culpability, and not the iniquities of an unjust system that calls out for transformation. Both the prophets of the Old Testament and Jesus in the New Testament espouse a theology of liberation that places God solidly on the side of the poor and oppressed over and against the powerful and mighty. For many Christian theologians and Islamic scholars, justice means right relationships, not only on an individual level but also in terms of the collective. For genuine reconciliation to take root among enemies requires changing unjust relationships at the structural level. Robert J. Schreiter argues that peaceful and just relations cannot exist within those structures that provoke, promote, and sustain violence.[169] Both of these world faiths, then, support the notion of reparations, which is a collective form of penance or restorative justice in action.[170]

In short, both Christianity and Islam have developed ideas that model peace-related values, including empathy, love for strangers, gestures of forgiveness, repentance, acknowledgment of past errors as a means for reconciliation, and the drive for social justice during times of transition.[171] These religious values—more so than the universal norms expressed in documents such as the Universal Declaration of Human Rights or international law—may have more appeal to religious leaders and their followers. They may also give an edge to approaches like a truth commission or other restorative approaches, for example, reparations or rituals that aim at reconciliation among enemies, over retributive approaches such as a tribunal that aims to punish a few ringleaders. The choice to forego trials and punishment—the cornerstones of Western notions of what are appropriate responses in the aftermath of atrocities—may spring from the "belief that there is a more-than-human agent, who is able and who intends to do justice beyond this world of space and time," thus freeing theists "to accept the limits of such justice as can be done here and now without compromising injustice."[172]

I turn in the following chapter to an examination of the traditional methods of conflict resolution practiced by the various ethnic groups in Sierra Leone, with a view to assessing their compatibility with the restorative justice ethos inherent in Christianity and Islam.

CHAPTER 6

TRADITIONAL RECONCILIATION PRACTICES

EXAMPLES OF AFRICAN INDIGENOUS METHODS

In addition to its requirement that the Commission seek assistance from clerics, the TRC Act directed it to reach out to traditional leaders in tacit acknowledgment that religion and tradition both provide deep resources in support of healing and reconciliation.[1] There was no dearth of precedents on the continent, where tradition had been employed as a means of conflict resolution.

The example of gacaca, a community-based justice system in Rwanda, is instructive.[2] The system, which had existed in some form since precolonial times, was resurrected and modified by the Tutsi-dominated government in 2001, to deal with the backlog of genocide suspects who had been languishing in prisons since 1994.[3] In traditional gacaca, the offender was brought before the community's elders to mediate infractions such as boundary, property, livestock, or inheritance disputes.[4] Ideally, the perpetrator would confess and beg for forgiveness, which would be granted, and the elders would determine appropriate compensation for the victim. This would be followed by a shared meal or drinks, usually provided by the offender, to symbolize the fact that reconciliation had occurred.[5]

Some (mostly Western) observers criticize the government of Rwanda for "inventing tradition" for crimes that gacaca historically had never addressed, questioning if modern gacaca was an appropriate forum for dealing with very serious crimes. They wonder whether indigenous conflict resolution methods can be appropriate vehicles of justice in the aftermath of gross human rights abuses and crimes against humanity.[6] They also fault gacaca for its lack of due process protections for defendants (no lawyers accompany suspects) and for sidelining legal professionals in favor of the community. (While there were elected judges who handed down the decisions, they were laypersons with six days of training, who relied on the community, the general assembly, to debate the issues.)

In addition to eliciting the truth about what happened, gacaca hearings offered both victims and perpetrators, the latter of whom were offered reduced prison sentences for a guilty plea, a space to talk about what had happened. Unlike in a conventional legal system, in a gacaca forum victims could directly question the suspect. Indeed, the entire community engaged in the dialogue, with the judges serving as mediators and final arbiters in a process that had reconciliation as the end goal.

In traditional gacaca, the reintegration of the offender into the community through apology and reparation, rather than retribution, was the priority in order to repair the social damage. Offenders were not sentenced to prison;[7] instead they would be allowed to regain their social standing in the community, once they had confessed and demonstrated a willingness to make the victims whole. Obviously, imposing prison sentences on the guilty departed from traditional gacaca, which led one critic to question modern gacaca's pretension to be restorative and to accuse it of being retributive at its core.[8]

Gacaca was also faulted for being a form of victor's justice, since cases were heard only against Hutu accused of acts during the genocide and not against Tutsi who were responsible for revenge killings against Hutu.[9] One may genuinely wonder how failing to deal with crimes of one ethnic group—which happens to be a minority in power—can lead to reconciliation. Moreover, unlike in the days of old, when gacaca was voluntary and did not involve political authorities, in modern gacaca villagers were required under threat of fine or imprisonment to attend hearings weekly to meet the requisite quorum, leading one critic to label it "unpopular participatory justice."[10]

In the face of these criticisms that gacaca was a "state-driven, state-owned, and top-down process with people abiding by the principles, mechanisms and discourses laid out for them,"[11] Clark has maintained that critics have overstated the degree of state coercion in the process.[12] He argued that government interference was in fact an uncommon occurrence and mostly happened in areas close to Kigali.[13] Overwhelmingly, Rwandans viewed themselves, and not the government, as the driving force behind gacaca, and surveys demonstrated enthusiasm and high support for the process.[14] Clark's extensive fieldwork uncovered the public's ability to shape gacaca in its own image to reflect its own goals, especially fulfilling their emotional and psychological needs, and it was often informed by people's religious beliefs,[15] emphasizing grace, mercy, atonement, and forgiveness.[16]

Tradition as a vehicle to promote reconciliation has been observed in Mozambique as well. Victor Igreja describes the rituals he witnessed in central Mozambique many years after the civil war between Frelimo and Renamo concluded in 1992. In these a *gamba* spirit, presenting himself as a dead victim, possessed the body of a survivor and the *gamba* healer reenacted war events while the spirit disclosed what happened to him or her, leading to acknowledgment and confession from the survivor and family for their wartime behaviors. Anyone who had suffered from the war could access *gamba* to give voice to his or her past trauma. Igreja believes that the strategy of amnesia implicit in the peace accord (which called neither for trials nor for a truth commission) indicated a complete lack of concern by state leaders for survivors who lived in remote areas, and whose "painful memories of violence and abuse did not fade away simply because of the authorities' unwillingness to address them officially."[17]

His position is at odds with the earlier assessment of anthropologist Alcinda Honwana, who argued that it was culturally inappropriate to vocalize what had happened during the war, since that would open the door for harmful spirits to penetrate the community. She asserted that talking about traumatic experiences does not help survivors come to terms with their distress.[18] Honwana, along with Carolyn Nordstrom, reported on the phenomenon of nonverbal rituals, performed by traditional healers, called *curandeiros*. These addressed the needs of perpetrator and victim alike to "remove the war," to symbolically break with the past, without actually giving voice to the harm done or blaming individuals.[19]

For a returning soldier, the *curandeiro* conducted a ceremony involving a series of symbolic procedures aimed at cutting his link to the past. Often this involved burning his military clothes and splashing the former fighter with water mixed with the leaves of the mululua tree.[20] Having thus placated the spirits of those killed, the former warrior was able to return to the community, where he was accepted even by the victims' relatives.[21] Similar community-based processes for victims were witnessed by Nordstrom, who describes a purification ceremony for a rape victim that included a ceremonial bath, accompanied by songs and stories about healing, and dressing the victim in specially prepared clothing. The ceremony concluded with a feast.[22]

Northern Uganda provides yet another example of traditional rituals being used to address crimes, in this case those committed during the twenty-five-year reign of terror by the Lord's Resistance Army (LRA) against the Acholi people. *Mato oput* involved mediation by elders to elicit confession and compensation. On acknowledgment of wrongdoing, the killer paid blood money to the family of the deceased to compensate for their loss; this was followed by a rite of reconciliation. A concoction of alcohol and the bitter extract from the roots of the oput tree were drunk from a single vessel by the killer and the deceased's family to wash away the evil. This was followed by the exchange of a ram's head, given to the family by the killer, with a goat's head, given to the killer by the deceased's kin. The ritual culminated in a shared meal, traditionally a bull, also provided by the killer.[23]

Another Ugandan ritual was *nyouo tong gweno* or "stepping on the egg," which was traditionally performed to welcome home someone who had been away for an extended time or had left after quarreling with the community. A raw egg was crushed underfoot, allowing the evil and violence to be transferred into the purity and innocence of the egg.[24] The idea here was that if the perpetrator were not cleansed, the spirits would bring harm to the entire community.[25]

A third ritual, *gumo tong* or "bending of the spears," required the conflicting parties to vow to end hostilities. Warring factions brought their weapons together, where they were bent or destroyed, rendering them unusable.[26] These northern Ugandan rituals are examples of a restorative justice approach in that they combine the elements of truth, accountability, compensation, and restoration of relationships, prioritizing reconciliation over justice.[27]

Not surprisingly, the restorative approach is at odds with Western preferences for justice through prosecutions. The international community and the Ugandan state both favored punishment, although they were divided on the proper locale, with the former preferring the International Criminal Court and the latter its own courts.[28] Yet they were united in their desire to punish just one side in the conflict, the LRA. Both the LRA and government forces (the National Resistance Army and the Uganda Peoples Defense Force) committed offenses resulting in loss of civilian lives and forced displacement, but punishment targeted one side alone.

Did all Acholi actually prefer traditional approaches over prosecution? The evidence is mixed. Although the leaders of the Acholi people asked the International Criminal Court to withdraw its arrest warrants against the LRA leaders, and to let Ugandans handle crimes through these traditional methods, a poll in 2005 indicated that people were ambivalent. A majority believed that perpetrators should be prosecuted, but paradoxically a majority also supported amnesty.[29] This ambivalence was reflected in a 2007 survey as well: of those polled, 59% said the LRA leaders should be tried and 55% believed the Uganda Peoples Defense Force should also be tried. But a majority of respondents also believed that amnesty should be granted, and fully half of those surveyed believed traditional methods *were* important mechanisms for the reintegration of perpetrators.[30]

Nevertheless, Tim Allen is skeptical about the use of these rituals as a way of dealing with crimes committed by the Lord's Resistance

Army, speculating that it sent the signal that "northern Ugandans need their own special justice measures, because they are not yet ready for modern ones."[31] For one thing he has argued they represented a convergence of interests between certain foreign humanitarian organizations with older Acholi men—both elders and churchmen—who wanted to reinforce their waning power with international support. Also, he notes that the revived rituals were unlike the traditional ones that involved a commitment to pay compensation.[32]

Critics believe there is a danger of appropriating "tradition" in a way that may trivialize serious acts. A perception may develop that certain people (i.e., Africans) get traditional cleansing rites and other rituals, while others (Westerners) get justice in terms of punishment of offenders. Comfort Ero argues that "It is . . . discriminatory to claim that African victims do not deserve to seek criminal accountability for serious international crimes with standing equal to that of other victims of grave abuse."[33] While this is certainly a widely held view in human rights and international law circles, it is not necessarily one endorsed by those who have survived the conflicts in Rwanda, Mozambique, and Uganda, and who generally support reconciliation through ritual. The people of Sierra Leone likewise have responded to a process of reconciliation that is more compatible with their traditional practices.

COMMISSIONING TRADITION

With these examples in mind, let us now consider the use of tradition in promoting reconciliation in Sierra Leone after the war. The United Nations High Commissioner for Human Rights, the Sierra Leone TRC's main funder, commissioned a report by the local NGO Manifesto 99 to examine the ways in which indigenous methods of conflict resolution could be adopted by the TRC. However, other than the weekly reconciliation ceremony at the conclusion of the district hearings, which was facilitated by religious and traditional leaders, little evidence shows that the TRC relied on tradition in its work. Mamoh Taziff Koroma, author of the Manifesto 99 study, said that instead of using the recommendation in his report to adopt local traditions, the TRC decided to "go another route."[34] Historian and TRC research director Joe Alie speculates that the TRC may have decided that traditional methods were too "backward" or "primitive" to be used.[35]

A partial explanation for the lack of traditional methods was the impact of the war itself on culture. The war occasioned mass movements of people from their homes in rural areas to either larger towns or camps for displaced persons, where adhering to cultural practices was difficult. Traditional leaders, the repositories of culture and tradition, were often targeted by the rebels, since they were viewed as part of the corrupt (and age hierarchical) system the insurgents were fighting to overthrow.

In addition, rebels defiled secret places in the bush where secret societies met, and they destroyed shrines and ceremonial objects. According to Elisabeth Hoffman, places of cultural significance, such as the sacred rock where villagers of Bormaru would gather to communicate with their ancestors, had not been visited since the war and were overgrown by the bush. In Kpaingbankordu, outside of Koindu, a structure in the village referred to as the "little house," where the spirits of the ancestors live and where people traditionally gather to resolve problems, had not been used in that way since the war. Throughout the country, special sites had been lost. Hoffman writes, "These traditions and practices speak to the cultural and relational infrastructure that was fractured along with the destruction of physical infrastructure during the war."[36] Alie concurs that "The impact of the conflict was incalculable, since these elders and institutions, which were methodically destroyed, were crucial to the effective functioning of these mechanisms. They consequently lost their prestige and relevance."[37]

Another explanation for why traditional structures were not used is that too many chiefs and village elders were implicated in the conflict and could not be neutral.[38] Corrupt chiefs imposed excessive cash levies, allocated land unfairly, required forced labor, and punished dissenters. These practices led to marginalization and bitterness among people, who then became susceptible to the blandishments of the RUF, and were highlighted as being among the causes of the war.[39]

Chiefs, for instance, often had multiple wives, while young men could not afford even one, dooming them to the status of "youth" indefinitely and deepening their shame.[40] (For that reason, and to bypass the chiefs, the Red Cross after the war helped form alternative local conflict reconciliation committees.)[41] The TRC itself highlighted the unsavory role of the chiefs as the reason it chose not to rely on traditional structures:

> The Commission was surprised by the number of complaints about the violations committed by many of the Chiefs during the conflict, for which they neither as a group nor individually expressed remorse or offered any explanation to their communities. In reality, while the Commission had to rely on the chiefs as leaders of their communities, and had to work closely with them, the Commission was cognizant of the fact that many chiefs have been discredited by their failure to explain the roles they played during the war. It is for this reason that the Commission has not felt entirely comfortable relying on traditional structures to help foster reconciliation.[42]

(Elsewhere in the report, the TRC claims also not to have relied on the Manifesto 99 report because of its poor quality.)[43]

SIERRA LEONE'S RESTORATIVE CULTURE

Most of the fourteen official ethnic groups in Sierra Leone have practices in place to deal with conflict. Usually these procedures involve apportioning blame, followed by eliciting apologies from the guilty party, and then encouraging forgiveness from the victim. Manifesto 99's report noted that indigenous methods historically were employed for crimes such as theft, family disputes, and rape, but there are no traditional methods for dealing with arson and amputation, two of the major crimes that were committed during the civil war.[44] Likewise, crimes such as murder are usually sent to the formal court systems rather than being handled at the local level through traditional means.

This raises the issue of whether local methods can be adapted to deal with serious crimes like sexual slavery, murder, and amputations.

Like Rwanda, Uganda, and Mozambique, Sierra Leone does have a restorative tradition that exists throughout the country, notwithstanding the potential problems in using tradition to deal with serious crimes, the danger of elite manipulation, and the question of whether all people actually prefer these methods to prosecution. A strong restorative tradition that is "negotiatory, deliberative, reparative, and reconciliatory" abides in the ethnic cultures of Sierra Leone, according to Park.[45] For example, peace huts (or court barrays) are important places, where community members typically gather to mediate community conflicts. There, the paramount chief consults with the Council of Elders to resolve conflicts. In many cases a mediator is brought in, one that is selected from either the Council of Elders or from other community leaders and local authorities, such as the village or section chief. The victim and alleged culprit are interrogated by these respected mediators. The mediators encourage the truth from both parties and an apology from the culprit, which is followed by restitution from the wrongdoer to the victim. In some cases the process is done publicly, but the Limbas employ conciliation in the secrecy of the Gbangbany Society, which is open only to members; the elders then inform the community of their findings, and their recommendations are followed.

Admission of guilt, forgiveness, and restitution are often followed by purification of the wrongdoers to cleanse themselves of their sins, protect them from the wrath of God and the ancestors, and reunite them with society.[46] Serious crimes such as accidental killing require cleansing of the perpetrator; crimes such as rape or incest require cleansing of both perpetrator and victim.[47] For "violating a bush"— which often refers to having sexual intercourse on land that could be used for farming in the future, or that is considered sacred and is believed to be inhabited by the spirits of ancestors—the bush itself (along with the perpetrator) is cleansed in order to avert the anger of the spirits.[48] In most of the ethnic groups (with the exception of the Creoles), secret societies exist that conduct cleansing ceremonies.[49] In some cases, professionals conduct cleansing ceremonies that are funded by the family of the transgressor. The purification represents new birth and allows the community to accept the offender.[50]

These ceremonies are often accompanied by the pouring of libation to appease the spirits and ancestors, who otherwise would be angry at not only the perpetrator but the entire community.[51] Libation involves pouring palm wine onto the ground to appease the ancestors, the dead, and the gods (a technique used in the closing ceremonies after district hearings of the TRC). Appeasement also requires that the offender give tokens such as rice, oil, a chicken, and a small amount of money to the offended party.[52] Compensating the victim, which is often overlooked by both truth commissions and tribunals, to repair the damage is central. (In some instances, truth commissions make recommendations for reparations from the government to victims, but this severs the link between the perpetrator and victim and eliminates the former's responsibility to repair the damage to the latter.)

It is striking how, contrary to Rosalind Shaw's analysis of a culture of silence (discussed below), many cultural practices require the verbal acknowledgment and apology of the wrongdoer as a necessary step. Even among the Temne, the group that Shaw observed, the culprits joined by their families and close relatives must "plead for pardon" once they are found culpable. This is also true for the Kissi and Loko.[53]

Shaw, however, argues that Sierra Leone jumped onto the truth commission bandwagon because it had appealed to "a very strong vocal minority" within the Freetown-based NGO community, church leaders and their congregations, and educated youth. She maintains that the TRC was very unpopular with people at large because it was at odds with the culture of secrecy, the desire for ambiguity, and the preference for forgetting that are the hallmarks of Sierra Leonean culture.[54] She believes that epochs of violence—including the Atlantic slave trade, the nineteenth-century (legitimate) trade wars, and the imposition of colonial rule—are remembered "nondiscursively in the landscape, ritual practice and visionary experience but rarely in discursive verbal form."[55] While people spoke of the violence when it was happening, Shaw argues that once it stopped healing took place through the practice of social forgetting. For Shaw, speaking of the violence, especially in public, is viewed as encouraging its return.[56]

Shaw contends that local practices of healing and reconciliation do not include verbalized remembering, which is anathema to the people she studied and is part and parcel of "Western memory culture,"[57] which is rooted in the Enlightenment emphasis on language, in twentieth-century enthusiasm for psychotherapy (the talking cure), in treatment of posttraumatic stress disorder (through verbal processing), and in the response to the Holocaust (which includes witnessing to the event) so that it is not repeated (as expressed in the phrase "Never again"). She believes the West has valorized a particular form of memory, in which the verbal recounting of the past is empowering and redemptive.[58]

Shaw's conclusion about the inefficacy of public truth-telling for Sierra Leone was formed on the basis of ethnographic studies of observing, listening, and talking to people. Recall that public polling had revealed high public support for the TRC. Her explanation is to discount "quantitative survey techniques," because scientific studies are problematic "in contexts in which people are emerging from mass violence and have historical reasons not to trust any exercise that resembles official information gathering."[59] Perhaps if she had demonstrated that the polls were unrepresentative of nonelites because they did not include people outside Freetown, her arguments would have more credence, but she does not indicate that.

In a 2007 article, Shaw soundly rejects the validity of poll results—in particular the PRIDE poll indicating that ex-combatants were willing to speak before the TRC—saying that people who view the organization as a potential source of assistance answer the questions in the way they perceive the organization wants.[60] She recounts how the people in a village near Makeni refused to cooperate when the TRC came to town. After "the *headman and other leaders*" [emphasis mine] warned them about the dangers of speaking to TRC officials, only three out of one thousand residents gave statements.[61] This, however, says more about authority figures' views than about actual grassroots perceptions. Her explanation is that villagers wanted to protect the young former combatants, many of whom had enlisted to fight with the CDF but were later abducted by the rebels and forced to inflict cruelties on the people in their own villages and on those in neighboring ones, who were their friends' children. She also says the people were fearful of retribution from former combatants and the government, which is not an indication of cultural aversion to testifying at all but rather a pragmatic calculation about security.

Finally, Shaw argues that speaking out about what the former combatants had done would have disrupted their own practices of reconciliation and reintegration. She describes the practices this way: "Instead of talking to the TRC, the village went to church."[62] Surprisingly, she describes the special services in the Catholic and Wesleyan churches in which the former combatants *"confessed what they had done and were prayed over by the congregation, who asked God to give both ex-combatants and themselves 'cool hearts'"* [emphasis mine].[63] She apparently does not recognize the irony here, having lambasted the truth-telling process of the TRC. Her distinction is this: truth-telling before the TRC was part of a legalistic process, whereas truth-telling in the village was part of a church service. She nevertheless concludes that the villagers in their church services "demobilized their memories of war" by refusing "to reproduce past violence through words," though it's unclear how they confessed without speaking.[64] Finally, she dilutes her original dogma that verbal discourse is culturally inappropriate, softening it to an assessment of the proper *balancing* between truth-telling and ritual: while the TRC devoted *most* of the four days of hearings to eliciting truth-telling, with only a *brief* reconciliation ceremony at the week's conclusion, the emphasis was reversed in the church services, where "the confession was merely the initial phase of a ritual process that gave *proportionately more attention* to ritualized reintegration and reconciliation" [emphasis mine].[65] This is a far cry from saying it is harmful culturally for people to speak about past violence.

Like Shaw, Park stresses that reintegration involves "ongoing observation" of the newly reintegrated persons to ensure their "proper behavior," making the point that reintegration and reconciliation are not isolated events but are part of a process.[66] Shaw, I believe, has it partially right: changed behavior ("a cool heart") rather than empty words is paramount.[67] But Shaw believes that acknowledgment of guilt is not only unimportant but in fact dangerous, and a changed behavior is all that is necessary for victims to accept former combatants. She recounts a case from Mamamah, a large village near Freetown, where one former combatant had settled after the war. He had been abducted by the AFRC when he had fled from Koidu in Kono in the east. Given the choice to join or have his arm amputated, he chose the former. When the war ended, he went through a disarmament, demobilization, and reintegration program and worked for an NGO in Mamamah. When that project was completed, he asked the local authorities for permission to settle there. Shaw writes, "Pa Usman and other elders did not ask about Amadu's experiences during the war, but instead emphasized present and future moral behavior in the community."[68] Perhaps verbal acknowledgment was unnecessary in this particular case because Amadu had not committed any atrocities in Mamamah. He had not harmed these people during the war, so no apology was expected. Something more than evidence of changed behavior would probably have been required of him had he raped, killed, and looted in Mamamah. In most cultural practices in Sierra Leone, verbal acknowledgment is the first step and is a critical component.

In addition to restorative approaches that bring victim and perpetrator together in a community to confess and forgive, traditional practices include punitive measures that may be at odds with basic human rights. For instance, giving testimony is accompanied by swearing/oath-taking as a way of instilling fear to get the victim and perpetrator to be truthful. Under threat of being struck with disease or calamity, including in some cases harm to one's offspring (e.g., death, barrenness, or ill luck), the perpetrator usually confesses.[69] The fear of offending the ancestors through perjury makes oath-taking especially effective. (Whether this is seen as a human rights offense depends on whether one believes that the failure to tell the truth actually causes the punishment of disease, misfortune, or death to befall the perpetrator.)[70] In any event, the TRC eschewed swearing/cursing/oath-taking to induce confessions, even though the Manifesto 99 report recommended that the TRC consider this practice.

There are other punitive measures at odds with international standards of human rights, which require respecting the dignity of the individual. For committing robbery, for example, in addition to requiring payment of fines or returning the goods, the Mende, Kono, Sherbro, Loko, Koranko, Limba, and Yalunka disgrace the culprit by dressing him in rags, tying him to a rope, and having him dance around the village. Beating the culprit is practiced among the Madingo, Kono, and Koranko.[71]

Sierra Leone cultural traditions also privilege men. Procedures for dealing with marital conflict, for instance, tend to favor the husbands. For the Temne, the woman is told to apologize even in cases in which the husband is at fault.[72] The Fullah too require the wife to beg for forgiveness from her husband, irrespective of who is at fault.[73] Alie points out that wronging a husband is not considered in the best interest of the family, even if he is guilty. Instead, the elders say soothing words to the wife and privately rebuke the husband. The aim is to restore the marriage.[74] More problematic for the protection of women's rights is that among the Mandingo rape victims are compelled to marry their rapists.[75] Restorative justice should not be about restoring unjust prior gender relations. For Park, "Restorative justice measures that are insensitive to women's and girl's needs threaten to restore inequality rather than restore dignity."[76]

Tradition-based measures privilege older people as well. Alie notes that "the over-reliance on elders for the settling of disputes . . . could be disadvantageous to other groups, for example, young people."[77] And Ferme, who studied the Mende, argues that reintegration into local communities after the war requires rejoining systems of dependency, which is not easy and possibly undesirable for youth grown used to wielding power over their elders during the war.[78] Stovel also considers problematic the use of traditional chiefs and elders for the reintegration of individuals back into the community, since these very structures were among the causes of the war, even though this was probably necessary for successful reintegration.[79] Recognizing this paradox, Alie urges that traditional methods provide for wider inclusion and participation for communities to adapt to respecting the rights of women and youth.[80]

THE IRC'S RECONCILIATION ACTIVITIES

During the final stage of the TRC, and with funding from the UNDP, the TRC invited the IRC to initiate local reconciliation activities in the country's fourteen districts and to set up structures that would operate beyond the time frame of the TRC. The IRC's members trained coordinators to implement activities in all the districts, and reconciliation support committees were established to encourage ongoing reconciliation activities. The program, which began on October 1, 2003, came to an end in August 2004.[81]

Each district coordinator was given a motorbike to get around his assigned district, where he met with the traditional leaders and elders in the community. As Marabel Mbayo, head of women's programs for the IRC, explains, "We did not go out there to propose it to them. [The district coordinator] asked [the community leaders], 'What can we do?' And so those coordinators brought different activities that people suggested. What we were able to finance, we did."[82] First holding a workshop and then working through the reconciliation support committee, the district coordinator was "not doing this unilaterally but was doing it in collaboration with the people on the ground," says Mbayo.[83] What is striking about these activities—and what sets them apart from the formal transitional justice measures (both the TRC and the Special Court)—is they were determined at the grassroots level. Khanu writes, "In every district and chiefdom, the communities proposed and implemented their own reconciliation activities."[84]

The preliminary workshops held in November 2003 in the districts highlighted some of the challenges and lingering issues: the marginalization of women and youth in decision making, discrimination against ex-combatants, noninvolvement of ex-combatants in decision making, and rejection of sexually abused women. Criticisms lodged against the TRC during the workshops were that it was too "official" and "a lot of people were unable to vent their opinions." Likewise, it was felt that perpetrators had "failed to show remorse."[85] As Mbayo explains, "At first the TRC was not so welcome; people feared it would open up wounds. But by the time it was near the end, people were ready to come forward, but it was too late."[86] It was also observed during the district workshops that many people only returned from the refugee camps after the statement-taking phase of the TRC and thus had not been able to share their stories.[87]

To meet the continued need for victims and perpetrators to share their stories, the reconciliation district coordinators encouraged one or two testimonies at each reconciliation event. Activities ran the gamut from marking mass graves to reintegrating former combatants and renaming bush children to holding cleansing ceremonies. The two major activities requested by the people were the proper burial of loved ones and football matches between former combatants and youth.[88]

The reports from the reconciliation committees highlighted the importance to the local communities of performing memorial ceremonies for those who had died during the war in order to appease the dead. In one report, this was characterized as "reconciliation between living and dead observed."[89] Bush wives (women taken as "wives" by rebels) and abducted children were also cleansed to remove the stigma, so that they would be accepted back into their communities. In one report, referring to the situation of bush wives, the outcome of the cleansing ritual is described as follows: "stigma removed, get husbands."[90] This refers to the impossibility for women perceived as nonvirgins to find husbands.[91] According to Ibrahim's study of postwar women in Sierra Leone, most women she interviewed wanted some sort of cleansing ceremony.[92] But neither Shepler in Mende-speaking areas nor Coulter in Kuranko-speaking Kabala found any women who had witnessed or undergone such cleansing rituals.[93]

In Sebehun, one hundred girls were initiated and "declared clean and [able to] marry."[94] The war had interfered with traditional rites of passage for boys and girls into secret societies, making them ineligible for their adult roles. In many cases, there was the renaming of the children born to bush wives. In addition, the bush, which had been contaminated through bloodshed during the war, was cleansed. In Kissy, the mosque also was purified.[95] The pouring of libation, the sacrificial offering of sheep, and the performing of traditional dances rounded out the reconciliation activities.

Ceremonial cleansing was performed on several former combatants, who apologized to the community. In Makka village, the former militia apologized to the citizens, and the people accepted the apology and embraced the young men.[96] Ex-combatants in Mende Town and Loko Masama publicly apologized to those communities, and the chiefs embraced them on behalf of the people.[97] In Bayorbor, confessions and apologies were offered by former fighters, who were reconciled with the community.[98] The military publicly apologized and begged for forgiveness in Makeni, and the chief accepted the apology on behalf of his people, which was followed by the sharing of a glass of water and kola nuts as symbols of peace.[99] In Matru village, members of the CDF and RUF made confessions, which were accepted.[100] Kamajors (of the CDF) apologized in Kpetewoma and were embraced by Sierra Leone Army officers.[101] Likewise, CDF atrocities committed in Masimera Town were publicly confessed, resulting in the reintegration of former CDF fighters into the community.[102] While the TRC failed in getting CDF fighters to confess, the local reconciliation committees were more successful. One case involved a conflict of allegiance between two neighboring villages in Tonkolili district: Rosangbel was under CDF control, while Romange was under RUF control. After a reconciliation ceremony conducted by religious leaders and the reading of the Quran, the two communities reconciled.[103]

An especially emotional reintegration involved Adama Saquee, a woman from Koidu Town in Kono, who had been a concubine of RUF leader Foday Sankoh and was in self-imposed exile, as she feared returning home because of her wartime activities. She had collaborated with the RUF by pointing out the locations of diamond mines and was associated with atrocities carried out there. She requested assistance from the IRC to broker her return. The IRC first met with women's groups, which included many victims of the war. At first, feelings of revenge were expressed, but the women eventually decided they would forgive her if she offered an apology. The women were encouraged to be "ambassadors of peace" and speak to others in the community.

Mbayo admitted it was difficult for the people at first: "They asked, 'Why is it so important we honor her when she did so many atrocities here?'"[104] Eventually the reconciliation committee was able to prepare the people to take her back. The ceremony, held in a public community hall, began with readings from the Bible and the Quran. An elder then poured a libation of a mixture of water, kola nut, and wine on to the ground and called on the forefathers. After speaking to the ancestors to remove the bad spirit, he chanted, "Please forgive and bring peace." The woman publicly apologized, noting that she had been a peaceful citizen before the war. Paramount chief Konobundor II accepted the apology on behalf of the Kono people, saying that "reconciliation was about love and forgiveness, rather than a refresher of bitter memories."[105] The ceremony concluded with traditional music and dancing.[106] Adama Saquee lives peacefully in Koidu Town today.

Sharing meals was also at the top of the list of desired activities. Mbayo explains, "When you eat together, it is a form of reconciliation, coming together once again, eating and drinking."[107] In Lumley and Juba in the Western Area, "cleaning of garbage site" was one reconciliation activity, as was rebuilding the road in Bo, which was performed by a youth association alongside former combatants.[108] In Mafindor Chiefdom, a land dispute between Yamandu and Koindu villages was settled after the pouring of libation. "After ten years, two villages came together."[109] All reconciliation activities were concluded with either Christian services or Muslim recitations or both.

The IRC also erected, in collaboration with the Council of Churches in Sierra Leone and Church World Service, the nation's first war memorial in Tumbudu, Kamara Chiefdom in Kono district.[110] (Several monuments were built to mark mass graves in many districts, and a national war memorial opened in 2012 in Freetown near the iconic Cotton Tree.) "When we went there," recounts Mbayo, "we found in the house a lot of skeletons holding hands."[111] Here it is alleged that more than one hundred people including infants were burned alive during the war. The IRC bought the property and the adjoining one for a war museum and put in glass cases for the skeletons. Later the people of Kono complained that the skeletons in the museum are a disgrace to the dead, who should have received a proper burial. Tamba Mansaray, the man in charge of the museum, believes that because the bones of the dead are nakedly exposed they are suffering. He said the ancestors are angry with them because of that.¹¹² Local opposition suggests that the activities may not always have been locally determined and organized. Did the IRC with every good intention force a museum of skulls on the community when it was culturally at odds with their beliefs?

FAMBUL TOK: COMMUNITY HEALING IN SIERRA LEONE

The IRC's reconciliation activities concluded in 2004, but there was the sense that much more needed to be done to heal the wounds of war. John Caulker, founder and executive director of the Forum of Conscience, developed Fambul Tok, Krio for *family talk*, in 2008.¹¹³ Caulker had been one of the TRC's biggest advocates and he worked tirelessly, albeit mostly unsuccessfully, to persuade the government to enact its recommendations. He directed the TRC Working Group, renamed the Truth and Reconciliation Working Group in 2002 to display a more independent, critical stance and to establish it as a means for continuing reconciliation work after the life of the TRC. Caulker nevertheless conceded that the TRC was viewed by rural villagers as a "foreign" institution that never really reached down into the small, remote areas.¹¹⁴

Drawing on Sierra Leone's family talk tradition of discussing and resolving issues within the family circle, Caulker envisioned Fambul Tok as a program that would work at the local level to assist people to organize an event that would include a truth-telling bonfire and a traditional cleansing ceremony—practices that many communities had not experienced since before the war—and would be more familiar to people than the overly "official" TRC had been.¹¹⁵ Conceived initially as a chiefdom-level program that would involve ceremonies in each of the 149 chiefdoms across the country, Fambul Tok quickly devolved to the level of the village and is helping people in the smallest locales to hold reconciliation ceremonies. Explaining this choice, Caulker says, "The TRC and Special Court did not operate at village level. . . . Our people did not benefit from the TRC and Special Court and have opted for village dialogue as a means of settling their conflicts."¹¹⁶

Consultations were held from December 2007 through March 2008 in all twelve provincial districts and were attended by victims, ex-combatants, women, youth, religious leaders, elders, cultural leaders, and local officials in order to assess people's readiness for reconciliation. From the consultations, it was evident that people continued to experience traumas from the war and to have difficulties living side by side with unrepentant perpetrators. It was also clear that local cultural traditions, dormant since the war, could be reawakened for social healing.[117] Caulker explained that former soldiers live alongside the women they had raped or whose husbands they had killed or mutilated through amputation, thereby creating a tense situation for villagers: "They didn't apologize, didn't acknowledge the past. They just moved back in."[118]

After nationwide consultations, Fambul Tok rolled out a pilot phase in Kailahun in March 2008.[119] "The choice of Kailahun District is significant," said Caulker. "This was where the war began in March 23, 1991 when rebels of the Revolutionary United Front crossed into Sierra Leone from Liberia."[120] At the first ceremony on the seventeenth anniversary of the start of the war in Bomaru, where the first shots of the war were fired, perpetrators initially remained silent, spooked by the half dozen white film crew members who were there to film a documentary. When the film crew left, the town chief, himself a former RUF fighter, made the first confession. Heartfelt apologies by former combatants who confessed to committing atrocities against their neighbors took place late into the night and early morning.[121]

In one village in Kailahun, the Fambul Tok ceremony marked the first time perpetrators met face to face with victims to apologize for the offenses they had committed during the conflict. "At last they have acknowledged their crimes," cried one man, who was on crutches from his wartime injuries.[122] Explaining the importance of the verbal confessions, Caulker said, "People will not forgive if someone does not come forward to them in person to acknowledge what they did. . . . Someone has to acknowledge that this person was hurt. That restores dignity to the victims."[123] Also in Kailahun, in the village of Daabu, a woman had lived in distress just one house away from the man who had killed her seven-year-old daughter. Never speaking, they had avoided each other until Fambul Tok arranged a reconciliation ceremony in which the killer apologized for his deed.[124]

A positive aspect of Fambul Tok is the degree to which women have felt free to speak out. Despite the cultural stigma of rape, women have told their stories and publicly accused their perpetrators at virtually all of the Fambul Tok bonfires.[125] According to a Fambul Tok staff member in Freetown, 44% of testimonies have come from women and 90% of their testimonies have been about sexual violations against them. In many cases, though, the perpetrators are not living in the same village as the women they raped, or the women were gang raped and cannot identify the actual perpetrators.[126] After the ceremonies in the districts where Fambul Tok operates took place, women set up women's support groups to discuss issues of common concern, engage in economic pursuits, and communicate issues to the nation. Fambul Tok has donated tape recorders to the groups, so they can tape themselves and broadcast their views about reconciliation, education, and community health on the radio.[127] In 2014, Fambul Tok distributed soap made by "peace mothers" of Pujehun and promoted handwashing in the districts in which Fambul Tok operates in an attempt to end the Ebola epidemic.[128]

Each village—or a cluster of no more than ten villages called a "section"—carries out the activities in its own way though the framework is similar. They include a truth-telling bonfire in the evening, during which victims and offenders share their stories before the community, followed by cleansing ceremonies the following day. The cleansing ceremonies draw on the particular traditions of the community and include communicating with the spirits and offering libations. According to Elisabeth Hoffman, president of the project's main financial supporter, Catalyst for Peace, each Fambul Tok process has these ingredients: "truth-telling, individuals taking responsibility and apologizing for offenses committed, forgiveness from victims, and collective activities aimed at drawing participants together into a reassertion of . . . their collective humanity."[129] Rooted in African sensibilities that emphasize the need for communities to become whole, rather than in Western traditions of crime and punishment, Fambul

Tok is designed to address the roots of conflict at the local level while emphasizing each person's important contribution toward peace.[130]

In a Fambul Tok ceremony in Mokaikono village, in the Moyamba district in March of 2009, former CDF fighters begged for forgiveness for previously unacknowledged crimes. A man whose wife was killed by a member of the CDF recounted how he had asked the soldier whether he could remember him, but the soldier had refused to acknowledge him. "But since Fambul Tok stresses forgiveness, I am ready to forgive those that wronged me." A woman in the village, who had lost all her belongings to a CDF fighter, said she kept away from him "because any time I saw him my heart pounded like a pestle in a mortar. The most unfortunate thing was that there was no forum to explain my ordeal. Fambul Tok has made it possible."[131]

But Andy Carl, executive director of Conciliation Services, warns of reifying African traditions: "We have to be careful about putting African traditions up on a pedestal, because they're also a construct. They're being reinvented all the time, and part of the war in Sierra Leone was about the failure of traditional institutions."[132] Fambul Tok departs from tradition in two significant ways: First, it involves women and youth—populations historically excluded from such ceremonies—and second, participation is voluntary. In the past, a community decision to reconcile made participation mandatory.[133] These two deviations address criticisms of those like Carl, who disapprove of traditional methods of conflict resolution when they do not adapt to respect the rights and agency of women and youth.

Caulker is quick to point out that chiefs are welcome to participate. If chiefs were part of the problem, he maintains, they need to be included in finding solutions since they are "part of the family."[134] However, no longer is the chief paid by the villagers for providing certain rituals; instead, the villagers go to the newly formed reconciliation committees for these reconciliation services. A reconciliation committee includes the mammy queen (female head of the secret society), a youth representative, a traditional leader (section chief), an imam, and a minister, all of whom have received training in human rights and conflict resolution. Since youths had been marginalized not only by traditional leaders but also the government, they play a new and important role in the reconciliation committee. Youths, both former combatants and victims, are proudly providing leadership and are doing most of the ground work for the reconciliation events.[135] The Youth Outreach Teams of five youth members from the different villages in the section spread the word and educate their communities about Fambul Tok.[136]

Youth have also been involved in Fambul Tok's postceremony initiatives such as radio-listening clubs. In each section in Kailahun where a ceremony has been held, the clubs get together one day each week to discuss reconciliation or development issues and to record the discussions, which are later broadcast by the Sierra Leone Broadcasting Service and by other networks. Football games are another youth-oriented activity. Fambul Tok has facilitated football matches between youths in the communities that have undergone reconciliation ceremonies. "In the spirit of Fambul Tok, communities work out conflicts that arise during the matches without quarreling or fighting."[137]

Caulker claims he saw more results from the first four months of Fambul Tok ceremonies than he witnessed during his decade as a human rights worker.[138] Although he worked tirelessly to promote the TRC—first as executive director of Forum of Conscience and then as director of the TRC Working Group—his recommendation (as far back as 1999) that Sierra Leone hold lots of "mini TRCs" throughout the country was rejected in favor of a more centralized approach, by which the TRC would be headquartered in Freetown and would devote only one week of hearings to provincial towns.[139] Some villages are located as far as eighty miles away from the provincial town and so were accessible only to those who could afford to travel.[140] Witnesses had enormous difficulty in getting to hearings in vehicles, which invariably broke down en route, and they often came alone without family support. For Caulker, the hurt during the war was to the whole family, and the TRC's emphasis on individual victims—inviting the victim to testify without the entire family—did not resonate with villagers.[141] Bishop George Biguzzi, the Catholic bishop of Makeni, explains, "[European philosophy] says 'I think, therefore I am.' Here, it's 'I'm related, therefore I am.' . . . They find strength in being together. They also find the courage to open up in the group, because somehow they know the group is there for healing."[142]

Healing and the restoration of relationships, not punishment, are the primary goals. According to Caulker, "We have found that there is little interest in Western notions of punishment at the community level. We have our own way of addressing justice . . . [and] it does not involve sending them to prison."[143]

RECONCILIATION AND DEVELOPMENT

The program recognizes that the ceremonies are only the beginning of the process. A novel component is that after the harm is addressed through confession and ritual, a group activity is undertaken to cement the relationships. In addition to group activities, such as friendly football matches, dances, and feasts, economic ventures, such as community farms, have been attempted. This is important since, as John Paul Lederach notes, the more ties people have with each other and the more they acknowledge their interdependence, the more likely they are to reconcile.[144]

In Kailahun, people have begun farming together again—something that had not been practiced since before the war. To encourage the people to work together as a symbol of unity, Fambul Tok donated rice seedlings and cassava trunks throughout Kailahun. Several villages that cultivated rice agreed to set aside some of the harvest for food for future reconciliation ceremonies. The remaining seeds were given to needy community members on loan, payable after the next harvest. Other communities that planted cassava together decided to process it into a popular dish, garri, to sell at market, using the proceeds to open a community account. Several communities in Kailahun with community farms have reported record harvests, which they attribute to the cleansing of the land that resulted from the reconciliation ceremonies. For the first time since the war, they do not have to import rice.[145] Following the examples of community farms in Kailahun district, Moyamba district after the Fambul Tok ceremonies also embarked on group farms, turning acres of swampland into productive rice farms. At the end of Fambul Tok's second year, thirty community farms, or "peace farms," had been established in the districts where Fambul Tok ceremonies had been held.[146]

In Kailahun's Golan village, the community worked together to construct a maternity home encouraged, said the town chief, by the Fambul Tok reconciliation ceremonies, which had inspired them to work together. In Madina village, using funds from their community farm, residents are buying cement to build a barray.[147] They also worked together to build a guesthouse to show strangers they are united in hospitality.[148] In Kenewa village, the people, aided by a donation of zinc from Fambul Tok, built a roof for the court barray where they come together to settle future disputes.[149] One village participant, whose father, the town chief, had been brutally tortured and killed by the rebels, made this link between reconciliation and development: "I decided we should forgive [because] the act has been done, and if we say we are going to [take] revenge, then there will be no peace in our community, there will be no development."[150]

Incidents of individual perpetrators assisting victims have been documented as well. For instance, the man from Daabu who had killed the seven-year-old daughter of his neighbor now looks for ways to assist the woman and her family. In Kono's Foindor village, using zinc and nails donated by Fambul Tok, a perpetrator is assisting in rebuilding his victim's house. These examples show how Fambul Tok has linked reparation to reconciliation, a connection that has been largely overlooked by tribunals and truth commissions, in ways that personalize the compensation, which may have a more reconciliatory impact long term.[151]

Fambul Tok has been established in Kailahun and Kono districts in the east; Koinadugu, Bombali, and Port Loko districts in the north; Moyamba and Pujehun districts in the south; and recently (2015) in the Western Area Rural district. In the first five years of the program, more than 155 ceremonies, with over 2,700 people testifying before 60,000 neighbors, took place.[152] At a cost of just $300 each, these ceremonies confirm Caulker's assertion that reconciliation need not be costly. Compared to the costs of both the Special Court, estimated at up to $300 million,[153] and its poor relation the TRC, which cost $5 million, Fambul Tok is extremely cost effective.[154] More significant than its low cost is its effectiveness in encouraging people at the grassroots to identify and to draw on their own traditions and resources to make themselves whole again.

CHAPTER 7

UNFINISHED BUSINESS

While cultural and religious resources were expected to assist in the process of reconciliation, structural reforms were also considered important, since many of the conditions that gave rise to the conflict still remained.[1] The TRC Act of 2000 had mandated that the TRC not only create an impartial historical record of the violations that occurred during the conflict but also to make recommendations for reforms that would prevent the repetition of violations, address impunity, respond to the needs of victims, and promote healing and reconciliation. The Act also required the government to implement the TRC's recommendations, which were substantial and accounted for some one hundred pages of its final report.[2] Finally, the Act mandated a follow-up committee to monitor the implementation of the recommendations and to submit quarterly and annual reports to the public evaluating the government's efforts.[3] These precedents made this truth commission the world's first to compel the government to enact its recommendations and to require that another group scrutinize the government's response[4]—a remarkable requirement for sure but one that has been woefully ignored.

In this chapter, I highlight the TRC's recommendations from the final report, which was presented to the president in October 2004.[5] I also present the government's official response to the TRC report, the June 2005 "White Paper on the Report of the Truth and Reconciliation Commission,"[6] which was "widely regarded as weak and inadequate,"[7] and analyze its activities in implementing the recommendations.

The Commission divided its recommendations to the government into three categories: *imperative, work toward,* and *seriously consider.* *Imperative* recommendations are considered urgent and should be implemented "immediately or as soon as possible."[8] The *work toward* recommendations require in-depth planning and the marshaling of resources and should be done within a "reasonable time period." The *seriously consider* recommendations are ones the government is expected to evaluate but is under no obligation to implement.[9] (A fourth category, *calls on*, deals with recommendations to other bodies outside government, such as NGOs and the international community.)[10] The focus of this chapter is on the *imperative* and *work toward* categories of recommendations, since these are the most urgent and enough time has passed to evaluate whether the government has been successful in implementing them.[11] The TRC concluded that decades of bad governance, of corruption, and of the denial of human rights were the major causes of the war. The recommendations, therefore, center broadly on building a human rights culture that is supported by good governance and accountability. The recommendations can be divided into the following subheadings: protection of human rights, establishment of the rule of law, security services, promoting good governance, fighting corruption, children, youth, women, external actors, mineral resources, and reconciliation and reparations.[12]

PROTECTION OF HUMAN RIGHTS

The Lome Peace Accord had mandated the creation of a human rights commission within ninety days of the signing. The TRC urged its immediate establishment with the power to subpoena and conduct interviews—an *imperative* recommendation.[13] It called for a public and open nomination process for the commissioners and recommended that the commission, while it would be accountable to Parliament and not the executive, advise all three branches of the state on how to meet their international obligations to incorporate human rights concepts into law.

The TRC also envisioned that the Human Rights Commission of Sierra Leone (HRCSL) would serve as the follow-up committee that had been mandated by the TRC Act to monitor the government's implementation of the recommendations. As a practical matter, the TRC decided it was *imperative* that the HRCSL be the official custodian of the Commission's documentation and materials. It recommended that the documents be organized to make future research possible, and it also required that the HRCSL *work toward* converting the statements and information into digitized form. Another *imperative* recommendation was that Parliament not pass legislation authorizing access to information in the archives that was provided in confidence, for instance, the identities of child combatants and victims of rape.[14]

In the White Paper, the government agreed to set up the follow-up committee to disseminate the report, archive its documentation, and "enforce the recommendations made by the Commission pertaining to the National Vision for Sierra Leone."[15] This statement startled observers, since it denoted a very limited view of its obligations under the TRC Act, which required the government to enact *all* the TRC's recommendations, not to handpick a few here and there. The National Vision Program had been launched by the TRC in October 2013, to elicit artistic and literary contributions from Sierra Leoneans about their expectations and aspirations for the country as a way of bringing people into the process. The TRC viewed recommendations surrounding it as less pressing, that is, not deemed *imperative* or *seriously consider*. Moreover, the follow-up committee was supposed to oversee the recommendations in all areas, not just those relating to the National Vision Program.[16]

One would have expected that by the time the government published its response some eight months after receiving the TRC's final report, it would already have set up the follow-up committee to oversee and monitor the government's implementation of the recommendations. The TRC Act had required that it be set up within ninety days after receipt of the final report. However, the government had clearly come to regret provisions of the law, which had been passed under international pressure. While Parliament had voted for the HRCSL in July 2004, and the White Paper had stated that "the appointment of members to this Commission is in process,"[17] it was only in October 2006, two years after the TRC had presented its recommendations, that Parliament finally appointed the five commissioners. The feeling among local NGOs was that the government used the long, drawn-out process of commissioner selection as an excuse to delay implementation of the recommendations since that body would be in charge of monitoring the government's performance on enacting them.[18]

The HRCSL also has not followed through on the recommendation that it issue quarterly updates and an annual report on how the government has implemented the TRC's recommendations. It did, however, hold a conference in 2008 on the status of the implementation of the TRC recommendations, and it published an accompanying matrix on the precise ways the government had or had not enacted the numerous recommendations.[19] The HRCSL, mandated by the TRC to be the official depository of the archives of the TRC, has placed those documents in the newly established Peace Museum located on the former Special Court campus.[20] As mandated by the TRC, those TRC documents that are not confidential have been digitized and are accessible to the public.

Among the TRC's proposed amendments to the 1991 Constitution of Sierra Leone were ones designed to enshrine the "right to human dignity" as a fundamental human right, and to incorporate the principle that the "right to life" is inviolable.[21] It recommended the abolition of the death penalty, and the immediate repeal by Parliament of all laws authorizing capital punishment, and urged that all pending death penalty sentences be commuted by the president—all *imperative* recommendations.[22]

However, the government in its White Paper denied the need to implement the recommendation to enshrine the right to human dignity as a human right in the Constitution, arguing that it can already be found there.[23] Although it claimed to accept the view expressed in the report that respect for human dignity and human rights must begin with respect for human life, it nevertheless refused to submit to the *imperative* recommendation that the government repeal the death penalty, arguing, "[The] Government wishes to state that Sierra Leone has just emerged from a decade-long armed conflict with attendant wanton killings of individuals and the commission of various atrocities, and as such does not accept the Commission's call for immediate abolition of [the] death penalty for persons guilty of heinous crimes."[24] It defended its position as being consistent with the provisions of the United Nations International Covenant on Civil and Political Rights, which provides that in countries that have not abolished the death penalty, it may be imposed only for the most serious crimes. It pointed out that the president, pursuant to section 63 of the Constitution, may pardon any person, including one sentenced to death. It did, however, agree to monitor and review its current position.[25]

In the post-TRC period, the government has sentenced twenty-two suspects to death. In December 2006, then president Ahmad Tejan Kabbah announced that the death penalty would no longer be carried out during his administration, which ended in July 2007, but it would be retained to serve as a deterrent. Although civil society organizations like the Sierra Leone Court Monitoring Project had lobbied the Constitutional Review Commission to recommend that the death penalty be abolished, the Commission in its long-anticipated draft report, submitted in 2007, saw fit to retain it, albeit acts of treason and other political crimes committed in the absence of loss of life were excluded.[26] In 2011, President Ernest Bai Koroma commuted the sentences of sixteen prisoners on death row to life imprisonment, but nine prisoners still remain on death row.[27]

Arbitrary arrest and detention without trial were roundly condemned, and the Commission enjoined the immediate release of detainees, making the *imperative* recommendation that such detentions be prohibited in the future.[28] It also recommended that the government *work toward* investigating cases in which previous regimes persecuted public officials deemed to be enemies of the government and restoring their good names if they were found innocent.[29] In response (in particular to the TRC's assertion that several detainees have been held without charge or trial since 2000),[30] the government insisted that "there are currently no arbitrarily arrested and incarcerated persons in the Country" and that it "has no intention to go against the practices identified and recognized both within national and international law."[31] But this assertion was disputed by human rights organizations. In 2006, 65% of prisoners were held in prolonged pretrial detention (up from 40% in 2005).[32] The HRCSL recorded two cases of suspects held at Pademba Road Prison, one since 1987 and another since 2004, without trial or indictment.[33] While a number of people, including soldiers in the Sierra Leone Army, detained after the war on suspicion of being rebels, collaborators, or both have been released, the question of arbitrary detention has not been addressed.[34]

Presidents have enjoyed wide latitude in using emergency powers to quell dissent and have exercised this power to move against political opponents. The TRC condemned the practice, directing that all emergency powers be subject to judicial review and a state of emergency be extended by Parliament for only three months, changes that would require a constitutional amendment. The TRC also recommended that clauses in the Constitution giving the president wide latitude to make regulations during a public emergency be removed and that the Constitution be amended to specify which rights are nonderogable.[35] These were all *imperative* recommendations.

The White Paper asserted in response that the government has the obligation to ensure law and order and to protect life and property: "Where the life and security of the Nation is threatened, it has the obligation to proclaim a state of emergency." It will only declare a state of emergency, however, in cases of "violent disturbance and demonstrations, or natural catastrophes, and during internal or international conflict that threaten the life of the Nation." Furthermore, it would not deviate from the international requirements pertaining to human rights, such as the right to life; the prohibition of torture; the principle of legality in criminal law; and freedom of thought, conscience, and religion that are identified in Article 4 (2) of the

International Covenant on Civil and Political Rights as nonderogable under any circumstances.[36]

The government did not respond to the particular recommendations that a state of emergency be subject to judicial review, or that the Constitution be amended to require such a review and regulate the wide powers given to the president to take such measures. In fact, President Koroma imposed a state of emergency as recently as July 2014 to give him more power to deal with the Ebola outbreak. Under the wide powers granted to him under the state of emergency, the president detained thirty-four people in Kono, seven of whom still remained in detention six months later, after a riot occurred when residents refused to hand over a ninety-year-old person suspected of being infected with Ebola.[37]

Serious deficiencies in both the police and judiciary have continued to undermine fundamental human rights according to Human Rights Watch. Police officers have been accused of using excessive force against alleged criminals. There have also been reports of bribe taking, extortion at checkpoints, and victims being forced to pay the police to file reports or conduct investigations. (Human Rights Watch did find that the police leadership is increasingly more willing to discipline and dismiss officers engaging in corrupt practices, noting that ninety-four police officers were fired in June 2008.)[38] In compliance with the TRC recommendations that the government *work toward* a compulsory program of human rights education in primary, secondary, and higher education, and *toward* human rights training for the army, police, and judicial recruits,[39] a six-month human rights–training course has been offered to recruits and refresher courses have been offered to other officers.[40]

The TRC called on the protection of freedom of expression, specifically the repeal of laws creating the offenses of criminal libel and sedition. Until the laws were repealed, it suggested a moratorium on all existing or pending prosecutions—an *imperative* recommendation.[41] But the seditious libel provisions in the Public Order Act of 1965 are still in effect to restrain journalists from reporting on official misconduct. In 2009, the publisher of *Awareness Times* was arrested for "ridiculing the President."[42] Likewise, the editor of the *Independent Observer* was charged with criminal libel when he accused the minister of Transport and Aviation of corruption. The Sierra Leone Association of Journalists sought to have seditious libel provisions nullified, arguing they are at odds with the freedom of expression protection in the Constitution, but the Supreme Court threw out the case in December 2009, ruling that the provisions were in line with the 1991 Constitution and "journalists were under no imminent threat."[43]

In October of 2013, two editors from the *Independent Observer* were charged with twenty-six counts, including criminally seditious libel for "bringing the name of his Excellency to disrepute and inciting hatred," according to the Criminal Investigations Department. The offending statement? "As the political father of the nation is regarded as an elephant but he behave [*sic*] like a rat and should be treated like one."[44] And in 2014, a radio journalist was also jailed for criticizing the government's handling of the Ebola crisis, including the possible misappropriation of aid money.[45]

A freedom of information act, which the TRC had urged the government to *work toward*,[46] was approved by the cabinet in November 2010 but stalled in Parliament, where parliamentarians were overwhelmingly antagonistic. Ironically, at the same time the two editors were being charged with seditious libel for calling the president a rat, Parliament unexpectedly passed the bill after years of foot dragging. Amanda Vragovich suggests that its passage was most likely driven by external actors and did not represent "a principled commitment to transparency and accountability."[47] She contends the government was seeking to qualify for membership in the Open Government Partnership, an international organization promoting transparency and accountability, and passing the legislation boosted its score to the bare minimum to join. Membership in the organization makes Sierra Leone eligible for a grant from the Millennium Challenge Corporation, another likely motivation for its passage. However, because of concerns over corruption, and despite the fact that the country moved up thirty-nine places (from 158 to 119 out of 177 countries) over five years on the Transparency International Perception of Corruption Index,[48] Sierra Leone ultimately failed to receive the grant for fiscal year 2014.

ESTABLISHMENT OF THE RULE OF LAW

Because the attorney general is the guardian of the public interest, he must be free from political influences. Hence, the TRC recommended that the Office of the Attorney General and the Minister of Justice be separated. This would require an amendment to the Constitution, and the government was urged to *work toward* this recommendation.[49] But the White Paper rejected this recommendation, arguing that the National Constitutional Review Commission of 1990 had deliberated on this very issue and had advised against including this in the 1991 Constitution.[50] It further suggested that since establishing the two posts in 1978, "there has been no occasion or history of conflict between the Attorney-General and Minister of Justice and the Chief Justice."[51] It emphatically rejected the view that the power to initiate, prosecute, or terminate criminal proceedings would be compromised because the Attorney General is also the Minister of Justice. It also pointed out that this situation is not unique to Sierra Leone but is shared by most Commonwealth countries. The government stated, it "will continue to encourage reforms in the Judiciary . . . to enhance the proper administration of justice and facilitate access to justice for all."[52]

Establishing the rule of law, the final report stated, begins with an impartial and autonomous judiciary with budgetary independence, which the government can *work toward*. Judges should be appointed for nonpartisan reasons and should reflect broadly the ethnic and gender composition of Sierra Leone. Representation needs to be expanded on the Judicial and Legal Services Commission that appoints judges to include one teacher of law and three members of Parliament, including a member of the opposition party.[53] Four practicing attorneys from the bar should be appointed to the Judicial and Legal Services Commission. These were *imperative* recommendations but to date representation on the Commission has not been broadened and the court does not have budgetary independence.

A code of conduct outlining principles of acceptable behavior for members of the bench was likewise an *imperative* recommendation.[54] Despite the passage in 2006 of a code of conduct for judges and magistrates, allegations of bribery and extortion appear in newspapers daily, making a mockery of a code. Perhaps that is because remuneration is low. Local court chairmen are paid so little there is a strong structural incentive for corruption. Hence, the TRC recommended that the government *work toward* incremental improvement of local court officials' remuneration.[55]

The TRC also recommended that the Judicial and Legal Services Commission incorporate the local courts into the judiciary, to be headed and supervised by the chief justice, and appoint a judicial/customary law officer in each district. Despite the TRC's recommendations to augment their numbers, there are still too few judges and attorneys. Only nineteen magistrates and thirteen prosecution lawyers serve the entire country. In its 2012 annual report, the HRCSL noted that Bonthe, Kenema, and Kailahun still did not have resident magistrates.[56]

Arguing that whatever rights may be enshrined in the Constitution are meaningless if access to the courts is lacking, the Commission recommended that the government *work toward* establishing public defenders in the main centers of the country,[57] but unfortunately there are no public defenders nationwide. Despite passage in 2012 of the Legal Aid Act, which provided for trained paralegals in each chiefdom, resources were not allocated in the annual budgets to fund the Legal Aid Board.[58] One positive sign, however, is that new courts have been built in a number of districts, others have been refurbished, and three new courts have been established in Freetown at Pademba Road.[59] Still, there need to be more, better-administered, and better-resourced courts, with Internet access for judges, which the TRC recommended. Since so many of the TRC's recommendations centered on law reform, the TRC advised that an effective Law Reform Commission must be equipped to modernize outdated laws.[60]

The TRC also advised that customary law should be adapted, although the Commission noted, "Some elements of customary law and Islamic law contradict basic human rights."[61] In cases when a customary law conflicts with rights enshrined in the Constitution, the

Commission said it should be declared illegal. This would require the repeal of some sections of the Constitution that exempt certain areas of family life from protection against discrimination. This was an *imperative* recommendation. Since customary law varies from place to place, and there is uncertainty about what customary law entails, the Commission instructed the government to *work toward* codifying it and said that a national dialogue on the codification of customary law, with special emphasis on the rights of women and children, should commence.[62]

SECURITY SERVICES

The TRC urged those in power to never again use national security as an excuse to deploy security forces for political ends. National security requires having only one military force, the Sierra Leone Army. It was deemed *imperative* that no member of a security service obey an illegal order or promote the interest of any political party. It enjoined the government to prohibit the existence of paramilitary forces that would in effect eliminate the Operational Support Division, which operates as a paramilitary force within the Sierra Leone Police. These national security principles must be enshrined in the Constitution—an *imperative* recommendation.[63]

The government, nevertheless, rejected the recommendation to disband the Operational Support Division, which the inspector general of the Sierra Leone Police in his submission to the TRC had described as an "instrument of tyranny and suppression" under Siaka Stevens.[64] The government insisted that "the increase in the crime rate in the aftermath of the decade-long war, the current unsettled situation in the sub-region and the primacy of State security which is now being transferred by UNAMSIL to Sierra Leonean security forces do not warrant an abolition of the OSD."[65] It "wishes to give assurances that whatever happened in the past as mentioned in the central findings of the Commission's Report will never be encouraged or tolerated again."[66] Why this might be and what institutional mechanisms have been put in place to prevent it were not explained. The Operational Support Division remains.

GOOD GOVERNANCE

The Commission had taken the issue of good governance very seriously, arguing "There is no option but to address bad governance and corruption head on. It would not be an overstatement to say that the survival of the nation depends on the success of society in confronting these issues."[67] Bad governance breeds corruption. The TRC, therefore, called on the culture of entitlement within the civil service to be stopped (153). According to the report, real economic development is not possible when corruption and bad governance are rife, as they lead to the inability to deliver services, which inevitably results in civil disorder (159).

An *imperative* recommendation was to include in the Constitution the requirement that Parliament publish a code of ethics setting out standards and rules to promote accountable government and the Constitution enjoin public servants not to act in any way inconsistent with their offices. Alleged breaches of ethics should be investigated. Parliament should disqualify someone from holding public office if he or she had ever been removed from office for a breach of ethics.[68] It urged the government to *work toward* ensuring that all levels of public administration accord with the principles of just administrative action and local government and that district councils also accord with certain core principles (156). The government chose to ignore these recommendations.

Another *imperative* recommendation was to make elections more free and fair by limiting the amount of contributions by individuals and groups to candidates, who would be required to disclose money raised and its sources.[69] There has been some movement on implementing the latter, since the Political Parties Registration Act requires parties to declare assets, expenditures, and sources of funds, and the parties' candidates complied with these rules in the last two elections.[70] But on the former recommendation, limiting contributions, there has been less compliance. Although the Political Parties Registration Act states that the Political Parties Registration Commission may make regulations limiting donations, it has not seen fit to do so.[71]

The TRC obligated the government to amend the laws to prevent secrecy and confidentiality provisions from stopping the exposure of corruption. It enjoined the government to amend the law so that whistle-blowers are not subject to charges, made under the cover of revealing state secrets, for exposing details of corruption; it also encouraged the government to provide legal protection to them—both *imperative* recommendations.[72] The requirement to protect whistle-blowers has been only partially met through amendments in 2008 to the Anti-Corruption Act which provided protection to whistle-blowers. And despite the promise of confidentiality, there have been recent allegations that informants' information and identities are being leaked to alleged perpetrators by moles within the Anti-Corruption Commission (ACC).[73]

An *imperative* recommendation was to require public officials to disclose their assets annually.[74] Following the lead of President Ernest Bai Koroma, the country's first head of state to declare his assets to the ACC, all senior government officials and parliamentarians have agreed to comply with the 2008 Anti-Corruption Act that requires public officers, their spouses, and children to declare their assets.[75] The ACC has started publishing an Asset Declarations Defaulters list of hundreds of names of government officials who have not declared their assets in order to shame them into compliance.

The TRC exhorted the government to be transparent about procurement, tenders, bids, the privatization process, and transportation because of the opportunities for personal enrichment.[76] It also insisted that the government *work toward* the publication of amounts sent to districts and communities for specific services and amenities. In response, President Koroma ordered a temporary ban on logging, while the process of leases could be investigated, and made efforts to address the lack of competitive bidding for contracts.[77] However, a 2011 Al Jazeera report showed footage of individuals claiming to represent Vice President Samuel Sumana soliciting bribes in exchange for conducting illegal timber operations.[78]

CORRUPTION

Fighting corruption, which was highlighted in the report as the major cause of the war, was high on the list of recommendations. The dissatisfaction of junior officers who witnessed high level officials' use of public resources for their private use led to two coups during the 1990s. Both were enacted in the name of rooting out corruption and provided ideological cover (at least initially) for the RUF, which claimed to be waging a revolution against a corrupt regime. Corruption not only caused the conflict, it helped to sustain it as soldiers on both sides—progovernment and rebels—were able to divert public resources (including diamond revenues) to sustain the war effort. The TRC acknowledged that the government's ACC was a good first step, but it insisted that the ACC should be able to pursue its own prosecutions without the involvement of the attorney general and free from political pressure (an *imperative* recommendation).[79]

At the time of the White Paper, observers believed that corruption was not being taken seriously by the government, even though Sierra Leoneans consider corruption the country's biggest challenge. They pointed to the fact that only 10% of the suspects investigated, and no high-level officials, had actually been charged by the ACC. In 2002, the ACC had indicted three of the five national election commissioners, but the government refused to prosecute them, indicating the ACC's lack of independence.[80] Impotence on the part of the ACC led TRC commissioner Laura Marcus-Jones to characterize it as "a barking dog with no teeth."[81] A 2004 study on perceptions of corruption found that 67% of service users reported having to pay bribes to obtain public services, and 42% of officials admitted to irregularities, including misappropriation of funds, in managing their budgets.[82] Regrettably, the SLPP government took few steps to stymie a culture of corruption.

Some steps were taken to improve the process under the APC government elected in 2007 and again in 2012. The new Anti-Corruption Act of 2008 empowered the ACC to pursue its own investigations and prosecutions rather than merely to advise the government about prosecutions through the presidentially appointed attorney general.

Although this legislation does allow the government to stop an ACC prosecution, this has not happened so far according to Sierra Leone Court Monitoring Project director Mohamed Suma.[83]

In 2008, three senior public officials, including the government ombudsman, were charged under the new act. In November 2009, two ministers were sacked for alleged graft. Eleven convictions were secured in 2009 (including that of the former ombudsman), and 2.8 billion leones were recovered.[84] In 2010, 171 investigations were initiated,[85] and several high-level officials were convicted, including the popular minister of Fisheries and Maritime for misappropriation of funds and kickbacks; the minister of Health and Sanitation for corruption in his handling of competitive contracts; the head of the school feeding program in the Ministry of Education; the director of procurement in the Ministry of Defense; and the former director of the Sierra Leone Road Transport Authority. Then head of the ACC Abdul Tejan-Cole[86] said that he was probing corruption not only among ordinary policemen seeking bribes but also among individuals at the highest level.[87]

Tejan-Cole's successor as head of the ACC, Joseph Fitzgerald Kamara, successfully convicted the mayor of Freetown and five other city officials for corruption and procurement violations.[88] However, the earlier conviction of the Fisheries and Maritime minister was overturned on appeal, and the ACC's case against officials in the health ministry, who allegedly misappropriated half a million dollars from the Bill and Melinda Gates Foundation that was meant for vaccines, resulted in acquittals in 2013. Kamara lamented, "It is a dark cloud over justice in Sierra Leone. The legal analysis applied by the judge was supported neither by law nor fact."[89]

CHILDREN

The TRC was mandated by its implementing legislation to pay special attention to the ways that children and women in particular suffered from the war. Thus, it comes as no surprise that most of the *imperative* recommendations dealt with these two groups (see chapter 3 for recommendations on women). The TRC recommended that a child rights bill incorporating provisions of the International Convention on the Rights of the Child be passed into law "as a matter of urgency."[90] The TRC's call was answered by 2007 legislation, the Child Rights Act, which was compatible with the Convention and its optional protocols. The Act among other things repealed the earlier Corporal Punishment Act, the repeal of which the TRC urged as *imperative*.[91] But according to Josephine Thompson Shaw, the contact person with the HRCSL overseeing the TRC's implementation, much more sensitization of teachers and parents to this issue is needed as corporal punishment remains commonplace.[92]

Also in the Child Rights Act was the requirement that eighteen be the minimum age for marriage, which was an *imperative* recommendation.[93] However, the HRCSL revealed in its 2008 report that, despite the Child Rights Act's prohibition of early marriage, the traditional practice of early marriage of girls persists nationwide.[94] The Child Rights Coalition estimates that 27% of girls marry before they turn fifteen, while 62% are younger than age eighteen.[95] And a loophole exists: the Registration of Customary Marriage and Divorce Act of 2007 (one of the three gender bills passed the same year) grants parents the right to give consent for their underage daughters to marry, and thus condones forced marriage, which is at odds with the Child Rights Bill.

The Commission recommended criminalizing the trafficking and sexual exploitation of children as soon as possible,[96] and the government responded with the Anti-Human Trafficking Act in 2005. Further attempts to stymie sexual exploitation of children were made in the Sexual Offenses Act of 2012. Responding, albeit belatedly, to the TRC's *imperative* recommendation that sex with a child under age sixteen be deemed statutory rape,[97] the act stipulates that no person under eighteen can give legal consent to sexual intercourse, thus consent will not be regarded as a defense.

Because of the number of war orphans, orphanages have proliferated. Accordingly, the TRC recommended that the government *work toward* passing legislation to regulate them and to ensure against abuse and child trafficking. It also suggested the government *work toward* reviewing the adoption laws to incorporate the practices of guardianship and fostering that exist in common law and practice. The Child Rights Act of 2007 gives the minister the power to oversee and regulate these homes and promulgate regulations on adoption.

The TRC insisted primary school education be free and compulsory for all children and not sending a child to primary school be made a criminal offense. It also directed the government to *work toward* removing all hidden charges (so-called chalk fees) for students. It also urged the government to *work toward* providing incentives for children to attend secondary school.[98]

The Child Rights Act makes primary education compulsory up to age fifteen and obligates parents to send their children to school, but there are no penalties for failing to do so.[99] Parents send their children off to do petty trading rather than to attend classes, and teachers, who are often unpaid by the government, exploit their students by sending them to their farms to work. And while primary education is in theory free and compulsory, the Education Act of 2004 does not actually require it. Instead, it merely makes it a government *policy* to provide free primary education to both boys and girls.[100] The UN Integrated Office for Sierra Leone notes that primary students are still expected to pay for "brooms, soaps, toilet papers, pamphlets, etc."[101]

The TRC suggested that the government *work toward* reviewing the practice of allowing children under age eighteen to be employed full time.[102] It also asked the government to promulgate regulations to prevent the employment of children in mines. It recommended ratifying the International Labor Organization conventions 138 on the Minimum Age of Employment and 182 on the Prohibition of the Worst Forms of Child Labor, both *imperative* recommendations. Those caught hiring children for the mines should have their licenses revoked, also an *imperative* recommendation. It advised the government to *work toward* spot checking mining sites to ensure that children were not employed. At the same time, it encouraged the government to *work toward* sensitizing families to the importance of foregoing income from child miners and stressing the important of education.[103]

Despite the Child Rights Act's prohibition against employing children under age fifteen for all work and under age eighteen for hazardous work, the employment of children is widespread. The US State Department estimates that 57% of children between the ages of five and fourteen are involved in child labor.[104]

YOUTH

Because youth—defined as young adults between the ages of eighteen and thirty-five—continue to languish in a "twilight zone of unemployment and despair," the TRC viewed the youth problem as a "national emergency that demands national mobilization."[105] It recommended the government *work toward* transforming the youth portfolio of the Ministry of Youth and Sports into a National Youth Commission that could raise funds locally and internationally and could spearhead private-public partnerships.[106]

The White Paper responded that the government was working to establish a youth commission that would address the problems and concerns of youth,[107] but it was not until December 2009 that the legislation finally concluded its arduous crawl through Parliament and the National Youth Commission was indeed established.

Since the denial of a meaningful voice had fueled the attraction by youth to rebel movements that espoused an antigovernment ideology, the TRC also suggested opening the political space for youth by requiring that at least 10% of candidates for all public elections be young people.[108] Despite it being an *imperative* recommendation, no quota was mandated for youth candidates for the elections in 2007 and 2012, and no legislation has been passed to require it. (Nevertheless, the APC government was commended in 2013 by the All Political Parties Youth Association for appointing five youths as ministers and other young people as heads of various parastatals.)[109] Nor is a youth serving on the HRCSL, although the TRC mandated that four representatives of civil society be among its members, including one youth.

EXTERNAL ACTORS

Although it offered no *imperative* recommendation regarding external actors, the Commission did suggest that the government work with Liberia to control the flow of small arms along the common border and harmonize the laws of Liberia and Sierra Leone regarding firearms.[110] The White Paper assured the public that the government will pursue working with neighboring countries to ensure adequate border security to prevent the proliferation of small arms.[111] But it did not say what these measures will be, except to note that a National Security Council has been established to direct all security measures involving the borders. In addition, the government "is giving active consideration" to reviewing the harmonization of small arms laws with neighboring states. Regarding the tracing of RUF assets, including those of Charles Taylor, in other countries—a recommendation under the category *call on*—the government said, "this matter is receiving active consideration" and it will solicit assistance from the international community "at the appropriate time."[112]

MINERAL RESOURCES

In addition to its injunction to ban child labor in the mines, the TRC ordered several reforms in the mining industry. It obligated the government to publish a regular account of how it spends the proceeds from diamonds. It further recommended that the bidding process for mineral exploitation licenses be fair and transparent. These were *imperative* recommendations. The TRC highlighted the need for more and better training for mine-monitoring officers and an increase in their remuneration to reduce the incentive for graft.[113] The Commission recommended that the ACC examine closely the issuing of licenses to relatives of public officials, an *imperative* recommendation.[114] The Ministry of Mineral Resources was urged to publish the names of all mining-related license holders annually, an *imperative* recommendation, and the government was told it must *work toward* conducting a review of the role played by chiefs in granting mining licenses.[115]

In response, the government stated that the revenues generated are collected in a transparent manner through the Ministry of Mines and the Government Gold and Diamond Office under the "watchful eyes of the International Monetary Fund."[116] It was silent, however, on how it would make the bidding process for the licenses fair and transparent, on the issue of public officials' relatives having an unfair advantage in receiving licenses, on the recommendation to publish the names of holders of all licenses, and on how it would go about prohibiting child labor in mines or revoking licenses for employers who do employ children. Whereas the TRC had required the government to publish a regular and detailed account of how it spends the proceeds generated from diamonds, the government responded simply by saying that the Ministry of Mines compiles and publishes sales returns and disbursements of minerals on a periodic basis and the "public is entitled and authorized to visit the Ministry to acquire the information it requires,"[117] thereby placing the burden on the citizen to uncover rather than on the government to reveal. To the recommendation that the Ministry of Mineral Resources conduct a review of the role played by chiefs in the granting of mining licenses, the response given in the White Paper was only "Government also wishes to add that a portion of revenues collected are specifically paid to chiefdoms of diamond mining areas to assist in the development of these areas, thus enhancing the socio-economic welfare of their people."[118] This completely missed the point of the recommendation that these chiefs need to be held accountable.

A new Mines and Minerals Act enacted in 2009 in theory makes the bidding process more transparent. But allegations that an iron ore contract given to African Minerals in Tonkolili violated the law have been raised by a local NGO, Society for Democratic Initiatives.[119] The Constitutional Review Commission recommended the inclusion in the Constitution of an Extractive Industries Transparency Commission.[120] If this makes its way into the next constitution, which will be voted in referendum, this will go some way toward making the industry more accountable. This could potentially aid in stemming the flow of untaxed diamonds; it is estimated that less than one half and possibly only one sixth of diamonds go through official channels.[121] In the meantime, the Mines and Mineral Resources minister announced in January 2012 that his ministry had designed a website showing payments made by mining companies and the status of license applications. This coincided with the opening of a transparency portal—a website showing data on the poverty-reduction projects and information on funding and disbursements—which the president said would bring about an "unprecedented level of openness" to government. Unfortunately, just 0.9% of the country's 5.4 million population has Internet access.[122]

REPARATIONS

The TRC's enabling act required it to make recommendations concerning the measures needed to respond to the needs of victims. The full implementation of reparations is something the government is mandated to *work toward*.[123] Not one recommendation for reparations is *imperative* because implementation would be costly and require in-depth planning. The report simply advises that the recommendations should be enacted "within a reasonable time period" (120).

The TRC proposed that a reparations program be coordinated by the National Commission for Social Action (NaCSA), which would administer the Special Fund for War Victims. The Special Fund for War Victims, which was mandated both by the Lome Accord and by the TRC Act, should be established within three months of the publication of the report.[124] It insisted that a national human rights commission perform the role of advisory committee to NaCSA, and it obligated NaCSA to "balance the needs of the victims with what government can afford" (194). It suggested possible funding sources, such as revenues generated from mineral resources (as provided for in Article 7 of the Lome Accord), a one-time tax on local and foreign corporate entities, and the pursuit of assets illegally removed from Sierra Leone during the conflict. Given the expense of many of the recommendations, the TRC urged NaCSA to collaborate with the international community to obtain additional funding (196).

Reparations were ordered in the areas of health, pensions, education, skills training, and microcredits. Certain categories of victims—amputees, war wounded, and victims of sexual violence—are entitled to free physical and mental health care for life. Existing mental health care programs need to be supported and expanded. Free prosthetic devices, free physiotherapy, and free occupational therapy should be offered to amputees. Other war wounded, and their wives and children, should be eligible for free health care if they have experienced a 50% or more reduction in earning capacity as a result of the injury. Organizations providing scar removal surgery for branded children should be supported.

In addition, the TRC called for free testing and treatment for HIV for all victims of sexual violence. Victims of sexual violence should receive free health care including fistula surgery. A monthly pension—in an amount to be determined by NaCSA—should be disbursed to all adult amputees and other war wounded with a 50% or more reduction in earning capacity and to victims of sexual abuse.[125] Free education (to the senior secondary level) should be provided for amputee children, other war wounded, victims of sexual violence, children who were abducted or conscripted, war orphans, children of amputees and other war wounded who experienced a 50% reduction in earning capacity, and children of victims of sexual violence (260–61). The TRC recommended skills training and microcredits for amputees, other war wounded, victims of sexual violence, and war widows. A business management course should be held for beneficiaries, and where feasible microcredits should be provided to those who successfully complete the program (262–63). Community reparations must aim at rebuilding infrastructure in areas most affected by the war, and groups must be consulted about what they need in community reparations (263).

Symbolic reparations including commemoration ceremonies and symbolic reburials for victims by traditional and religious leaders should be initiated. Monuments, renaming of buildings or locations, and the transformation of sites of conflict into useful spaces were recommended. At minimum, the government should build one national war monument.[126] Other reconciliation activities should include apologies by all actors (including national and political leaders), traditional and religious ceremonies, social and recreational events, trauma counseling, and government support for the efforts of the district reconciliation and support committees set up by the TRC and the IRC (see chapter 6 for a discussion of these). A national reconciliation day to commemorate the day in 2002 when three thousand weapons were symbolically burned at Lungi to herald the end of the war should be held annually on January 18.[127]

The government assured the public in its White Paper that it would fully implement the recommendations on advancing reconciliation, though it didn't say specifically what steps it had taken or planned to take. Because of their expense, and the effort required to implement them, the recommendations on reparations were not made *imperative* but *work toward*, and it appears that the government has used this as an excuse to do nothing. While it accepted "in principle" the findings and recommendations, it would only implement the various programs "subject to the means available to the State" from its own resources and assistance from the international community.[128] It said nothing specifically about its plans to offer free health care or pensions to the targeted categories of victims. In fact, it was silent about any specifics.

The TRC had mandated that the reparations program be coordinated by NaCSA, since it was the government agency charged with administering the Special Fund for War Victims. The Special Fund was to be established within three months of the publication of the report, and NaCSA was directed by the TRC to complete the implementation program within six years with the proviso that some programs, including pensions and health care to certain categories of victims such as amputees, war wounded, and victims of sexual violence, would continue throughout their lives. Given the price tag of pensions, free education, skills training, and microcredit to victims, it came as no surprise that the government did not rush forward to implement the recommendations.

Still, it was not until August 2006 that the government finally authorized NaCSA as the implementing agency, leaving the impression that a systematic reparations policy was not high on the list of government priorities. An often-heard complaint is that more has been done for perpetrators through the Disarmament, Demobilization, and Reintegration Program for ex-combatants than for victims, who had been left to suffer alone.[129] In response to the government's stonewalling, members of four separate victims' organizations—the Amputees, the War Wounded, the Vision for the Blind, and the Ex-service Wounded in Action Personnel Organization—formed in September 2006 the Coalition of War Disabled in Sierra Leone. One member, an amputee, complained that the government had already done a lot for the perpetrators but was allowing the amputees to suffer.[130] At the end of 2006—more than two years after the report was submitted—the SLPP government announced the establishment of the Special Fund for War Victims with a modest outlay of $100,000.[131]

The TRC's recommendation for reparations was categorized as *work toward* because of its expense. To be sure, the needs of victims are great, and paying for programs in the areas of health, pensions, education, and skills training for amputees, war wounded, and victims of sexual violence is daunting for a country that is consistently ranked on the UN Human Development Index as one of the poorest countries in the world and was economically devastated by a decade-long civil war. Still, the small initial investment in the fund suggests that a systematic reparation policy is off the government's agenda.

In 2008 the UN Peacebuilding Fund contributed $3,000,000 to jump-start the government's efforts. That contribution made possible a one-year project. The conditions of the Peacebuilding Fund grant were twofold: the monies had to be used within one year and 75% of the funds had to be spent to directly benefit victims.[132] NaCSA registered 29,733 victims from December 1, 2008, through June 30, 2009, in this project, although it was estimated that there were as many as 55,500 victims (4). There were lower numbers of registrants in rural districts such as Kailahun (although this district was particularly hard hit during the war) and among women who had been victims of sexual violence (5).

During the one-year project, money was to be spent on educational support to child amputees, on the war wounded, on victims of sexual violence, on abductees, on those who had been conscripted, on children born of rape and orphans, on fistula surgeries and HIV testing for victims of sexual violence, on free health care for direct victims, and on counseling for all categories of victims. NaCSA did implement emergency medical care for a limited number of victims, including 31 individuals who received medical operations. It also arranged for 235 victims of sexual violence to be examined on Mercy Ships, a few of whom were provided with fistula surgery.[133]

The original plan for the first year was for the reimbursement of money paid for school fees, uniforms, and books for child victims in primary or middle school. Although classes began in September 2009, no special educational support was forthcoming by that date. In any event, the plan had been criticized, since reimbursement, unlike direct payment of school-related fees, benefits only those who are already in school. The International Center for Transitional Justice also criticized the plan, since to be truly reparatory it would provide reimbursement at the secondary level. Providing money for the primary levels was a "socio-economic right to which all school children are entitled."[134]

In practice, most of the funds were limited to relief money and were not directed in a comprehensive approach. To the 20,107 victims who had registered through December 2009, most of the money was disbursed in small amounts (300,000 leones or approximately $75) in one-time interim payments to individual amputees, war wounded (with 50% incapacity), and victims of sexual violence.[135] Ibrahim Kamara, NaCSA's outreach coordinator, defended the grants, noting that the money would help victims improve their lives as they waited for services: "We are doing this because the services that we are to provide for them are still being worked out by the commission."[136] It was anticipated that the funds, though small, would at least help to initiate the process of developing a five-year strategic plan for reparations.[137] But one-time grants were not what the TRC had recommended; instead it had advised awarding ongoing pensions and services to victims.[138] The International Center for Transitional Justice estimates on the basis of the number of registered victims and the annual cost of pensions that the cost to the government to comply would be 6,305 million leones, not an inconsiderable amount but "not insurmountable."[139] Adding additional classes of victims, such as war widows—widows of military personnel had already received pensions—would raise the cost to 7,940 million leones per year.[140]

When President Koroma officially launched the War Victims Trust Fund on December 5, 2009,[141] director of reparations, Buya Kamara, announced that the fund would continue what the Peacebuilding Fund had begun.[142] The International Center for Transitional Justice stressed the importance of finding internal sources of funding before turning to the international community, noting there is "little precedent of international donors funding international [reparation] programmes."[143] Sadly, the government that year saw fit to contribute a mere $246,000.[144] Implementation came to a standstill because of lack of funds.[145] A second payment of 300,000 leones to each of 330 beneficiaries came from the government only in 2011. That year the UN Peacebuilding Fund also contributed $450,000 for microgrants and emergency medical assistance to 2,310 individuals. 1,172 beneficiaries who had not received the initial grant in 2009 each received 300,000 leones. Grants of 940,125 leones each were awarded to 1,138 amputees and 1,055 war wounded and sexually violated women. UN Women also provided 296 sexually violated women with skills training, tool kits, and a $500 grant.[146] A third installment worth $860,240 came in 2012, again through the UN Peacebuilding Fund. The funds were dispersed to 10,753 victims in payments of around $80 to each victim.[147] A fourth and possibly final installment was disbursed in 2013 as rehabilitation grants to some 1,138 amputees and 152 seriously wounded victims.[148]

Beginning with the government's tepid reaction in the White Paper to the recommendations, the follow-up phase got off to an inauspicious start. This is not unusual; the historical record of governments actually implementing recommendations from truth commissions is poor.[149] But there had been high hopes in Sierra Leone that since the Parliament had legislated that the government must implement the recommendations things would be different here.

According to Howard Varney, former head of the investigative unit of the TRC, "The government wants to sweep the report under the carpet—civil society needs to put it on the agenda."[150] If the TRC is to fulfill its mandate, it must deal with the root causes that led to the conflict in the first place and address the financial needs of victims. Distributive justice demands nothing less. But more than a decade after the war ended, the root causes—corruption, poor governance, lack of human rights—remain, and the needs of victims have been mainly unfulfilled.

CONCLUSION

(STILL) A WESTERN PREFERENCE FOR PROSECUTION

I had not set out originally to study the workings of the Special Court or its legacy, preferring to leave that to the legion of international lawyers and human rights advocates who are its main supporters. However, I quickly found there was no way to investigate the TRC, or the issues of restorative justice more broadly, in a vacuum. For better or for worse, the Special Court was an imposing presence casting a long shadow over its stepsister institution. It is one marker of the international community's increasing commitment to prosecute war crimes and crimes against humanity (part of what Lutz and Sikkink have called the "justice cascade"[1]), which began with the Nuremburg and Tokyo tribunals after World War II and continued with the ad-hoc International Criminal Tribunals for Yugoslavia and Rwanda of the 1990s; the establishment of the International Criminal Court (ICC) in 1998; national efforts to claim "universal jurisdiction" (e.g., Spain's attempt to extradite Pinochet and Belgium's prosecution of Rwandan genocidists); and, most recently, the creation of hybrid courts not only in Sierra Leone but also in places like Cambodia and Timor-Leste.

Human rights activists and international lawyers like Diane Orentlicher famously promoted the view that there is a "duty" under international law "to prosecute."[2] In the shadow of the Latin American self-amnesties, she viewed calls for "reconciliation" as veiled watchwords for "impunity."[3] Restorative approaches such as truth commissions, amnesties, or local practices were seen at the time to be, if not a complete sacrifice of justice, then surely a "second best" alternative to justice; they were usually viewed as a necessary evil formed purely on the basis of pragmatic political considerations.

The trend now is to see these two processes—trials and truth commissions—not as distinct options but as complementary choices. There is excitement in some quarters about pulling from the toolkit of transitional justice an array of fixes for a transitioning country: a tribunal for the very bad guys, a truth commission for everyone else, reparations for victims, and some institutional reforms. Debates center more often not on which to choose but on the order in which they should be sequenced. Even Orentlicher has conceded that the passage of time has altered her views in favor of a "comprehensive approach" to address abuses of the past in which "various measures—among them truth commissions; trials; institutional, social and economic reforms; and reparations programmes—play a distinct and unique part." And the United Nations has come to embrace the idea of truth commissions, though not amnesties for war crimes, crimes against humanity, and genocide (which is problematic since these are exactly the kinds of crimes that are often committed during a civil war), and has incorporated one into virtually every peace agreement it has been involved in since the early 1990s. In his report to the UN Security Council in 2004, Kofi Annan stressed the need "to eschew one-size-fits-all formulas and the importation of foreign models, and, instead, base our support on national assessments, national participation, and national needs and aspirations." He went on to argue that due regard should be given as well to "indigenous and informal traditions" in settling disputes.[4] Fine words indeed, but how sincere?

While truth commissions and local traditional rituals are becoming increasingly more acceptable to the international community, they are still deemed so only when they are used *in addition to* punitive measures and never *in place of* trials. Those same scholars who once denounced truth commissions see a role for them, albeit one lacking in any reconciliatory purpose in my view, and that is to collect evidence for future trials. The Argentine and Chilean truth commissions collected evidence that decades later provided the basis for trials of previous regime leaders (though originally they were protected by amnesty agreements).[5] But it was the Peruvian truth commission that first created a unit within the commission dedicated to preparing cases for prosecution. While the commission was still under way, it submitted four cases to the prosecutor and in its final report recommended the prosecutions of forty-three additional people.[6] Closer to home in Liberia it was understood that the work of their truth and reconciliation commission would be followed by prosecutions; in its final report in 2009, it recommended that 116 "most notorious perpetrators" be prosecuted in a special hybrid tribunal and 44 more be tried domestically.[7]

PREFERENCE FOR RESTORATIVE APPROACHES IN SIERRA LEONE

This new embrace of truth commissions fails to grasp the true value of these institutions, which is not merely to uncover the truth (factual truth) but more importantly to reconcile former enemies through telling and hearing the truth (dialogical truth).[8] For many people in transitioning countries, restoring right relationships, through a process of acknowledgment and forgiveness, is a more important achievement than securing convictions in a court of law.

I am reminded of a derisive op-ed piece, "Justice or Therapy?," penned by Kenneth Roth and Alison Des Forges in response to Helena Cobban,[9] whose *Boston Review* article had put forth her view on the limits of Western punitive justice in postconflict nations.[10] In the case of survivors who are coping in the aftermath of unspeakable traumas, I along with Cobban would wager that they may actually prefer therapeutic healing through truth commissions and local rituals than justice through trials.

Is there evidence for the healing power of truth? Just as the evidence is mixed on the nexus between deterrence and trials or the promotion of human rights and trials (addressed below), neither has it been scientifically established that speaking out in a truth commission or in a traditional forum promotes healing.[11] During the South African Truth and Reconciliation Commission, the *New York Times* reported that the Trauma Center for Victims of Violence and Torture in Cape Town found that 60% of witnesses felt worse after testifying because it brought back feelings of anger and sorrow.[12] A later study indicated that testifying actually had a negative impact on the willingness to forgive. Those who had submitted a statement or testified were less willing to forgive than those who had not.[13]

It struck me when reading the study that victims' disenchantment may have had more to do with their not receiving reparations for their suffering than any supposed post-traumatic stress that may have been induced from testifying. Public hearings perhaps raised expectations for victims that remained unfulfilled when the government decided it could not afford the ample reparations that the TRC had recommended. What I deduce from this is not that speaking in a truth commission is necessarily harmful in itself but that it can be harmful in the absence of reparations, which should go hand-in-hand with this process as an official acknowledgment of the victims' suffering.

Rosalind Shaw, on the basis of the polling from South Africa, had suggested that in Sierra Leone people would be worse off psychologically after testifying.[14] Yet when she later interviewed those victims from Bombali, who had testified earlier before the TRC, none claimed to have felt worse after testifying and all but one said he or she felt better. They were, however, disappointed that they did not receive compensation for sharing their painful past experiences.[15] Because of Sierra Leoneans' religious perspectives and traditional worldview, they did not find speaking out in a truth commission or within a local structure psychologically destructive, though it may have been in another context.

COMPLEMENTARY INSTITUTIONS?

For Sierra Leone, the two contemporaneous post-transition institutions were not complementary or "synergistic" as William Schabas described the relationship but rather fundamentally contradictory, that is, based on "incompatible mandates."[16] But despite the admitted strain in the relationship between the Special Court of Sierra Leone and the TRC, international analysts refuse to acknowledge that the two institutions were at cross-purposes. Special Court prosecutor David Crane in fact bragged that he had convinced the ICC prosecutor of the brilliance of Sierra Leone's experiment as a model for the ICC.[17] But the advisability of running concurrent retributive and restorative justice mechanisms—or for that matter of using truth commissions as investigative tools for future prosecutions as was done in Liberia and Peru—needs to be revisited.

There is the nightmarish prospect of transitioning countries holding truth commissions, domestic trials, and ICC prosecutions at the same time. This is not such a farfetched notion, since Africa has been the locale of all the ICC indictments to date (cases are open in the Democratic Republic of Congo, Uganda, the Central African Republic, Kenya, Ivory Coast, Sudan, Libya, and Mali)[18] and has hosted nine truth commissions since 2002 (Sierra Leone, Ghana, Morocco, Liberia, DRC, Kenya, Mauritius, Togo, and Ivory Coast). In addition, Africa has been the scene of one international "ad-hoc" tribunal, the International Criminal Tribunal for Rwanda, and one international "hybrid" court, the Special Court for Sierra Leone. Add to this the unusual case of Senegal's prosecution of Hissene Habre, the former leader of Chad. If one can learn anything from the Sierra Leone example, it is that concurrent retributive and restorative justice mechanisms are counterproductive. They certainly harden the resistance of perpetrators to speaking frankly in a truth and reconciliation commission venue, and they also induce witnesses to fear speaking out. Without the promise of amnesty, perpetrators are unlikely to be honest about sharing their stories. Unfortunately, most truth commissions are not accompanied by amnesties. And the United Nations since 1999 has refused to cooperate with those countries that offer amnesty for serious crimes.[19]

THE COST OF JUSTICE

The sheer expense of international justice also should give policy makers pause. Is punishment such an important value that it trumps all others? Given the limited amount of finances available for post-conflict reconstruction of all sorts, do we want the lion share's to be devoted to trying a handful of ringleaders of a conflict, especially when the choice of defendants is contested? Penfold has lambasted the Special Court as a highly expensive enterprise, noting that the electricity used to light and air-condition the cavernous space could light up a third of Freetown.[20] Gberie has also criticized its swollen budget, which is more than that of the entire government's civil service.[21] The Special Court had been envisioned as a less expensive alternative to the ad-hoc tribunals that had preceded it[22]—the international criminal tribunals of Yugoslavia and Rwanda both cost in the neighborhood of $100 million per year[23]—yet its estimated price tag was a mind-boggling $250–$300 million by the conclusion of the Charles Taylor trial and appeal.[24] The cost of punitive justice was a staggering $30 million for each defendant tried in Freetown, with another $50 million spent on the Charles Taylor trial in the Hague, estimates the former prosecutor Stephen Rapp.[25] By contrast, the more restorative justice approach of the TRC, which received 7,706 statements from victims and perpetrators,[26] has cost just $650 per statement-giver, surely a more cost-efficient mechanism.

Punishment, especially if it diverts funds that could be used toward reconciliation activities, monetary reparations, and institutional reforms, may be valued highly by an international community committed to the "rule of law," "no impunity," and the "duty to prosecute" but not so much by locals. Only 2% of victims who submitted statements to the TRC, for example, said they wanted "justice."[27] Nevertheless, the value of restorative as opposed to retributive justice is given mere lip service by the international community.

This priority is reflected in the significant commitment of resources to tribunals, compared to the smaller amounts allocated for restorative measures, such as truth commissions, and the even lesser amounts for traditional methods of conflict resolution. This is despite Braithwaite's observation that legal systems based on retributive justice are the ones that are an anomaly across time and culture, whereas restorative justice "has been the dominant model of criminal justice throughout most of human history for all the world's people."[28]

EMPIRICAL EVIDENCE?

Supporters of tribunals argue they build a culture of respect for human rights and also serve as a deterrent against future abuses. Does the evidence justify these claims? On the issue of human rights, the evidence is mixed. Kim and Sikkunk's study shows a positive correlation between post-transition trials and lower levels of human rights violations,[29] but Sikkunk's and Walling's study indicates that lower levels of human rights violations require both truth commissions and trials, rather than trials alone.[30] The evidence is inconclusive as well on deterrence. Do harsh punishments deter crime? Kim and Sikkunk's study finds little evidence that is the case for major human rights violations.[31] Snyder and Vinjamuri also conclude that trials do little to deter future violence.[32] In terms of deterrence, "Neither history nor its observers have yet shown that international criminal courts deter human rights violations," observes Minow.[33]

In the absence of empirical proof that punishment through tribunals leads to deterrence and the promotion of a culture of human rights, policy makers should move cautiously before allocating large postconflict funds to these institutions.[34] Surely when the choice of defendants appears to be arbitrary, and the compensation of witnesses is viewed as creating an incentive to lie, courts may serve to inspire only cynicism among locals rather than a commitment to democracy and human rights.

Especially in Africa, restorative justice approaches based on religion and tradition are well accepted. According to Deng, "At heart,

Africans are deeply spiritual people. To fail to draw on this reality is to fail to see the limitation of secular approaches to peacemaking."[35] It would therefore behoove the international community in future post-conflict settings to consult more widely with survivors about what they need to become whole. Even the staunchest early supporter of the duty to prosecute, Diane Orentlicher, in her retrospective of how her thinking has changed from the early years of transitional justice, now concedes that "staying the hand of prosecution in deference to local preferences . . . should be considered."[36] Outsiders might be surprised that punishing offenders is not always at the top of the victims' lists of preferences. Rather they want the right to receive apologies, the right to acknowledgment of guilt, the right to education, the right to reparations, the right to employment, and so forth. On the day the guilty verdict for Charles Taylor was announced by the Special Court, punishment was not foremost on the mind of amputee James Kpomgbo: "I will reflect on the suffering we suffered today but I want to forget. We have known all along CT is guilty. Today is just another day when we must find food."[37]

Culture shapes how various peoples prioritize punishment and reconciliation. If transitional justice systems do not resonate culturally, they will have a limited impact and legacy. Sierra Leoneans respond to notions of reconciliation, apology, and forgiveness. They are values that have meaning for them, notwithstanding negative critiques of such concepts by those who do not always share the same faith commitments or worldviews. Critics may assert that an ethic of resentment is more appropriate than one of forgiveness, and retributive justice is more valuable than reconciliation.[38] But all the world's great religions—and I would include African traditions—elevate reconciliation over justice. Unfortunately, many scholars and practitioners of transitional justice tend to relegate reconciliation and forgiveness to the realm of private morality, opting for retributive justice as the more appropriate public response to mass atrocity. They worry that "reconciliation" is a cover for impunity and can threaten individual rights while placing unreasonable burdens on victims, who are expected to forgive and empathize with their victimizers. By pushing religious and traditional understandings aside to formulate transitional justice mechanisms of accountability, countries that follow the advice of (mainly international) consultants risk losing one of their more valuable assets in peacebuilding. While concepts such as reconciliation, forgiveness, and mercy can certainly be manipulated, they also have the capacity to revitalize victims and perpetrators alike as they struggle to live together at the end of conflict.

PROSPECTS FOR RECONCILIATION: LOOKING FORWARD

Volkan writes about the intransigence of "chosen traumas," wherein one group (usually ethnic or religious) harbors deep resentments toward another group, incorporates the sense of being victimized by the out-group into its defining narrative of identity, and passes that sense of grievance on to subsequent generations.[39] Sierra Leone largely avoided the ethnic divisions that fuel so many domestic conflicts. Each combatant group—the RUF, AFRC, the CDF, and the Sierra Leone Armed Forces—recruited, conscripted, and abducted people from towns and villages all over the country with no regard for ethnicity or region. It was a war waged not between ethnic or regional groups but one fought at the local level.[40]

The war was not caused by a Temne-Mende conflict, a north-south struggle, Muslim-Christian hostility, or even a city-rural division. The political parties have, however, tended to be ethnically and geographically based, with the APC garnering support from mainly Temne Muslims in the north and the SLPP appealing to Mende Christians in the south. In addition, the provinces felt they were at a disadvantage relative to Freetown in terms of government services and attention.[41] Reconciliation between and among different identity groups is therefore possible to achieve in Sierra Leone, since people have more conflicts with their own neighbors than with other groups, toward which they harbor a "chosen trauma." Especially because the war was not waged on the basis of religion—a major divider in many multireligious countries—the IRC was able to make a more positive contribution than would have been possible had the conflict been religiously driven.[42]

The war lacked an ideological basis as well—there was no one ideologically inspired group pitted against another equally inspired group that was committed to fight to the end for survival or for a grand cause. Indeed, one reason it lasted so long was that nationalism provided insufficient inspiration to the soldiers to sacrifice to save the nation, and the material incentives were sufficient for certain people to want to prolong the war. There was no group cause that inspired transcendent loyalty. Without the motivations of ideology, religion, or ethnicity, the conflict was simply, as Gurr suggests, "predatory warfare and armed banditry."[43] Human Rights Watch notes that "Because of the lack of an ideological aspect and the limited ethnic dimension to the civil war in Sierra Leone and the all-pervasiveness of the abuse, victims of human rights abuses, including survivors of sexual violence, generally feel free to talk openly about their experiences."[44] This absence of deep group hostilities, coupled with the impossibility of any one group being able to claim exclusive "victim" status, bodes well for stopping the intergenerational transmission of traumas to future generations.

CONTINUED NEED FOR ACKNOWLEDGMENT: FROM TRC TO FAMBUL TOK

Reconciliation for the individual may occur at three levels: intrapersonal, interpersonal, and intracommunity. The intrapersonal level for victims means reconciliation with oneself, the healing of memories, and psychological closure.[45] For perpetrators, too, intrapersonal reconciliation may mean realizing and expressing how they were hurt and dehumanized by what they did to others and coming to terms with their experiences. At the TRC, victims usually described their experiences in the absence of their perpetrators, who feared testifying. Those few perpetrators who did testify often claimed they were also victims, as many were abducted and forced to commit egregious acts, but they were less forthcoming in admitting their own responsibility.

At the interpersonal level, reconciliation means renewed relationships between victim and perpetrator. When the TRC knew that a victim was planning to name his or her perpetrator, it offered the perpetrator a chance to respond and responses actually did happen, albeit infrequently. The TRC also occasionally mediated between individual perpetrators and their victims. While the majority of statement-givers had indicated they wanted to meet with their perpetrators and/or victims, this rarely happened, again due to budgetary and time constraints.

The third level of reconciliation for the individual is with his or her community, which is often overlooked in the peacebuilding literature but has enormous relevance in the Sierra Leonean context. Zehr notes that perpetrators and victims alike often feel disconnected from their communities.[46] This is especially true for child soldiers, other former combatants, rape victims, and combatant women, who have all had enormous difficulties returning to their homes because of the stigma attached to their wartime status. The TRC hoped to bring attention to their plights, to pave the way for their acceptance in their communities, but most perpetrators settled outside their communities.

Although the TRC hearings began the process of storytelling and the empathetic listening that is central to reconciliation, there was little actual acknowledgment of wrongdoing during the hearings (unfortunately, just 1% of the testimonies came from perpetrators). At the district hearings in Port Loko, the TRC was unable to muster even a single perpetrator to give a testimony.[47] Even among the small number of perpetrators who testified, very few actually admitted doing anything wrong. Typical was the statement of one RUF rebel: "I am apologizing for what the war did."[48]

Kelsall points out that while there was very little "truth" or acknowledgment from perpetrators at the TRC hearings, the ritual aspects of their prostrating themselves and asking for forgiveness at the weekly reconciliation ceremony seemed to have a profound effect on the crowd.[49] His conclusion—that in Sierra Leone, the verbal truth-telling aspect of truth commissions may be inappropriate or unnecessary and the ritual aspect is relevant—misses the point, however. The TRC, unlike many former truth commissions, did not unearth truths that had been hidden, such as facts about the "disappeared" and torture in secret chambers, because the conflict in Sierra Leone had been waged in the open. Women were raped in full public view, boys and girls suffered amputations in front of their families, and so forth. The "facts" of the war, in short, are widely known.[50] This does not mean as Kelsall and Shaw maintain, however, that vocalizing what one did, or what was done to oneself, is unimportant to people. As Nagel so aptly put it, there is a difference between knowledge of the facts, which people mostly knew,[51] and acknowledgment of deeds;[52] what they want is the acknowledgment.

The TRC was only partially successful in promoting acknowledgment of wrongdoing owing to many factors, such as budgetary constraints that limited the hearings in the district towns to just five days, and the simultaneous operation of the Special Court, which confused and frightened perpetrators. These are more plausible explanations for the lack of truth-telling at the TRC hearings than the cultural ones (a tradition of secrecy and obfuscation/dissimulation, as posited by Shaw and Kelsall).[53]

RELIGION AND THE PROMOTION OF RESTORATIVE JUSTICE

I started this project thinking that the religious communities were major sources of restorative justice ideas that supported the TRC, and I end it with that belief reaffirmed. Surely, the role of the IRC in brokering the peace by pushing for amnesty rather than continued warfare cannot be overemphasized. Rebels, soldiers, government officials, and civilians alike respected religious leaders as neutral arbiters.[54] Equally significant, religious leaders connected to perpetrators on a personal level, recognizing and respecting them as God's children, fellow brothers and sisters, who could be redeemed. For the rebels who struck out against civilians out of a sense of shame, if one accepts Keen's interpretation, violence provided a way to overcome that shame. The weak for the first time became powerful—"big men" so to speak. They demanded respect, often making victims applaud them as they killed and maimed.[55] For once, they had power over the chiefs, the elders, the well to do, or even their neighbors, who had diminished them in the past. Religious leaders in no way condoned their egregious acts, but they empathized with them and told them they understood their feelings about government corruption and neglect. They recognized the rebels' legitimate complaints about uncaring government officials who devalued them, and limited their opportunities, while enriching themselves. They accepted them as valuable human beings equal in the sight of God/Allah. "God loves you no matter what you have done" is a radical and healing message.

According to Stovel, the officials responsible for disarmament, demobilization, and reintegration had stressed in the early phase of reintegration that former combatants were not responsible for their actions.[56] Certainly, this is an understandable stance, when so many perpetrators were abducted and forced to commit atrocities. Asserting their lack of culpability may have facilitated their communities' willingness to accept them. However, not acknowledging their complicity may have impeded meaningful reconciliation, as perpetrators need to accept some measure of responsibility for their own personal healing, and victims long to hear a sincere acknowledgment and apology from perpetrators.

Christianity and Islam provided theological underpinnings for the TRC, which aimed at eliciting confessions (truth) from perpetrators in exchange for forgiveness by victims. In both religions, no one is an irredeemable devil. For Christians, this is because the atoning death of Christ saved all of humankind from sin, and for Muslims this is because they reject the very notion of original sin. In Islam, Christ's redemptive death was not necessary because humankind is not so depraved that Christ's sacrificial death was required. Because humans' original nature is one of moral innocence, humans are entirely capable of be(com)ing good.[57]

Both religions elevate restorative over punitive approaches. In Philpott's careful analysis of Christian and Muslim foundational texts, he finds that the meaning of *reconciliation*—"the restoration of relationships that wrongs have ruptured"—turns out "to be virtually the same" as the meaning of *justice*. In both religions, *justice* is a state of right relationships and a process through which right relationships can be restored after wrongdoing. It follows, then, that "justice is identical to reconciliation."[58] This insight is not lost on Sierra Leoneans—neither the religious leaders whom I interviewed nor the people at the grassroots for whom tradition emphasizes the restorative approach.

TRADITION AND RESTORATIVE JUSTICE

Over the course of this project, I came to discover that tradition also provides a basis for the promotion of restorative justice. Along with religion, it provides a rich resource for what John and Valerie Braithwaite call "reintegrative shaming," defined as "treating the wrongdoer respectfully and empathically as a good person who has done a bad act and making special efforts to show the wrongdoer how valued they are after the wrongful act has been committed."[59] Deng, who has studied indigenous methods of conflict resolution on the African continent, agrees that both modern restorative justice approaches and African tradition "prioritize the need to salvage and affirm the moral worth and dignity of everyone involved."[60] In Sierra Leone, this view is expressed in the often-quoted Krio expression, "There is no bad bush to throw away a bad child."

The reconciliation events initially sponsored by the IRC, and later by Fambul Tok after the TRC's conclusion, point to the importance of verbal acknowledgment and ritual to local communities for effective reconciliation among enemies. Ritual is important as it "captures the . . . sense of divine intervention that is part of the African healing process," but, according to Odama, it is preceded by verbal acknowledgment of wrongdoing.[61] Hamber and Wilson argue for a "diversity of memory processes outside of national commissions."[62] I agree with this assessment, but not with the conclusion that acknowledging guilt can be bypassed in the pursuit of reconciliation.

Walter Fisher reminds us that humankind is essentially "homo narrans."[63] Narrative is an impulse that is "international, transhistorical, transcultural."[64] According to Hayden White, "So natural is the impulse to narrate, so inevitable is the form of narrative for any report on the way things really happened, that narrativity could appear problematical only in a culture in which it was absent or . . . programmatically refused."[65] The process of telling and observing one's story being heard allows survivors to become subjects again.[66] This is especially so when the act of telling one's story invites a response. But a caveat is in order: storytelling as a means of reconciliation is best done at the local level. Coulter reminds us, "There is a great difference between telling one's story in a circle of friends and family, within a particular storytelling tradition, and telling one's story in the formal venues provided by the demobilization programmes, the TRC, and the Special Court, all of which operate within a very different 'storytelling tradition.'"[67] One glaring weakness of the TRC was that, despite its best intentions, it did not get deep into the countryside to operate at the village level.

The IRC's reconciliation events, and later the Fambul Tok ceremonies, have done much to redress that deficit by bringing individuals together locally to share their stories. This can be empowering for victims, who are pointing accusingly at their perpetrators and demanding an apology. Those who used the war to settle old scores are taking the opportunity now to confess and be absolved. Sierra Leoneans' traditional and religious resources are making this a reality, so that people don't get stuck in the past with unrepentant or unforgiving hearts. On the importance of genuine remorse, Keen wrote, "If people can be encouraged to feel and acknowledge a genuine sense of shame or guilt or remorse at what they have done, this holds the potential for making violence less likely."[68] Furthermore, the income-generating activities that Fambul Tok has promoted will go a long way toward cementing reconciliation, if one accepts Lederach's view that the more people acknowledge their interdependence and the more ties they have, the more likely they will be to reconcile.[69]

NATIONAL RECONCILIATION?

Outside observers express amazement at how quickly people seem to have moved on. I believe the explanation is that for most people the real enemy is the government, rather than their neighbors, who got sucked into the war by force, for profit, or out of despair. Neglect, abuse, corruption, and poor governance were the causes of the war, for which people hold the government responsible. There is much more anger at corrupt government officials than at those who actually committed wartime atrocities. This is promising in terms of the prospect of people being able to live together again in communities where former combatants wreaked such havoc during the war. As Keen notes, "Where the common enemy is not civilians in general but rather a particular kind of political system, the potential for positive change may be significant."[70]

Reconciliation, to the extent that it is proceeding, has been mainly at the individual and community levels because of the nature of the conflict. Fambul Tok seems to be succeeding locally in helping villagers overcome the traumas of war, elicit apologies and forgiveness, and develop structures to deal with present and future conflicts. Daly and Sarkin stress the importance of a ground-up, as opposed to a top-down, approach: "If reconciliation is going to have a deterrent effect, it must be reconciliation among the people, not just between the leaders."[71] But if Fambul Tok is succeeding at the local level, how does this translate into national reconciliation? Caulker is convinced that change will come "from the bottom up" but is vague about precisely how this will happen.[72] Will the outcome of Fambul Tok be psychologically healed individuals? Not to minimize individual healing, which Daly and Sarkin argue is a requirement for healthy democracies, but how can this process at the community level lead to national reconciliation—that is, to strong, transparent, equitable institutions?[73] Daly and Sarkin posit that there is "no evidence that individual transformations even if frequently replicated, translate into national reconciliation."[74] Whether more and more communities setting up reconciliation committees as permanent bodies to mediate ongoing conflicts, and developing a network of community committees, will have ramifications at the national level is not certain.

One senses that, in the absence of government responsiveness to the TRC's recommendations, Caulker envisions people taking ownership of their own trauma healing, their own reconciliation, and even their own economic development. Anthropologist Michael Jackson has noted that in Sierra Leone healing was sought through "things": "Fees to send children to school. Cement and roofing iron to rebuild houses. Grain. Micro-credit. Food. Medicines."[75] For national reconciliation to take root, "the material means that are needed to sustain life, and ensure a future for one's children" are required.[76]

If national or political reconciliation means trusting the government and its institutions to provide material goods fairly, then Sierra Leone is hardly reconciled. If Kriesberg is correct in saying that positive peace requires a "minimal level of equity,"[77] Sierra Leone has far to go, and this aspect of reconciliation remains an enormous challenge. Restorative justice requires not just healing individuals but also addressing the root causes of conflict. Witnesses before the TRC often highlighted the larger issue of corruption as the cause of the war. Abdul Kamara, for instance, testified, "You talk about sustainable peace when people are stealing government money. They are the rebels!"[78] The personal dimension of reconciliation cannot be minimized, but alongside that is the need for structural change at the national level. National reconciliation requires dealing with the causes of the war and transforming institutions to make them responsive to the people's grievances and needs.

And that is where a truth commission has the advantage over localized efforts. In addition to holding hearings where victims and perpetrators can share their individual stories—which in the case of Sierra Leone was not entirely successful—truth commissions gather together many voices, including institutional ones, in an effort "to get a clear picture of the past."[79] A major task of truth commissions is to create an historical record, address the root causes of conflict, and make recommendations to the government to prevent a recurrence. Even though most people knew what had happened during the decade-long war, publishing a history of the events serves as an official acknowledgment by the government of the people's suffering, with a promise that such conflicts will not happen again. Before the TRC, political, military, and rebel leaders spoke about their deeds and motivations, and, while these people were not always honest or entirely forthcoming, researchers in the investigative unit filled in the analysis for the report. In addition, thematic hearings were held on good governance, management of mineral resources, and corruption, and recommendations for the future made their way into the final report. The final report, *Witness to Truth*, remains an important advocacy tool for civil society groups pushing the government to enact the enumerated reforms to prevent future conflict.

ECONOMICS AND RECONCILIATION

The economic aspect of reconciliation should not be minimized. Shaw suggests that victims who had participated in the TRC's therapeutic-redemptive model of storytelling did so solely in exchange for material benefits, even though she claims it was culturally at odds with their memory practices. She argues (along with Kelsall) that because most of the testimony was dry and clinical rather than emotional, speaking out publicly was neither cathartic and healing nor culturally appropriate, as Sierra Leoneans had devised over the centuries a particular form of directed forgetting to cope with violence. Those who agreed to speak out, rather than to forget, did so under the assumption they would be rewarded with material benefits from the government and/or international community.[80]

While I reject her view that speaking out was culturally inappropriate and psychologically harmful—something her own research inadvertently disproves[81]—I accept Shaw's point that witnesses often came forward with the expectation they would receive help from the TRC or government. Millar's study in Makeni, for instance, revealed that most people (the uneducated nonelites) expected the TRC to provide money in exchange for stories and were disappointed in the process when it did not.[82] The point that economic assistance is crucial for reconciliation is well taken and has been confirmed by scholars,[83] by activists,[84] and by the witnesses themselves. In a review of the transcripts of the public hearings, I found that nearly all witnesses, when asked what they wanted, responded with some sort of material gain such as education, microcredits, and jobs. As Shaw posits, testifying did seem to imply a quid pro quo bargain. As one witness stated, "Yes, now that we have honored your invitation by coming to testify we are urging you to seek assistance for NGOs to help us rebuild our community."[85] One woman whose home was burned down and whose father suffered an amputation said, "I have now got my house, my toilet, some people are helping my children and that is why I say I am ready to forgive." She continued, "So you please help us so that we can forgive with all our hearts."[86]

The sources of conflict in Africa vary, but according to Villa-Vicencio, "They almost always include economic inequality." Sierra Leone poses no exception to this observation. He continues, "To the extent that the transitional justice debate neglects the economic side of this transition, it undermines its own principled commitment to sustainable peace."[87] This is where religion can contribute. Religion provides a basis for advocating for the equitable sharing of resources. In Islam, peace is understood not simply as the absence of war but as the elimination of the conditions, including economic inequality, that lead to conflict. Islam therefore requires its adherents to work toward establishing a just social reality and to reject oppression, not only at the personal but also at the structural level.[88] Abu-Nimer argues that, for Islam, "A nation cannot survive without making fair and adequate arrangements for the sustenance and welfare of all the poor, underprivileged, and destitute members of every community. The ultimate goal would be the elimination of their suffering and poverty."[89] Christianity also teaches the importance of economic justice, in particular liberation theology's emphasis on God's preferential option for the poor. While Christian teaching emphasizes charity on the personal level, it also advocates justice as a communal effort—the transformation of institutional structures that contribute to suffering and injustice.

Will the IRC be the prophetic voice to speak truth to power and stand with the poor and marginalized in their quest for social and economic justice? During the war, an NGO worker said, "As a result of the conflict, a lot of expatriates have left. A lot of the Church people didn't run. This puts them in a position of authority."[90] The IRC began to flex its muscle, for the first time speaking truth to power like the Old Testament prophets of old—first to the AFRC regime by asking it to step down and second to the SLPP government by asking it to negotiate with the RUF. But even the IRC's secretary general in his 2003 report voiced the concern that the heyday of the IRC had passed: "It would seem that the satisfaction of the IRCSL success in the peace process brought with it some lethargy to the point that members' attendance at meetings dropped considerably and thus important decisions were either delayed or not taken."[91] In part this was inevitable. To the degree that religious peacemakers are effective in the three phases of conflict transformation, which Scott Appleby terms conflict management, conflict resolution, and structural reform,[92] they appear to be least effective in the last phase. Part of this has to do with the simple fact that funds are limited. The founding of the IRC as a national chapter of the World Conference of Religions for Peace was immediately followed by the AFRC coup. As a result of this crisis, the body received significant funding from the World Conference of Religions of Peace, which facilitated the IRC's wartime efforts at mediation (Appleby's "conflict resolution" stage) but curtailed its contributions significantly when the war concluded, hampering further efforts at "structural reform."[93] Not surprisingly, Fambul Tok, with funding from its international partner Catalyst for Peace, has replaced the IRC in terms of influence in the postconflict period.

Can the faith community resurrect the role it had established during the war? One priest conceded, "We ... [are] thinking too much in terms of compassion and not enough dealing with structures that are corrupt or inadequate. You need to look at the structures that institutionalize sin, in line with liberation theology."[94] This view is refreshing but is a minority one among the religious leaders I interviewed in 2006 and 2007, most of whom mildly suggested, "I'm sure the government is doing what it can," "All governments are corrupt," and so forth.

In his presentation to the TRC in 2003, IRC secretary general Alimamy Koroma (who served at the same time as the general secretary of the Council of Churches in Sierra Leone) contrasted the Council's work in education, health, and social services before the war to its more robust approach during the war through the IRC. He highlighted the faith community's engagement in "prophetic advocacy" that "acts in solidarity with the oppressed and marginalized."[95]

Koroma, appointed minister of Works, Housing, and Infrastructure in the APC government, conceded that the faith community, even while still involved in working on the issues that led to the war and actively participating in civic education, voter education, and election monitoring, is no longer at the center of activism: "[Internationals] don't visit CCSL and IRC offices anymore. There are other organizations, other key players, like the Human Rights Commission."[96]

But despite its weakened position, and even in the absence of a vibrant theology of liberation, the faith community by default still has the most clout as the voice for the voiceless and is in a strategic position to push the government to provide reparations and enact necessary reforms. Both church and mosque have much to draw on from their teachings about economic justice, fairness, and equality, and the faith community also has the international linkages to rely on for resources and assistance for advocacy.

Religion and tradition are the strongest resources for restorative justice in Sierra Leone today. Traditional methods that "are homegrown, locally owned, culturally embedded"[97] are the most likely to resonate with people, especially "upcountry" in the provinces. A cautionary note is in order, however. One of the main dangers surrounding recognition of the value of African traditional practices is that the state may try to incorporate them into a legal framework and by codifying them may cause what are dynamic practices to stagnate. These practices may become less effective when they are placed in the service of a concrete political outcome, such as national unity and reconciliation. Or, as in the example of Rwanda, a state may be tempted to deviate from its original intention and take a traditional practice like gacaca and turn it into a more punitive enterprise. Perhaps the success of a tradition-based enterprise like Fambul Tok relies on local ownership and lack of government involvement or oversight.

At the same time, the faith community, with structures in place and educated leaders to advocate effectively with the government in Freetown, is a potentially important lobby to push for needed reforms that address the causes of the war. Even without international support in the postwar era, religious leaders are well respected and credible actors. Working in tandem, religion and tradition—that "treasure trove called culture"[98]—provide abundant resources for the ongoing work of transitional justice. While the Sierra Leonean example suggests that restorative approaches like truth commissions and local ceremonies are crucial, and should be considered by other transitioning countries in search of guidance, countries without either strong, active religious leadership that is independent from the state or reconciliatory traditions may find themselves, like the West, preferring to punish rather than pardon.

APPENDIX I

THE INSTRUMENT

What is your understanding of the concept of reconciliation? How closely is it tied to the need for acknowledgment of wrong on the one hand and forgiveness on the other?

Is there a difference in the religious and secular approaches to reconciliation?

What is needed in [Sierra Leone] to achieve reconciliation?

To what extent and in what ways has the TRC contributed to national reconciliation?

To what extent have [perpetrators] come to accept personal and social responsibility for [the war] as a result of TRC hearings?

To what extent have the survivors of gross human rights violations benefited from the TRC?

Was it helpful to have a religious person on the TRC which was a national government appointed body?

What can and what does the religious community do to foster reconciliation? As far as your specific faith group is concerned, are the commitment, energy and resources available? Or are there other priorities?

What is the task of the religious communities at this time in [Sierra Leone]?

In your view, how important is confession to reconciliation? Can rituals replace apologies? Should local understandings of reconciliation be taken into account when devising a national truth commission?

How do you compare the value of what the Special Court is doing with what the TRC accomplished? What in your opinion is the relationship between justice and reconciliation?

How important is it that the government enact the TRC's recommendations? Which recommendations do you believe are most important to advance reconciliation?

Any other comments on the reconciliation process?

APPENDIX 2

INTERVIEWS OF RELIGIOUS LEADERS

Umaru Sillah Bah, national president, Supreme Islamic Council, July 3, 2007
A. A. Bangura, general secretary, Emmanuel Baptist Convention, July 24, 2007
Marie Barnett, pastor, Evangelical Lutheran Church, July 24, 2007
Tom Barnett, bishop, Evangelical Lutheran Church, July 18, 2007
George Biguzzi, bishop, Catholic Church, Diocese of Makeni, July 12, 2006
Prince Charles Brainard, secretary general, Catholic Bishops Conference of the Gambia and Sierra Leone, July 3, 2007
Abu Bakarr Conteh, chief imam, Hamdallah Mosque, United Council of Imams; former missionary, Muslim World League; and senior lecturer, Freetown Teacher's College, July 5, 2006
Daniel Desay, pastor, Pentecostal Church, July 13, 2006
Reuben Dove, general superintendent, Countess of Huntingdon Connexion, July 31, 2007
M. O. Ekemode, evangelist, Christ Apostolic Church, July 24, 2007

Aiah D. Foday-Khabenje, general secretary, Evangelical Fellowship of Sierra Leone, August 1, 2007

Usman Fornah, interim secretary general, Inter-Religious Council, June 28, 2007

Joseph Humper, bishop, United Methodist Church, and former Chairman of the TRC, July 4, 2006

Alie Kallay, senior cleric, Sierra Leone Muslim Missionary Union, August 1, 2007

Solomon Kampbell, general secretary, Baptist Convention of Sierra Leone, July 23, 2007

Abdul Babatunde Karim, secretary general, Sierra Leone Muslim Congress; and professor, Fourah Bay College, July 30, 2007

Moses Khanu, former director, Inter-Religious Council; and commissioner, Human Rights Commission, July 17, 2007

S. Paul Khazali, founder and head, National Christian Evangelical Mission, July 19, 2007

Joseph Konteh, national superintendent, Wesleyan Church, July 5, 2007

Abdul Karim Koroma, Muslim Brotherhood Islamic Mission, August 6, 2007

Tamba Koroma, general superintendent, National Pentecostal Mission, August 6, 2007

Bankole Large, pastor, African Methodist Episcopal Church, July 26, 2007

J. O. P. Lynch, bishop, Anglican Church, Diocese of Freetown, July 14, 2006

Mariatu Mahdi, president, Federation of Muslim Women's Associations of Sierra Leone, July 6, 2006

Milton Marah, pastor, Missionary Church of Africa—Sierra Leone, August 8, 2007

Mabel Mbayo, Women's Desk, Inter-Religious Council, August 2, 2007

John P. Meindy, national field secretary, Church of God of Prophecy Mission, July 19, 2007

Francis S. Nabieu, bishop, Methodist Church of Sierra Leone, July 23, 2007

F. T. C. Randall, canon in residence, St. George's Anglican Church, July 11, 2006

Sahr Kemoore Salia, general secretary, Council of Churches in Sierra Leone, July 3, 2006

Henry C. Samuels, pastor, Vine Memorial Baptist Mission, July 25, 2007

Paul M. Sandi, chancellor, Catholic Archdiocese of Freetown and Bo, July 11, 2006

Ahmed Tejan Sillah, chief imam, Freetown Central Mosque; United Council of Imams, July 5, 2006

Billy K. Simbo, general superintendent, United Brethren in Christ Church, September 10, 2007

D. M. Speck, general superintendent, West African Methodist Church, July 24, 2007

Fomba Abubakar Swaray, chief imam, Madingo Central Mosque; Sierra Leone Muslim Missionary Union; and station manager of Voice of Islam radio station, August 1, 2007

NOTES

Preface

1. See Lyn S. Graybill, *Truth and Reconciliation in South Africa: Miracle or Model?* (Boulder: Lynne Rienner, 2002).
2. Harold Strachan, letter to the editor, *Mail and Guardian*, July 25, 1997.
3. Quoted in Wilhelm Verwoerd, "Forgiving the Torturer but Not the Torture," *Sunday Independent*, December 14, 1998.
4. Richard Wilson, "Reconciliation and Revenge in Post-apartheid South Africa: Rethinking Legal Pluralism and Human Rights" (paper presented at the Truth and Reconciliation Conference on Commissioning the Past, University of Witwatersrand, Johannesburg, June 1999).
5. Quoted in Mark Gevisser, "The Ultimate Test of Faith," *Mail and Guardian*, April 12, 1996.
6. Richard Wilson, *The Politics of Truth and Reconciliation in South Africa: Legitimizing the Post-apartheid State* (Cambridge: Cambridge University Press, 2001), 11.
7. Daniel Philpott, *Just and Unjust Peace: An Ethic of Political Reconciliation* (New York: Oxford University Press, 2012), 2.

Introduction: Postwar Transitional Justice

1. Statute of the Special Court for Sierra Leone, January 16, 2002.
2. Bishop Joseph Humper, quoted in William A. Schabas, "The Relationship between Truth Commissions and International Courts: The Case of Sierra Leone," *Human Rights Quarterly* 25 (2003): 1038.
3. Thomas Mark Turay, "Civil Society and Peacebuilding: The Role of the Inter-Religious Council of Sierra Leone," *Accord* 9 (2000): 50.
4. See Audrey R. Chapman and Bernard Spong, eds., *Religion and Reconciliation in South Africa: Voices of Religious Leaders* (Philadelphia: Templeton Press, 2003).

5. Ibid., 17–18.

6. Rosalind Shaw, "Memory Wars: Commissioning Truth and Reconciliation in Sierra Leone" (unpublished paper, n.d.).

7. Alcinda Honwana, "Sealing the Past, Facing the Future: Trauma Healing in Rural Mozambique," *Accord* 3 (1998): 75–80; and Alcinda Honwana, "The Collective Body: Challenging Western Concepts of Trauma and Healing," *Track Two* 8, no. 1 (1999): 30–35. For a critique see Lyn S. Graybill, "Pardon, Punishment, and Amnesia: Three African Post-conflict Methods," *Third World Quarterly* 25, no. 6 (2004): 1117–30.

8. Rosalind Shaw, "Rethinking Truth and Reconciliation Commissions: Lessons from Sierra Leone," USIP Special Report 130 (February 2005).

9. Tim Kelsall, "Truth, Lies, Ritual: Preliminary Reflections on the Truth and Reconciliation Commission in Sierra Leone," *Human Rights Quarterly* 27, no. 2 (2005): 361–91.

10. Wilson, *Politics of Truth*.

11. Graybill, *South Africa*, 25–37.

12. Luc Huyse, "Introduction: Tradition-Based Approaches in Peacemaking, Transitional Justice and Reconciliation Policies," in *Traditional Justice and Reconciliation after Violent Conflict: Learning from African Experiences*, eds. Luc Huyse and Mark Salter (Stockholm: IDEA, 2008), 5.

13. Erin Daly and Jeremy Sarkin, *Reconciliation in Divided Societies: Finding Common Ground* (Philadelphia: University of Pennsylvania Press, 2006), 61.

14. Desmond Tutu, *No Future without Forgiveness* (New York: Doubleday, 1999), 51.

15. See for example Martha Minow, "Making History or Making Peace: When Prosecutions Should Give Way to Truth Commissions and Peace Negotiations," *Journal of Human Rights* 7, no. 2 (2008): 174–85.

Chapter 1. Role of the Inter-Religious Council

1. Many of the insurgents were part of Taylor's National Patriot Front of Liberia rebel forces, which included Liberian and Burkinabe mercenaries. See Sierra Leone Truth and Reconciliation Commission, *Witness to Truth: Report of the Sierra Leone Truth & Reconciliation Commission* (Accra: Graphic Packaging, 2004), 3A:120. See also Joe A. D. Alie, "Reconciliation and Traditional Justice: Tradition-Based Practices of the Kpaa Mende in Sierra Leone," in Huyse and Salter, *Traditional Justice and Reconciliation*, 123.

2. See Revolutionary United Front, "Footpaths to Democracy: Toward a New Sierra Leone," 1995. This was written, however, in 1995 to give ex post facto ideological justification for the invasion.

3. Alie, "Reconciliation and Traditional Justice," 127.

4. Two different views of the RUF's rebellion are expressed in the works of Robert Kaplan, who characterizes it as senseless, irrational banditry and barbarism, and Paul Richards, who argues for a more principled, rational opposition originating from excluded intellectuals. See Robert Kaplan, "The Coming Anarchy: How Scarcity, Crime, Over-Population and Diseases Are Rapidly Destroying Our Planet," *Atlantic Monthly*, February 1994; and Paul Richards, *Fighting for the Rain Forest: War, Youth, and Resources in Sierra Leone* (Portsmouth, NH: Heinemann, 1996).

5. Under the APC, the army was largely a "ceremonial" one, unequipped to defeat the RUF. The forces numbered just four thousand, with the "cream of the crop" deployed with the Economic Community of West African States Monitoring Group (ECOMOG) in Liberia. See Sierra Leone Truth and Reconciliation Commission, *Witness*, 3A:149–50. The coup had as much to do with the resentment of junior officers against senior officers—anger about the back pay they were owed and poor conditions on the battlefield—as with a commitment to ending the war.

6. Ibid., 3A:159.

7. For a good summary of how certain elements colluded in the war because they benefited from the war's continuation, see David Keen, *Conflict and Collusion in Sierra Leone* (Oxford: James Currey, 2005).

8. While the *Kamajors* operated mainly in the east and south, the *Tamaboros* operated in the far north, the *Gbettis* in the north, and the *Donzos* in the far east. See Human Rights Watch, "We'll Kill You If You Cry: Sexual Violence in the Sierra Leone Conflict," *Human Rights Watch* 15, no. 1-A (2003): 10.

9. Alie, "Reconciliation and Traditional Justice," 127.

10. Sierra Leone Truth and Reconciliation Commission, *Witness*, 3A:223.

11. See Keen, *Conflict and Collusion*, 117. See also Sierra Leone Truth and Reconciliation Commission, *Witness*, 3A:228.

12. Lansana Gberie, *A Dirty War in West Africa: The RUF and the Destruction of Sierra Leone* (Bloomington: Indiana University Press, 2005), 95.

13. Quoted in Keen, *Conflict and Collusion*, 154.

14. The SLPP ruled from 1961–67 but was defeated in 1967 by the APC, which was in power until the coup in 1992.

15. Sierra Leone Truth and Reconciliation Commission, *Witness*, 3A:285.

16. Alie, "Reconciliation and Traditional Justice," 125.

17. Sierra Leone Truth and Reconciliation Commission, *Witness*, 3A:329.

18. Ibid., 3A:319–20.

19. Key commanders of the AFRC junta launched the attack and were joined only later by the RUF. See Sierra Leone Truth and Reconciliation Commission, *Witness*, 3A:317.

20. Ibid., 3A:329.

21. Tom Kamara, *Sierra Leone: A Search for Peace against the Odds* (Geneva: UNHCR, 2000), 5.

22. Sierra Leone Truth and Reconciliation Commission, *Witness*, 3A:389, 433.

23. Statistics are from the Crimes of War Education Project.

24. John L. Hirsch, *Sierra Leone: Diamonds and the Struggle for Democracy* (Boulder: Lynne Rienner, 2001), 29.

25. Moses Benson Khanu, "The Role of the Inter-Religious Council in the Sierra Leone Peace Process (1977–2003)" (master's thesis, Fourah Bay College, 2005), 11.

26. Sierra Leone Truth and Reconciliation Commission, *Witness*, 3A:69.

27. Ibid., 3A:70.

28. J. Peter Pham, "Liberia and Sierra Leone: A Study of Comparative Human Rights Approaches by Civil Society Actors," *Interdisciplinary Journal of Human Rights Law* 1, no. 1 (2006): 87.

29. Turay, "Civil Society," 50.

30. Alimamy P. Koroma, at the Tanenbaum Center's Peacemakers in Action Retreat, Amman, Jordan, May 3–5, 2004, quoted in David Little, "The Power of Organization: Alimamy Koroma," in *Peacemakers in Action: Profiles of Religion in Conflict Resolution*, ed. David Little (New York: Cambridge University, 2007), 288.

31. Turay, "Civil Society and Peacebuilding," 51.

32. Cynthia Sampson, "'To Make Real the Bond between Us All': Quaker Conciliation during the Nigerian Civil War," in *Religion, the Missing Dimension of Statecraft*, ed. Douglas Johnston and Cynthia Sampson (New York: Oxford University Press, 1994), 110–11.

33. Ibid., 111.

34. Monica Duffy Toft, Daniel Philpott, and Timothy Samuel Shah, *God's Century: Resurgent Religion and Global Politics* (New York: W. W. Norton, 2011), 192.

35. Ibid., 175.

36. R. Scott Appleby, *The Ambivalence of the Sacred: Religion, Violence, and Reconciliation* (Lanham, MD: Rowman and Littlefield, 2000), 158–65.

37. For a firsthand account, see Susan Collins Marks, *Watching the Wind: Conflict Resolution during South Africa's Transition to Democracy* (Washington, DC: USIP Press, 2000).

38. William Vendley, "Exploring Strategies to Enhance Interfaith Cooperation for Sustainable Peace: The Experience of Religions for Peace," Conference on Interfaith Cooperation for Peace, United Nations, June 22, 2005, 1.

39. Toft, Philpott, and Shah, *God's Century*, 185.

40. David R. Smock, ed., "Religious Contributions to Peacemaking: When Religion Brings Peace, Not War," *Peaceworks* no. 55 (January 2006): 2.

41. Religions for Peace, Commission on Conflict Transformation, Eighth World Assembly, Kyoto, Japan, August 2006.

42. The IRC had been preceded by PROCMURA (Project for Christians and Muslims) in the 1980s as a way to avoid the inter-religious violence of Nigeria.

43. The Catholic Church is made up of the Archdiocese of Freetown, and the Dioceses of Bo, Kenema, and Makeni. Until 2011, the Archdiocese of Freetown included Bo.

44. Conflict Transformation Working Group, "Building Peace from the Ground Up: A Call to the U.N. for Stronger Collaboration with Civil Society" (New York: CTWG, 2002), 11.

45. L. A. Foullah and Macsood Gibril Sesay, "Peaceful Co-existence in a Multi-religious Society" (Freetown: Council of Churches in Sierra Leone, 2006), 9.

46. Cynthia Sampson, "Religion and Peacebuilding," in *Peacemaking in International Conflict: Methods and Techniques*, ed. I. William Zartman (Washington, DC: USIP Press, 2007), 275.

47. Alimamy Koroma, quoted in Little, "Power of Organization," 290.

48. Vendley, "Exploring Strategies," 2.

49. Khanu, "Role," 57.

50. Turay, "Civil Society and Peacebuilding," 51.

51. Alimamy Koroma, the minister of Works, Housing and Infrastructure in the APC government at the time of my interview (April 21, 2010), says he "was invited by the police" to come to headquarters.

52. Pham, "Liberia and Sierra Leone," 88.

53. Khanu, "Role," 60–61.

54. Ibid., 64–65.

55. Turay, "Civil Society," 51.

56. Pham, "Liberia and Sierra Leone," 88.

57. Peter Penfold, "Faith in Resolving Sierra Leone's Bloody Conflict," *Round Table* 94, no. 382 (2005): 552.

58. Khanu, "Role," 72.

59. Turay, "Civil Society," 51.

60. Moses Khanu, former director, Inter-Religious Council, interview, July 17, 2007.

61. Penfold, "Sierra Leone's Bloody Conflict," 552.

62. Turay, "Civil Society," 52.

63. I could not get an interview with Ganda, and I was told that he has never spoken of his ordeal.

64. Penfold, "Sierra Leone's Bloody Conflict," 553.

65. J. Peter Pham, "Lazarus Rising: Civil Society and Sierra Leone's Return from the Grave," *International Journal of Not for Profit Law* 7, no.1 (November 2004): 59.

66. It should be noted that ECOMOG, as well as progovernment forces, also perpetrated grave human rights abuses, including the summary execution of suspected rebel sympathizers and aerial attacks on civilian targets. See Michael O'Flaherty, "Sierra Leone's Peace Process: The Role of the Human Rights Community," *Human Rights Quarterly* 26 (2004): 32.

67. Penfold, "Sierra Leone's Bloody Conflict," 553.

68. Gberie, *Dirty War*, 130.

69. Abu Bakarr Conteh (chief imam, Hamdallah Mosque, United Council of Imams; former missionary, Muslim World League), interview, July 5, 2006.

70. The bishop was a known supporter of the SLPP government.

71. Joseph Humper (bishop, United Methodist Church, and former chairman of the TRC), interview, July 4, 2006.

72. J. O. P. Lynch (bishop, Anglican Church, Diocese of Freetown), interview, July 14, 2006.

73. Gberie, *Dirty War*, 60, 136.

74. Revolutionary United Front, "Footpaths to Democracy," 12.

75. Richards, *Fighting for the Rain Forest*, 179.

76. Alimamy Koroma, interview, July 21, 2010.

77. Keen, *Conflict and Collusion*, 44, 61.

78. See Keen (ibid., 229–41) on the notion of shame and on attempts to overcome it.

79. Quoted in ibid., 292.

80. The paramount chiefs had been uprooted during the war and were residing in Freetown.

81. Jane Lampman, "Faith's Unbreakable Force," *Christian Science Monitor*, December 23, 1999.
82. Inter-Religious Council, communique, February 25, 1999.
83. Khanu, "Role," 86.
84. Ibid., 77.
85. Ibid.
86. Ibid., 78.
87. Ibid., 89–90.
88. Little, "Power of Organization," 292.
89. Lampman, "Faith's Unbreakable Force."
90. Alimamy Koroma, quoted in Little, " Power of Organization," 293.
91. Ibid.
92. Khanu, "Role," 90.
93. O'Flaherty, "Sierra Leone's Peace Process," 51.
94. Khanu, "Role," 91.
95. Turay, "Civil Society," 52.
96. Moses Khanu, interview, July 17, 2007.
97. Khanu, "Role," 92.
98. Turay, "Civil Society," 53.
99. Lampman, "Faith's Unbreakable Force."
100. Ibid.
101. Turay, "Civil Society," 53.
102. Peter Penfold argues that the main objection of civil society was to power sharing. Under the Accord, RUF was given four minister posts and four deputy minister posts. Under pressure from the United States, Sankoh was made chairman of strategic resources, in effect putting him in control of the diamonds. See Peter Penfold, *Atrocities, Diamonds and Diplomacy: The Inside Story of the Conflict in Sierra Leone* (Barnley, UK: Pen and Sword Books, 2012), 148–51.
103. Corinna Schuler, "Sierra Leone's 'See No Evil' Pact," *Christian Science Monitor*, September 15, 1999.
104. Turay, "Civil Society," 53.
105. Penfold, "Sierra Leone's Bloody Conflict," 555.
106. Lampman, "Faith's Unbreakable Force."
107. Alimamy Koroma, quoted in Little, "Power of Organization," 295.
108. Khanu, "Role," 98.
109. Ibid.

Chapter 2. The Sierra Leone Truth and Reconciliation Commission

1. Lome Peace Accord, "Pardon and Amnesty," art. 9 (3), July 7, 1999.

2. A new, democratically elected government in Nigeria had decided the cost—$1 million a day in addition to high casualties—would prevent it from maintaining its soldiers in ECOMOG.

3. More problematic than amnesty for most people was power-sharing with the RUF. Penfold argues that Kabbah was under extreme pressure from the international community, especially the United States, to seek a power-sharing arrangement with the rebels. Jesse Jackson, Clinton's special envoy, referred to Sankoh as the "Nelson Mandela of West Africa." See Peter Penfold, "The Special Court for Sierra Leone: A Critical Analysis," in *Rescuing a Fragile State: Sierra Leone 2002–2008*, ed. Lansana Gberie (Waterloo, ON: Wilfrid Laurier University Press, 2009), 54.

4. Interestingly, the UN had not opposed the amnesty agreements in the Abidjan Accord in 1996. That is most likely the reason the temporal jurisdiction of the Court begins after the Abidjan Accord; crimes committed before the Accord were covered by an amnesty.

5. Lome Peace Accord, "Post-War Rehabilitation and Reconstruction," art. 28.

6. Penfold, "Special Court," 53.

7. The Kenyan Truth, Justice, and Reconciliation Commission's long-awaited final report was released on May 2, 2013.

8. Penfold, "Special Court," 54.

9. International Crisis Group, "The Special Court for Sierra Leone: Promises and Pitfalls of a 'New Model,'" Report no. 16, August 4, 2003, 16.

10. Statute of the Special Court for Sierra Leone, art. 1, January 16, 2002.

11. The eight indictees who were tried in Freetown have been convicted and sentenced and are serving their sentences in Rwanda. They are Alex Tamba Brima (AFRC), Brima Bazzy Kamara (AFRC), Santigie Borbor Kanu (AFRC), Moinina Fofana (CDF), Allieu Kondewa (CDF), Issa Sessay (RUF), Morris Kallon (RUF), and Augustine Gbao (RUF).

12. Richard Bennett, "The Evolution of the Sierra Leone Truth and Reconciliation Commission," in *Truth and Reconciliation in Sierra Leone: A Compilation of Articles on the Sierra Leone Truth and Reconciliation Commission*, Freetown: United Nations Mission in Sierra Leone, 2001.

13. "Recommendations Adopted by the Human Rights Committee," February 19, 1999.

14. Sierra Leone Truth and Reconciliation Commission, *Witness*, 1:28.

15. Pham, "Liberia and Sierra Leone," 92.

16. Alimamy Koroma (former IRC secretary general), interview, April 21, 2010.

17. International Center for Transitional Justice, "The Sierra Leone Truth and Reconciliation Commission: Reviewing Its First Year" (New York: ICTJ, 2004), 2.

18. Rosalind Shaw, "Rethinking Truth and Reconciliation," 4.

19. The four Sierra Leonean commissioners were Bishop Joseph Humper, head of the IRC; Deputy Chair Laura Marcus-Jones, a former judge of the Sierra Leone High Court; Professor John Kamara, a former principal of Njala University College and a veterinary surgeon; and Sylvanus Torto, a teaching fellow at the Institute of Public Administration and Management of the University of Sierra Leone. The international commissioners were Ajaaratou Satang Jow, former minister of education in the Gambia; William Schabas, Canadian human rights lawyer and head of the Irish Centre for Human Rights; and Yasmin Louise Sooka, director of the Foundation for Human Rights in South Africa, former commissioner from the South African Truth and Reconciliation Commission, and a human rights lawyer. Haiti and Guatemala provided precedents for including international commissioners.

20. It is not unusual for truth commissions to be constrained by limited finances, or to run out of money during the process. See Priscilla Hayner, *Unspeakable Truths: Confronting State Terror and Atrocity* (New York: Routledge, 2001), 223–24.

21. Sierra Leone Truth and Reconciliation Commission, *Witness*, 1:9, 60.

22. International Crisis Group, "Sierra Leone's Truth and Reconciliation Commission: A Fresh Start?," December 20, 2002, 5.

23. Beth K. Dougherty, "Searching for Answers: Sierra Leone's Truth and Reconciliation Commission," *African Studies Quarterly* 8, no. 1 (2004): 43.

24. Yasmin Jusu-Sheriff (executive secretary, TRC), interview, July 9, 2007. Jesu-Sheriff claimed her background as an attorney did not prepare her adequately for the administrative duties her new role entailed, but she had been assured by Humper that the United Nations would assist her with running things, which she found to be untrue.

25. International Crisis Group, "Sierra Leone's Truth," 9.

26. In addition to the IRC, other groups on the selection committee had included the National Forum for Human Rights, RUF, and the National Commission for Democracy and Human Rights. The same selection panel was consulted by OHCHR regarding the international commissioner appointments.

27. International Center for Transitional Justice, "Sierra Leone," 2.

28. The advantage of having both national and international commissioners is it allows "national familiarity and international expertise to complement one another." See Hayner, *Unspeakable Truths*, 220.

29. Joseph Humper (chair, TRC), interview, July 4, 2006; Sylvanus Torto (commissioner), interview, July 25, 2007; Laura Marcus-Jones (deputy chair, TRC), interview, August 2, 2007.

30. Yasmin Jusu-Sheriff, interview, July 9, 2007.

31. Ibid.

32. According to the International Center for Transitional Justice, most of the staff were Sierra Leoneans, although most of the department heads were foreigners. See International Center for Transitional Justice, "Sierra Leone," 3.

33. Yasmin Jusu-Sheriff, interview, July 9, 2007.

34. Dougherty, "Searching for Answers," 42.

35. Jusu-Sheriff concedes that she was not experienced in administration but had been told by President Kabbah (her godfather) not to worry because the United Nations would be in charge of providing the staff. She said she would have been better suited for a commissioner position rather than that of executive secretary, but she was encouraged by the president to take this position. Yasmin Jusu-Sheriff, interview, July 9, 2007.

36. Ibid.

37. Sierra Leone Truth and Reconciliation Commission, *Witness*, 1:97.

38. William A. Schabas, "The Sierra Leone Truth and Reconciliation Commission," in *Transitional Justice in the Twenty-First Century: Beyond Truth versus Justice*, ed. Naomi Roht-Arriaza and Javier Mariezcurrenta (New York: Cambridge University Press, 2006), 23.

39. Ibid., 39.

40. The TRC's final report indicates that there were 14,995 victims and 40,242 individual violations noted in their database. See Sierra Leone Truth and Reconciliation Commission, *Witness*, CD-ROM, statistics.

41. Public hearings were held in Kabala, Makeni, Magburaka, Port Loko, and Kambia in the Northern Province; Bo, Mayamba, Bonthe, and Pujehun in the Southern Province; Kenema, Koidu, and Kailahun in the Eastern Province, and Freetown in the Western Area. The TRC was unable to get statements in 9 of the 149 chiefdoms.

42. Cambodia has since established both tribunal and truth commission, and in Timor-Leste, the Commission for Reception, Truth and Reconciliation (CAVR) has functioned at the same time as the Serious Crimes Unit

(SCU), which was mandated to prosecute those responsible for violence surrounding the preindependence referendum in 1999.

43. Schabas, "Relationship," 1038.

44. On the difference in the two approaches, see Tutu, *No Future;* Howard Zehr and Harry Mika, "Fundamental Concepts of Restorative Justice," *Contemporary Justice Review* 1, no. 1 (1998): 47–55; Mark Amstutz, "Restorative Justice, Political Forgiveness, and the Possibility of Political Reconciliation, in *The Politics of Past Evil: Religion, Reconciliation, and the Dilemmas of Transitional Justice*, ed. Daniel Philpott (Notre Dame, IN: University of Notre Dame Press, 2006), 151–88.

45. Robert Vincent, "Punishment and Forgiveness in Sierra Leone—A Response to Peter Penfold," *Observer*, November 3, 2002.

46. See Graybill, *South Africa*.

47. Unlike his inspiring South African counterpart, Humper has been described as "a somewhat uncharismatic and little known . . . Bishop." See Lansana Gberie, "Briefing: The Special Court of Sierra Leone," *African Affairs* 102, no. 409 (2003): 640. John Caulker felt that the choice of Humper was regrettable, and had the chair been someone like the dynamic bishop of Makeni, George Biguzzi, the TRC would have been more successful because former rebels, who knew and trusted him, would have felt safe in testifying. According to Caulker, "there was no one on the Commission that the rebels saw as sympathetic" (John Caulker, founder and executive director, Fambul Tok, interview, June 28, 2007).

48. Quoted in Turay, "Civil Society," 53.

49. Tutu, *No Future*.

50. The exceptions were Germany and Timor-Leste, where religious leaders strongly advocated punitive justice. See Toft, Philpott, and Shah, *God's Century*, 199.

51. In theory, where an outgoing regime maintains a certain level of power, its leaders will not be prosecuted. Where an outgoing regime is defeated, on the other hand, there will be prosecutions. See, for example, Samuel P. Huntington, *The Third Wave: Democratization in the Late Twentieth Century* (Norman: University of Oklahoma Press, 1991). Philpott, however, argues that there are too many variances to the model of outgoing power to explain all post-transition choices: There were cases in which there were trials in the absence of a clear victor (e.g., Timor-Leste, Yugoslavia, and eventually Chile); cases in which truth commissions followed a regime's defeat (Germany, Argentina, and Brazil); and hybrid cases of both trials and truth

commissions (Sierra Leone, Timor-Leste, Germany, and Argentina). See Philpott, *Just and Unjust*, 75–79.

52. Daniel Philpott, "When Faith Meets History: The Influence of Religion on Transitional Justice," in *The Religious in Responses to Mass Atrocity: Interdisciplinary Perspectives*, ed. Thomas Brudholm and Thomas Cushman (London: Cambridge University Press, 2009), 181.

53. Sierra Leone Truth and Reconciliation Commission Act, 2000.

54. *Religion and Ethics Newsweekly*, "Sierra Leone: Truth and Reconciliation," January 10, 2003.

55. Sierra Leone Truth and Reconciliation Commission, *Witness*, 1:182.

56. Graybill, *South Africa*, 49–50.

57. Sierra Leone Truth and Reconciliation Commission, *Witness*, 3B:434.

58. Laura Stovel, "Long Way Home: Building Reconciliation and Trust in Post-conflict Sierra Leone" (PhD diss., Simon Fraser University, 2006), 192.

59. On the value of empathy for reconciliation, see Jodi Halpern and Harvey M. Weinstein, "Rehumanizing the Other: Empathy and Reconciliation," *Human Rights Quarterly* 26 (2004): 561–83.

60. Solomon Berewa, "Addressing Impunity Using Divergent Approaches: The Truth and Reconciliation Commission and the Special Court," in *Truth and Reconciliation in Sierra Leone: A Compilation of Articles on the Sierra Leone Truth and Reconciliation Commission* (Freetown: United Nations Mission in Sierra Leone, 2001), 3–4.

61. Africa News Service, "Amputees to Take Part in Reconciliation Hearings," September 6, 2002.

62. Jusu Jaka (national chairman of the Amputees and War Wounded Association in Sierra Leone), interview, July 8, 2006.

63. Sierra Leone Truth and Reconciliation Commission, *Witness*, transcripts of the TRC Hearings, Freetown, April 14, 2003, CD-ROM, appendix: 1–5.

64. Schabas, "The Sierra Leone Truth and Reconciliation Commission," 31.

65. Of all the statements received, 36% were from women. See Truth and Reconciliation Commission, *Witness*, 1:170.

66. Shaw, "Memory Wars," 4.

67. Ibid.

68. Tim Kelsall, "Truth, Lies, Ritual," 68.

69. Dougherty, "Searching for Answers," 49.

70. That is the number that went through the Disarmament, Demobilization, and Reintegration process (DDR). (See International Crisis Group, "Sierra Leone after Elections: Politics as Usual?," July 15, 2002.) But Peter Andersen, Special Court public affairs officer, believes the actual number of combatants was closer to fifty thousand (interview, July 4, 2006).

71. For a description of the South African children's hearings, see Lyn S. Graybill, "Honoring the Voices of Children at the Truth and Reconciliation Commission," *Iris* 39 (Fall 1999): 32–35.

72. Gberie, *A War*, 8.

73. There had been speculation about whether the Special Court would indict youths, since the act allowed for those over fifteen years old to be indicted, but Prosecutor Crane put this notion to rest when he announced he had no intention of indicting children. See Schabas, "Relationship," 1045.

74. Sierra Leone Truth and Reconciliation Commission, *Witness*, 1:99.

75. Samuel Hinga Norman died in custody on February 22, 2007. The other three who were indicted and are now dead, or are presumed dead, are RUF leader Foday Sankoh and his military commander, Sam Bockarie; and Johnny Paul Koroma, the former AFRC junta leader, whose bloody coup in 1997 led to the Nigerian-led ECOMOG intervention.

76. The government denied it had reneged on the amnesty agreement. President Kabbah told the TRC that the government considered amnesty applicable only in national courts. (Sierra Leone Truth and Reconciliation Commission, *Witness*, Thematic Hearing on Reconciliation, Freetown, August 5, 2003, CD-ROM.) Some RUF defendants have been tried in state courts, but only for acts that occurred after the signing of the Lome Peace Accord and are unprotected by that accord. And of course the United Nations in its written caveat to the Lome Accord noted that it did not consider amnesty applicable for international crimes.

77. Rumors circulated that there was a secret underground passageway between the TRC and the Special Court, and they were sharing information. Some personnel who worked for the TRC were later seen in the employ of the Special Court, which fueled suspicion that they were colluding.

78. Sierra Leone Truth and Reconciliation Commission *Witness*, Statistical Report, CD-ROM, appendix, 3. The International Center for Transitional Justice had erroneously reported that 13% of all testimonies were from perpetrators, a higher percentage than for any previous truth commission (International Center for Transitional Justice, "Sierra Leone," 4).

79. Commissioner William Schabas noted, "*in some cases* [they asked] pardon or forgiveness of their victims" (emphasis mine) (Schabas, "Relationship," 1051).

80. Rosalind Shaw, "Transitional Subjectivities: Reconciling Ex-combatants in Northern Sierra Leone" (unpublished paper, n.d.).

81. Some observers doubt he would have apologized, since he had pled not guilty in the Special Court. Regardless, Mohamed Suma argues that, even if he had publicly apologized, it was too late in the process to set an example for his followers, since by the time he expressed interest in testifying, the hearings were winding up (Mohamed Suma, director of the Sierra Leone Court Monitoring Project, interview, July 4, 2007).

82. The CDF's rules forbid sexual intercourse before battle, but once the CDF moved from their native areas, the internal discipline was weakened. See Mariane C. Ferme and Danny Hoffman, "Hunter Militias and the International Human Rights Discourse in Sierra Leone and Beyond," *Africa Today* 50, no. 4 (2004): 75.

83. Hirsch, *Sierra Leone*, 45.

84. Of victims, 88% wanted to meet with their perpetrators; of perpetrators, 86% wanted to meet with their victims (Sierra Leone Truth and Reconciliation Commission, *Witness*, Statistical Report, CD-ROM, appendix, 36).

85. Moses Khanu (co-founder, IRC), interview, July 17, 2007.

86. Tim Kelsall, "Truth, Lies, Ritual," 378–80.

87. Quoted in Sierra Leone Truth and Reconciliation Commission, *Witness*, 3B:485.

88. Ahmad Tejan Kabbah, "Unity, Freedom and Justice" (Address to the Nation on the Occasion of the Thirty-Ninth Anniversary of Sierra Leone's Independence, Freetown, Sierra Leone, April 27, 2000).

89. William A. Schabas, "A Synergistic Relationship: The Sierra Leone Truth and Reconciliation Commission and the Special Court for Sierra Leone," *Criminal Law Forum* 15, no. 1–2 (2004): 3.

90. Ibid., 54.

91. Ibid.

92. Schabas, "Synergistic Relationship," 42. The reason there were so few amnesty applications in South Africa surely had to do with the concern about how the criteria for amnesty might be interpreted by the amnesty committee. Conditions for amnesty included a political motivation, proportionality, and full disclosure. In addition, the act had to be committed "without malice." Amnesty was not automatically granted, it had to be applied for individually, and there were many examples of seeming inconsistencies (See

Graybill, *South Africa*, 69–73). That said, there were still over seven thousand amnesty applicants, not an inconsiderable number.

93. Letter from PRIDE to the International Center for Transitional Justice, quoted in Schabas, "Synergistic Relationship," 28.

94. Sierra Leone Truth and Reconciliation Commission, *Witness*, 3B:376.

95. Ibid., 3B:382.

96. Ibid., 3B:383.

97. Ibid., 3B:399.

98. Quoted in ibid., 3B:413.

99. Ibid., 3B:425.

100. Jasmin Jusu-Sheriff, interview, July 9, 2007.

101. Mohamed Suma, interview, July 4, 2007.

102. Sierra Leone Working Group on Truth and Reconciliation, "Searching for Truth and Reconciliation in Sierra Leone: An Initial Study of the Performance and Impact of the Truth and Reconciliation Commission," 2006, 26. Later a poll was commissioned by the Special Court. Its results showed such high support for the Court that its methodology and accuracy were called into question. It is not available on the Special Court's website (Lotta Teale, legal program officer with the International Rescue Committee, interview, March 11, 2010).

103. Sigall Horovitz, "Transitional Criminal Justice in Sierra Leone," in *Transitional Justice in the Twenty-First Century: Beyond Truth versus Justice*, ed. Naomi Roht-Arriaza and Javier Mariezcurrenta (New York: Cambridge University Press, 2006), 60.

104. Alfred Carew (executive secretary of the National Forum for Human Rights), interview, July 4, 2007.

105. Horovitz, "Transitional Criminal Justice," 49.

106. Peter Penfold, "Is This Justice? Sierra Leone's Special Court Drags On," *Znet*, January 20, 2005.

107. Keen, *Conflict and Collusion*, 319.

108. UN News Service, "UN Names Local Lawyer to Top Post in Court Trying War Crimes in His Homeland," September 8, 2009.

109. Under the statute, the UN secretary general selects the chief prosecutor, and the government selects a Sierra Leonean to serve as the deputy prosecutor. There is no requirement that the prosecutor be an American.

110. Courtenay Griffiths, "Interview with Taylor's Lead Counsel Courtenay Griffiths QC in the Hague," by Angela Stavrianou, *Monitor* 40 (October–November, 2009): 15.

111. Albert Carew, interview, July 4, 2007.

112. The Sierra Leone Court Monitoring Project was reconstituted as the Centre for Accountability and Rule of Law in 2010.

113. Mohamed Suma, interview, July 4, 2007.

114. Penfold, "Is This Justice?"

115. Peter Penfold, "An Interview with Peter Penfold," by Lansana Gberie, *African Affairs* 104, no. 414 (2005): 123.

116. Lauren Gelfand, "As Sentencing Approaches, Cynicism about Sierra Leone Tribunal Lingers," *World Politics Review*, July 12, 2007.

117. Tim Kelsall, *Culture under Cross-Examination: International Justice and the Special Court for Sierra Leone* (New York: Cambridge University Press, 2009).

118. Ibid., 257.

119. Ibid., 211.

120. Ibid., 261.

121. This figure is disputed by Special Court official Peter Andersen, who claims it is closer to $185 million—still a huge amount. Peter Andersen, in discussion with the author, February 7, 2010.

122. Stephen Rapp succeeded Desmond de Silva, who had succeeded David Crane.

123. Sulakshana Gupta, "Stephen Rapp: Obama's Point Man on War Crimes," *Time International*, September 14, 2009.

Chapter 3. Women and Transitional Justice

1. Human Rights Watch, "We'll Kill You," 25–26.

2. Physicians for Human Rights, *War-Related Sexual Violence in Sierra Leone: A Population Based Assessment* (New York: Physicians for Human Rights, 2002), 2.

3. Human Rights Watch, "We'll Kill You," 35.

4. Susan McKay and Dyan Mazurana, *Where Are the Girls? Girls in Fighting Forces in Northern Uganda, Sierra Leone and Mozambique: Their Lives during and after War* (Montreal: International Center for Human Rights and Democratic Developments, 2004), 92.

5. One explanation is the younger the girl, the less likely she would have been HIV infected.

6. Sierra Leone Truth and Reconciliation Commission, *Witness*, 3B:159.

7. According to Coulter, girls needed to be perceived as virgins, whether they were actual virgins or not. She makes the distinction between social and actual virginity and argues that virginity is a concept that is negotiable. Chris

Coulter, *Being a Bush Wife: Women's Lives through War and Peace in Northern Sierra Leone* (Uppsala: Uppsala University, 2006), 355–57.

8. Ironically, the only armed group not to be implicated in human rights abuses was the mercenary group Executive Outcomes, a South African–based company that was hired by the Sierra Leonean government to repel the rebel forces.

9. The ICTR was established by the UN Security Council in 1994, whereas the Special Court was established in 2000, by treaty between the government of Sierra Leone and the United Nations.

10. Because of pressure from women's groups, the indictment against the former mayor of Taba, Jean-Paul Akayesu, was amended to include rape as a crime against humanity and as a means of committing genocide. He was convicted in September 1998.

11. Jamesina King asserts the Special Court and the TRC focused on gender crimes because before the hearings commenced women's groups and other civil society groups had formed the Women's Task Force on the Role of Women in the TRC and the Special Court to ensure that gender crimes were adequately identified and addressed. See Jamesina King, "Gender and Reparations in Sierra Leone: The Wounds of War Remain Open," in *What Happened to the Women? Gender and Reparations for Human Rights Violations*, ed. Ruth Rubio-Marin (New York: Social Science Research Council, 2006), 254.

12. Statute of the Special Court for Sierra Leone, January 16, 2002.

13. Since the war was not ethnically based, and no attempts to eliminate one ethnic group were attempted, genocide was not listed as a chargeable offense in the statute of the Special Court. See Shana Eaton, "Sierra Leone: The Proving Ground for Prosecuting Rape as a War Crime," *Georgetown Journal of International Law* 35, no. 4 (2004): 909.

14. Binaifer Nowrojee, "Making the Invisible War Crimes Visible: Post-conflict Justice for Sierra Leone's Rape Victims," *Harvard Human Rights Journal* 18 (Spring 2005): 100.

15. See Binaifer Nowrojee, "'Your Justice Is Too Slow': Will the ICTR Fail Rwandan's Rape Victims?," Occasional Paper 10, United Nations Research Institute for Social Development, November 2005.

16. Statute of the Special Court for Sierra Leone, art. 15 (14), January 16, 2002.

17. King, "Gender and Reparations," 256.

18. See, for example, Gerard Prunier, *The Rwanda Crisis* (New York: Columbia University Press, 1995), 356–89; Alison Des Forges, *Leave None*

to Tell the Story: Genocide in Rwanda (New York: Human Rights Watch, 1999), 692–735; and Amnesty International, "Rwanda: Reports of Killings and Abductions by the Rwandese Patriotic Army, April–August 1994," index no. AFR 47/016/1994, October 20, 1994.

19. The RUF defendants were Issa Sesay, Morris Kallon, and Augustine Gbao. The AFRC defendants were Alex Tamba Brima, Brima Bazzy Kamara, and Santigie Borbor Kanu.

20. Special Court for Sierra Leone, "Guilty Verdict in the Trial of the AFRC Accused," Press Release, June 20, 2007.

21. Special Court for Sierra Leone, Office of the Prosecutor, Press Release, February 25, 2009.

22. *AllAfrica*, "Sierra Leone: 'Forced Marriage' Conviction a First," February 26, 2009.

23. The CDF defendants were Samuel Hinga Norman (whose case was closed when he died in 2007), Moinina Fofana, and Allieu Kondewa.

24. See Sara Kendall and Michelle Staggs, "Silencing Sexual Violence: Recent Developments in the CDF Case at the Special Court for Sierra Leone," War Crimes Study Center, University of California at Berkeley, June 28, 2005.

25. Michelle Staggs Kelsall and Shanee Stepakoff, "'When We Wanted to Talk about Rape': Silencing Sexual Violence at the Special Court for Sierra Leone," *International Journal of Transitional Justice* 1, no. 3 (2007): 356.

26. Kelsall and Stepakoff argue that the Court failed to fully appreciate the difficulties in gathering evidence against the CDF from women victims, since the CDF members committed rape against women who continued to live in the same communities as the perpetrators. Surely, women feared reprisals since the CDF defendants were considered by many Sierra Leoneans to be national heroes, which made evidence gathering in a timely manner difficult (see Kelsall and Stepakoff, "'Talk about Rape,'" 361).

27. Ibid., 366, 368.

28. The two domestic crimes the Court could have prosecuted were arson and sex with a person under age fourteen, but instead it chose to prosecute under international law, perhaps to avoid the amnesty controversy. The Special Court claims that it does not recognize amnesty for *international* crimes.

29. Human Rights Watch, "We'll Kill You," 24.

30. Nowrojee, "War Crimes," 88.

31. For instance, the first successful rape case in Sierra Leone was only prosecuted in 1999. See Coulter, *Bush Wife*, 359.

32. Eaton, "Sierra Leone," 913.

33. Julie Mertus, "The War Crimes Tribunal: Triumph of the 'International Community,' Pain of the Survivors," *Mind and Human Interaction* 8, no. 1 (1997): 51.

34. Human Rights Watch, "Justice in Motion: The Trial Phase of the Special Court for Sierra Leone," *Human Rights Watch* 17, no. 14A (2005): 8.

35. Kelsall and Stepakoff, "Talk about Rape," 372.

36. Human Rights Watch, "Justice in Motion," 35.

37. Sierra Leone Truth and Reconciliation Commission, *Witness*, 1:170.

38. A distant second reason for not wanting perpetrators to be punished was "fear of reprisal/revenge" (25%). See Physicians for Human Rights, *Sexual Violence*, 53–54.

39. Lome Peace Accord, art. 28.

40. Sierra Leone Truth and Reconciliation Commission Act, 2000.

41. Colleen Duggan and Adila Abusharaf, "Reparation of Sexual Violence in Democratic Transitions: The Search for Gender Justice," in *The Handbook of Reparations*, ed. Pablo de Greiff (New York: Oxford University Press, 2006), 636.

42. Under pressure from women's organizations and after a submission by Beth Goldblatt and Sheila Meintjes to the TRC that urged it to consider gender in its operation, the TRC attempted to refocus its work to make sure women's voices and experiences were heard, by holding special women's hearings to investigate the special ways in which women were targeted. See Beth Goldblatt and Sheila Meintjes, "Gender and the Truth and Reconciliation Commission," submission to the South African Truth and Reconciliation Commission, 2006.

43. Nowrojee, "War Crimes," 93.

44. Sierra Leone Truth and Reconciliation Commission, *Witness*, l:165.

45. See Lyn S. Graybill, "The Contribution of the Truth and Reconciliation Commission toward the Promotion of Women's Rights in South Africa," *Women's Studies International Forum* 24, no. 1 (2001): 1–10.

46. Nowrojee, "War Crimes," 86. The third woman, Laura Marcus-Jones, was a retired high court judge in Sierra Leone.

47. Sierra Leone Truth and Reconciliation Commission, *Witness*, 3B:90.

48. Nowrojee, "War Crimes," 95.

49. Ibid.

50. Schabas, "Sierra Leone Truth," 31. See also Sierra Leone Truth and Reconciliation Commission, *Witness*, 1:183.

51. Stovel, "Long Way Home," 202.

52. The CDF's rules forbid sexual intercourse before battle since sex would remove their power of immunity from bullets, but once the CDF moved from their native areas, the internal discipline was weakened.

53. Sierra Leone Truth and Reconciliation Commission, *Witness*, 3B:176.

54. According to the statute of the Special Court, the sending country has primary jurisdiction over prosecution of its troops: "In the event the sending State is unwilling or unable genuinely to carry out an investigation or prosecution, the Court may, if authorized by the Security Council or the proposal of any state, exercise jurisdiction over such persons" (art. 1 [3]).

55. Sierra Leone Truth and Reconciliation Commission, *Witness*, 1:170.

56. US Department of State, Country Reports on Human Rights Practices for 2005: Sierra Leone, (Washington, DC: Bureau of Democracy, Human Rights, and Labor, 2006). Coulter found that some women felt loyalty and love for their bush husbands and wanted to stay with them (see Coulter, *Bush Wife*, 237, 332).

57. Myriam S. Denov, "Wartime Sexual Violations: Assessing a Human Security Response to War-Affected Girls in Sierra Leone," *Security Dialogue* 37, no. 3 (2006): 335–36.

58. See Coulter, *Bush Wife*; and Khristopher Carlson and Dyan Mazurana, *From Combat to Community: Women and Girls of Sierra Leone* (Washington, DC: Women Waging Peace, 2004).

59. Johanna Boersch-Supan, "What the Communities Say: The Crossroads between Integration and Reconciliation: What Can Be Learned from the Sierra Leone Experience?" (master's thesis, St. Cross College, Oxford University, 2008).

60. Carlson and Mazurana, *Combat to Community*.

61. Rosalind Shaw, "Memory Wars." See also Shaw, "Rethinking Truth and Reconciliation."

62. Rosalind Shaw, "Memory Wars," 26.

63. King, "Gender and Reparations," 257.

64. Augustine S. J. Park, "'Other Inhumane Acts': Forced Marriage, Girl Soldiers and the Special Court for Sierra Leone," *Social and Legal Studies* 15, no. 3 (2006): 330.

65. There were some prosecutions of RUF combatants in the state courts, but no defendants were charged with rape. See Lotta Teale, "Addressing Gender-Based Violence in the Sierra Leone Conflict: Notes from the Field," *African Journal on Conflict Resolution* 9, no. 2 (2009): 75.

66. Ibid., 81.

67. Lotta Teale, interview, March 11, 2010.

68. Jamesina King (commissioner, Human Rights Commission of Sierra Leone), interview, July 13, 2007.

69. Sierra Leone Truth and Reconciliation Commission, *Witness*, 2:115–224.

70. Ibid., 2:168. Perpetrators have had an easier time returning to their communities than victims of sexual violence have. See ibid., 3B:191.

71. Ibid., 2:169.

72. Ibid., 2:255–56. Other categories of victims eligible for free mental and physical health care are amputees and war wounded.

73. Ibid., 2:259.

74. Ibid., 2:170. The TRC had four categories of recommendations: imperative, work toward, seriously consider, and call on. *Imperative* recommendations are urgent and ought to be implemented immediately or as soon as possible. *Work toward* recommendations require in-depth planning, and the marshaling of resources, and should be done within a "reasonable time period." *Seriously consider* recommendations are those the government is expected to evaluate but is under no obligation to implement. *Calls on* recommendations deal with recommendations to other bodies such as NGOs and the international community that do not make up the executive or legislative arms of government.

75. Ibid., 2:170.

76. Ibid., 2:169.

77. Ibid., 2:168, 170–71.

78. Ibid., 2:173.

79. Ibid., 2:172.

80. Ibid., 1:17.

81. Sierra Leone Truth and Reconciliation Commission Act, 2000, pt. 5, no. 17.

82. Government of Sierra Leone, "White Paper on the Report of the Truth and Reconciliation Commission" (June 27, 2005), 8–10.

83. King, "Gender and Reparations," 253.

84. Government of Sierra Leone, "White Paper," 9.

85. Ibid.

86. *Concord Times*, "Sierra Leone Women Sidelined in Upcoming Campaign," June 29, 2007.

87. See Katy Gabel and Courtney Hess, "Sierra Leone: Women Aim for the Presidency by 2012," *AllAfrica*, October 28, 2007.

88. Human Rights Commission of Sierra Leone, *The State of Human Rights in Sierra Leone: 2008* (Freetown: HRCSL, 2009).

89. European Union Election Observation Mission, "Final Report: Presidential, Parliamentary and Local Council Elections, November 17, 2012," 29.

90. *Standard Times*, "Coalition of Women's Organisations in Sierra Leone Writes Attorney General and Minister of Justice," March 2, 2009.

91. World Bank, *Education in Sierra Leone: Present Challenges, Future Opportunities*, Africa Human Development Series, in collaboration with the Ministry of Education, Science and Technology of Sierra Leone (Washington, DC: World Bank, 2006).

92. UNICEF Global Databases, "Education: Secondary Net Attendance Ratio—Percentage," October 2015.

93. Irinnews, "Sierra Leone: Fighting Gender Bias Ahead of Elections," June 13, 2007.

94. UNICEF Global Databases, "Adult Literacy," October 2015.

95. Lotta Teale, "The Gender Bills: An Update," Sierra Leone Court Monitoring Project, March 26, 2007.

96. According to then US ambassador Thomas Hull, these bills were not popular with male Sierra Leoneans. They were passed, since 80% of the MPs were not running for re-election and did not have to worry about how their votes would be received (interview, July 6, 2007).

97. See Lotta Teale, "Sierra Leone Passes the Gender Bills into Law," *Monitor* 24 (June 2007): 11–12.

98. Temitope Adeyemi, "Summary of the Strategic Roll-Out Plan for Implementation of the Three Gender Acts," Sierra Leone Court Monitoring Project, March 20, 2009.

99. Human Rights Commission of Sierra Leone, *State of Human Rights in Sierra Leone: 2008*.

100. Teale, "Gender-Based Violence," 80.

101. Santigie Kamara, "Human Rights Issues," *Standard Times*, April 9, 2010.

102. The law also entitles victims to free medical treatment and a medical report, the latter of which is required for prosecution.

103. Irinnews, "Fighting Gender-Based Violence in Sierra Leone," November 6, 2013.

104. Irinnews, "Sex Crimes Up amid Ebola Outbreak in Sierra Leone," February 4, 2015.

105. According to Teale, the gender activists not only mobilized around the TRC recommendations, they were responsible for presenting the

recommendations to the TRC, which accepted them for inclusion in the final report. Lotta Teale, interview, March 11, 2010.

106. Lisa Denney and Aisha Fofana Ibrahim, "Violence against Women in Sierra Leone: How Women Seek Redress" (London: Overseas Development Institute, December 2012), 6.

107. King, "Gender and Reparations," 250.

108. As a result of the war, HIV rates may be much higher than the official figure of 1.6% (UNAIDS, *Global Report: UNAIDS Report on the Global Epidemic* [Geneva: UNAIDS, 2010]), 181. The fact that 90% of women have undergone genital cutting means HIV infection is much more likely.

109. USAID Office of Women in Development, "Gender Matters," Information Bulletin no. 9 (December 2000).

110. *TerraViva News*, "Sierra Leone: No End to Rape," December 15, 2004.

111. Nairobi Declaration on Women's and Girls' Right to a Remedy and Reparation, 2007.

112. Carolyn Nordstrom, *Girls and Warzones: Troubling Questions* (Uppsala: Life and Peace Institute, 1997), 1.

113. Helene Cobban compares the cost of "justice" with "reconciliation" in countries like Rwanda (which pursued justice through an expensive ICTR) and South Africa (which pursued reconciliation more cheaply through a truth and reconciliation commission). She also points out that distributive justice is often overlooked in postconflict countries. See Helene Cobban, *Amnesty after Atrocity? Healing Nations after Genocide and War Crimes* (Boulder: Paradigm, 2007).

114. Coulter, *Bush Wife*, 293–330.

115. Sara L. Zeigler and Gregory Gilbert Gunderson, "The Gendered Dimensions of Conflict's Aftermath: A Victim-Centered Approach to Compensation," *Ethics and International Affairs* 20, no. 2 (2006): 191.

116. Quoted in Teale, "Gender-Based Violence," 76.

117. *Standard Times*, "President Koroma Consoles 11,000 War Widows," April 1, 2010.

118. Ibid. See also Mohamed Suma and Cristian Correa, "Report and Proposals for the Implementation of Reparations in Sierra Leone" (New York: International Center for Transitional Justice, December 2009), 5.

119. The Centre for Accountability and the Rule of Law was formerly the Sierra Leone Court Monitoring Project.

120. Mohamed Suma, interview, December 14, 2009.

Chapter 4. Popular Views of the TRC and the Special Court

1. Manifesto 99, "Traditional Methods of Conflict Management/Resolution of Possible Complementary Value to the Proposed Sierra Leone Truth and Reconciliation Commission" (Freetown, 2002).

2. While the Special Court had been authorized by UN Resolution 1315 in August 2000, it was not until January 16, 2002, that it was officially established by enabling legislation and a treaty between the government and United Nations. The TRC, authorized under the 1999 Lome Accord, was established by law in 2000 but only commenced in July 2002, with the swearing in of commissioners.

3. Manifesto 99, "Traditional Methods," 57–58.

4. Ibid., 58.

5. Ibid., 59.

6. Ibid., 56.

7. Ibid., 55–56.

8. PRIDE, *Ex-combatant Views of the Truth and Reconciliation Commission and the Special Court in Sierra Leone* (Freetown: PRIDE, September 12, 2002), 24.

9. Focus groups of selected ex-combatants followed.

10. PRIDE, *Ex-combatant Views*, 44.

11. Macartan Humphreys and Jeremy Weinstein, "What the Fighters Say: A Survey of Ex-combatants in Sierra Leone" (CGSD Working Paper 20, Columbia Global Centers, Columbia University, NY, August 2004), 4, 39.

12. Ibid., 40.

13. Ibid.

14. Ibid.

15. Penfold, "Interview," 122.

16. David Crane, conversation with the author at the Jackson Symposium Conference: Sixty Years after Nuremberg, Chautauqua, New York, September 28, 2005.

17. PRIDE, *Ex-combatant Views*, 58.

18. Donna E. Arzt, "Views on the Ground: The Local Perception of International Criminal Tribunals in the Former Yugoslavia and Sierra Leone," *Annals of the American Academy of Political and Social Science* 603, no. 226 (2006): 234.

19. Rosalind Shaw, "Rethinking Truth and Reconciliation," 4.

20. The number that went through disarmament, demobilization, and reintegration programs is 76,000. See Humphreys and Weinstein, "Fighters," 9.

21. PRIDE, *Ex-combatant Views*, 11.
22. Ibid., 23.
23. Ibid., 11.
24. Manifesto 99, "Traditional Methods," 48.
25. Ibid., 47.
26. Ibid., 49.
27. Campaign for Good Governance, *Opinion Poll Report on the TRC and Special Court* (Freetown: Campaign for Good Governance, 2003), 12, 14.
28. Ibid., 11.
29. Ibid.
30. Ibid.
31. Ibid., 14.
32. Eight cases were concluded; Norman died before a verdict was issued. The indictment against Foday Sankoh, leader of the RUF, was withdrawn after his death in custody in 2003. The indictment against Sam Bockarie, commander of the RUF, was also dropped after his death in Liberia in 2003. Johnny Paul Koroma, leader of the AFRC, is presumed dead.
33. Colin Waugh, "Charles Taylor—The Long Wait for Justice Almost at an End," African Arguments, May 31, 2012.
34. Sierra Leone Working Group on Truth and Reconciliation, "Searching for Truth," 7.
35. Ibid., 8.
36. Ibid., 5.
37. Ibid., 9.
38. Ibid., 10.
39. Ibid., 11.
40. Edward Sawyer and Tim Kelsall, "Truth vs. Justice? Popular Views on the Truth and Reconciliation Commission and the Special Court for Sierra Leone," *Online Journal of Peace and Conflict Resolution* 7 no. 1 (2007): 47.
41. Rosalind Shaw, "Rethinking Truth and Reconciliation," 4.
42. This information comes from Sawyer's polling, which was included in his university thesis but did not find its way into his copublished article with Tim Kelsall. Edward Sawyer, "Restoration, Retribution, Post-conflict Development: Grassroots Perceptions of Transitional Justice in Sierra Leone" (undergraduate thesis, Newcastle University, 2006).
43. Ibid.
44. Human Rights Watch, "We'll Kill You," 25–26.
45. See Richards, *Fighting for the Rain Forest*.

46. Sawyer, "Restoration."
47. Ibid.
48. Ibid.
49. Sesay defends the choice, arguing that the capital is a microcosm of the country, since many refugees flooded there during the war for safe haven, and many remained, giving the city "an ethnic mix that is rich enough for the study" (Amadu Sesay, "Does One Size Fit All? The Sierra Leone Truth and Reconciliation Commission Revisited," Discussion Paper 36, Uppsala, Nordiska Afrikainstitutet, 2007, 7).
50. Ibid., 34.
51. Ibid., 35.
52. Ibid., 37.
53. Ibid., 36.
54. Ibid., 42.
55. Ibid.
56. See Graybill, *South Africa*, 49–50. See also Audrey Chapman, "Perspectives on the Role of Forgiveness in the Human Rights Violations Hearings," in *Truth and Reconciliation in South Africa: Did the TRC Deliver?*, ed. Audrey R. Chapman and Hugo van der Merwe (Philadelphia: University of Pennsylvania Press, 2008), 77.
57. Sesay, "Does One Size?," 42.
58. BBC World Service Trust and Search for Common Ground, "Building a Better Tomorrow: A Survey of Knowledge and Attitudes for Transitional Justice in Sierra Leone," August 2008, 1–37.
59. The survey also queried people about their views on security reform and the role of media.
60. BBC World Service Trust and Search for Common Ground, "Building a Better Tomorrow," 19.
61. Those with the most education knew the most about the recommendations.
62. BBC World Service Trust and Search for Common Ground, "Building a Better Tomorrow," 23.
63. Ibid.
64. Ibid., 24–25.
65. Ibid., 18.
66. Ibid.
67. Boersch-Supan, "What the Communities Say," 87.
68. Ibid., 30.
69. Ibid., 35.

70. Ibid., 43.
71. Ibid., 57.
72. Rosalind Shaw, "Rethinking Truth and Reconciliation," 11.
73. Boersch-Supan, "What the Communities Say," 58.
74. Ibid., 35.
75. Physicians for Human Rights, *Sexual Violence*, 53–54.
76. Boersch-Supan, "What the Communities Say," 59.
77. Sierra Leone Truth and Reconciliation Commission, *Witness*, 2:235.
78. Gearoid Millar, "Assessing Local Experiences of Truth-Telling in Sierra Leone: Getting to 'Why' through a Qualitative Case Study Analysis," *International Journal of Transitional Justice* 4, no. 3 (2010): 477–96.
79. Ibid., 492.
80. Ibid., 490.
81. Ibid., 493.
82. No Peace Without Justice, *Making Justice Count: Assessing the Impact and Legacy of the Special Court for Sierra Leone in Sierra Leone and Liberia*, Survey (New York: No Peace Without Justice, 2013), 12.
83. Kirsten Ainley, Simone Datzberger, Rebekka Friedman, and Chris Mahoney, *Ten Years On: Transitional Justice in Post-conflict Sierra Leone*, Report and analysis of a conference held at Goodenough College, London, December 2012 (London: London School of Economics, 2013), 10–16.
84. As the Court was transitioning into the Residual Special Court phase, it wanted to demonstrate its accomplishments. Hence the deadline for the report was an arbitrary, self-imposed one that led to a less-than-professional piece of work. The deadline was chosen in the hope of taking advantage of a surge in the public's positive opinion after the sentencing of the one living defendant whom most Sierra Leoneans believed was clearly among those most responsible for the violence.
85. No Peace Without Justice, "Making Justice Count," 10.
86. Charles Taylor was sentenced on May 30, 2012. The polls were conducted in June and July of 2012.
87. No Peace Without Justice, "Making Justice Count," 10–11.
88. Ibid., 1.
89. Ibid., 26.
90. Ibid., 47.
91. Other options were military court; truth and reconciliation commission; other truth mechanism; traditional (customary) justice; put them in jail; conflict resolution projects; grant amnesty, forgive; dialogue, unity; God; no means; revenge; don't know; other. See ibid., 15.

92. Ainley, Datzberger, Friedman, and Mahoney, "Ten Years On," 11.
93. No Peace Without Justice, "Making Justice Count," 48.
94. Ibid., 43.
95. Ibid., 15.
96. Ibid., 56.

Chapter 5. Perceptions of Religious Leaders

1. See appendix 2 for a list of religious leaders who were interviewed.
2. Audrey Chapman granted permission to replicate the interview instrument she and Bernard Spong developed for their study on religious views of reconciliation in South Africa. See appendix 1 for the instrument.
3. Graybill, *South Africa*, 27–28.
4. Usman Fornah, interim secretary general of the Inter-Religious Council, interview, June 28, 2007.
5. M. O. Ekemode, evangelist, Christ Apostolic Church, interview, July 24, 2007.
6. Mariatu Mahdi, president, Federation of Muslim Women's Associations of Sierra Leone, interview, July 6, 2006.
7. Abdul Babatunde Karim, secretary general, Sierra Leone Muslim Congress, interview, July 30, 2007.
8. Henry C. Samuels, pastor, Vine Memorial Baptist Mission, interview, July 25, 2007.
9. Abdul Karim Koroma, Muslim Brotherhood Islamic Mission, interview, August 6, 2007.
10. Bankole Large, pastor, African Methodist Episcopal Church, interview, July 26, 2007.
11. Reuben Dove, general superintendent, Countess of Huntingdon Connexion, interview, July 31, 2007.
12. Joseph Konteh, national superintendent, Wesleyan Church, interview, July 5, 2007.
13. A. A. Bangura, general secretary, Emmanuel Baptist Convention, interview, July 24, 2007.
14. Tom Barnett, bishop, Evangelical Lutheran Church, interview, July 18, 2007.
15. J. O. P. Lynch, bishop, Anglican Church, diocese of Freetown, interview, July 14, 2006.
16. Henry C. Samuels, interview, July 25, 2007.

17. Francis S. Nabieu, bishop, Methodist Church of Sierra Leone, interview, July 23, 2007.

18. Abdul Karim Koroma, interview, August 6, 2007.

19. Fomba Abubakar Swaray, chief imam, Madingo Central Mosque, Sierra Leone Muslim Missionary Union, interview, August 1, 2007.

20. Abu Bakarr Conteh, chief imam, Hamdallah Mosque, United Council of Imams, interview, July 5, 2006.

21. Fomba Abubakar Swaray, interview, August 1, 2007.

22. Ibid.

23. Abu Bakarr Conteh, interview, July 5, 2006.

24. Ahmed Tejan Sillah, chief imam, Freetown Central Mosque, United Council of Imams, interview, July 5, 2006.

25. Henry C. Samuels, interview, July 25, 2007.

26. John P. Meindy, national field secretary, Church of God of Prophecy Mission, interview, July 19, 2007.

27. Abdul Karim Koroma, interview, August 6, 2007.

28. Prince Charles Brainard, secretary general, Catholic Bishops Conference of the Gambia and Sierra Leone, interview, July 3, 2007.

29. Tom Barnett, interview, July 18, 2007.

30. Reuben Dove, interview, July 31, 2007.

31. F. T. C. Randall, canon in residence, St. George's Anglican Church, interview, July 11, 2006.

32. Joseph Humper, bishop, United Methodist Church, and former chairman of the TRC, interview, July 4, 2006.

33. Billy K. Simbo, general superintendent, United Brethren in Christ Church, interview, September 10, 2007.

34. Joseph Konteh, interview, July 5, 2007.

35. Usman Fornah, interview, June 28, 2007.

36. Solomon Kampbell, general secretary, Baptist Convention of Sierra Leone, interview, July 23, 2007.

37. Aiah D. Foday-Khabenje, general secretary, Evangelical Fellowship of Sierra Leone, interview, August 1, 2007.

38. Milton Marah, pastor, Missionary Church of Africa—Sierra Leone, interview, August 8, 2007.

39. M. O. Ekemode, interview, July 24, 2007.

40. Prince Charles Brainard, interview, July 3, 2007.

41. Abdul Babatunde Karim, interview, July 30, 2007.

42. George Biguzzi, bishop, Catholic Church, diocese of Makeni, interview, July 12, 2006.

43. Billy K. Simbo, interview, September 10, 2007.
44. Joseph Humper, interview, July 4, 2006.
45. Usman Fornah, interview, June 28, 2007.
46. Bankole Large, interview, July 26, 2007.
47. Marie Barnett, pastor, Evangelical Lutheran Church, interview, July 24, 2007.
48. Mariatu Mahdi, interview, July 6, 2006.
49. Reuben Dove, interview, July 31, 2007.
50. Marie Barnett, interview, July 24, 2007.
51. Tom Barnett, interview, July 18, 2007.
52. Abdul Karim Koroma, interview, August 6, 2007.
53. John P. Meindy, interview, July 19, 2007.
54. Milton Marah, interview, August 8, 2007.
55. Billy K. Simbo, interview, September 10, 2007.
56. Daniel Desay, pastor, Pentecostal Church, interview, July 13, 2006.
57. Usman Fornah, interview, June 28, 2007.
58. Francis S. Nabieu, interview, July 23, 2007.
59. Aiah D. Foday-Khabenje, interview, August 1, 2007.
60. Bankole Large, interview, July 26, 2007.
61. Joseph Konteh, interview, July 5, 2007.
62. Billy K. Simbo, interview, September 10, 2007.
63. Ibid.
64. Moses Khanu, former director of Inter-Religious Council, and commissioner of the Human Rights Commission, interview, July 17, 2007.
65. Milton Marah, interview, August 8, 2007.
66. Tom Barnett, interview, July 18, 2007.
67. Milton Marah, interview, August 8, 2007.
68. Abdul Babatunde Karim, interview, July 30, 2007.
69. Mabel Mbayo, Women's Desk, Inter-Religious Council, interview, August 2, 2007.
70. D. M. Speck, general superintendent, West African Methodist Church, interview, July 24, 2007.
71. Prince Charles Brainard, interview, July 3, 2007.
72. Ahmed Tejan Sillah, interview, July 5, 2006.
73. Solomon Kampbell, interview, July 23, 2007.
74. Billy K. Simbo, interview, September 10, 2007.
75. A. A. Bangura, interview, July 24, 2007.
76. Marie Barnett, interview, July 24, 2007.

77. Tom Barnett, interview, July 18, 2007.
78. Reuben Dove, interview, July 31, 2007.
79. Bankole Large, interview, July 26, 2007.
80. Usman Fornah, interview, June 28, 2007.
81. Milton Marah, interview, August 8, 2007.
82. Joseph Humper, interview, July 4, 2006.
83. Billy K. Simbo, interview, September 10, 2007.
84. Aiah D. Foday-Khabenje, interview, August 1, 2007.
85. Billy K. Simbo, interview, September 10, 2007.
86. Francis S. Nabieu, interview, July 23, 2007.
87. The clerics who especially emphasized the importance of implementing the TRC's recommendations included George Biguzzi, J. O. P. Lynch, Usman Fornah, Joseph Humper, Francis S. Nabieu, Billy K. Simbo, John P. Meindy, M. O. Ekemode, Marie Barnett, Milton Marah, Joseph Konteh, Henry C. Samuels, and Tamba Koroma.
88. Abdul Karim Koroma, interview, August 6, 2007.
89. Bankole Large, interview, July 26, 2007.
90. Usman Fornah, interview, June 28, 2007.
91. Joseph Humper, interview, July 4, 2006.
92. J. O. P. Lynch, interview, July 14, 2006.
93. George Biguzzi, interview, July 12, 2006.
94. Daniel Desay, interview, July 13, 2006.
95. Usman Fornah, interview, June 28, 2007.
96. J. O. P. Lynch, interview, July 14, 2006.
97. Milton Marah, interview, August 8, 2007.
98. Joseph Humper, interview, July 4, 2006.
99. J. O. P. Lynch, interview, July 14, 2006.
100. Paul M. Sandi, chancellor, Catholic Archdiocese of Freetown and Bo, interview, July 11, 2006.
101. D. M. Speck, interview, July 24, 2007.
102. Abu Bakarr Conteh, interview, July 5, 2006.
103. Ahmed Tejan Sillah, interview, July 5, 2006.
104. Aiah D. Foday-Khabenje, interview, August 1, 2007.
105. Daniel Desay, interview, July 13, 2006.
106. Ibid.
107. Prince Charles Brainard, interview, July 3, 2007.
108. Tom Barnett, interview, July 18, 2007.
109. Ahmed Tejan Sillah, interview, July 5, 2006.

110. Aiah D. Foday-Khabenje, interview, August 1, 2007.
111. Tamba Koroma, general superintendent, National Pentecostal Mission, interview, August 6, 2007.
112. A. A. Bangura, interview, July 24, 2007.
113. F. T. C. Randall, interview, July 11, 2006.
114. Marie Barnett, interview, July 24, 2007.
115. At the time of the interview, no monies had been disbursed. The Reparations Fund for Victims was not launched until January 2009.
116. Usman Fornah, interview, June 28, 2007.
117. Abdul Karim Koroma, interview, August 6, 2007.
118. S. Paul Khazali, founder and head, National Christian Evangelical Mission, interview, July 19, 2007.
119. Abdul Karim Koroma, interview, August 6, 2007.
120. Ibid.
121. Henry C. Samuels, interview, July 25, 2007.
122. Francis S. Nabieu, interview, July 23, 2007.
123. Billy K. Simbo, interview, September 10, 2007.
124. Reuben Dove, interview, July 31, 2007.
125. Abu Bakarr Conteh, interview, July 5, 2006.
126. Sahr Kemoore Salia, general secretary of the Council of Churches in Sierra Leone, interview, July 3, 2006.
127. Solomon Kampbell, interview, July 23, 2007.
128. Aiah D. Foday-Khabenje, interview, August 1, 2007.
129. Bankole Large, interview, July 26, 2007.
130. Francis S. Nabieu, interview, July 23, 2007.
131. Tamba Koroma, interview, August 6, 2007.
132. Joseph Konteh, interview, July 5, 2007.
133. Milton Marah, interview, August 8, 2007.
134. Usman Fornah, interview, June 28, 2007.
135. Moses Khanu, interview, July 17, 2007.
136. Abdul Karim Koroma, interview, August 6, 2007.
137. George Biguzzi, interview, July 12, 2006.
138. A. A. Bangura, interview, July 24, 2007.
139. Tom Barnett, interview, July 18, 2007.
140. Daan Bronkhorst, *Truth and Reconciliation: Obstacles and Opportunities for Human Rights* (Amsterdam: Amnesty International Dutch Section, 1995), 38.
141. Marc Gopin, "Forgiveness as an Element of Conflict Resolution in Religious Cultures: Walking the Tightrope of Reconciliation and Justice," in

Reconciliation, Justice, and Coexistence: Theory and Practice, ed. Mohammed Abu-Nimer (New York: Lexington Books, 2001), 87.

142. Luke 23:34.

143. Matt. 18:22.

144. Matt. 18:21–35.

145. Mohammed Abu-Nimer, "Islamic Principles of Nonviolence and Peacebuilding," in *Nonviolence and Peacebuilding in Islam: Theory and Practice*, ed. Mohammed Abu-Nimer (Gainesville: University of Florida Press, 2003), 67.

146. Carol Shersten LaHurd, "So That the Sinner Will Repent: Forgiveness in Islam and Christianity," *Dialog* 35, no. 4 (1996): 288.

147. Quoted in Gopin, "Forgiveness," 93.

148. Abu-Nimer, "Islamic Principles," 67.

149. LaHurd, "The Sinner Will Repent," 291.

150. John W. De Gruchy, *Reconciliation: Restoring Justice* (Minneapolis: Fortress Press, 2002), 133.

151. Abu-Nimer, "Islamic Principles," 68.

152. De Gruchy, *Reconciliation*, 132–33.

153. Philpott, *Just and Unjust*, 159.

154. Ibid., 160.

155. Inter-Religious Council of Sierra Leone, *Report of the Secretary General* (Freetown: IRCSL, 2003), 7.

156. Abu-Nimer, "Islamic Principles," 51.

157. Majid Khadduri, *The Islamic Conception of Justice* (New York: Johns Hopkins University Press, 1984): 3–12, quoted in Daniel Philpott, "Religion, Reconciliation, and Transitional Justice: The State of the Field" (SSRC Working Paper, October 17, 2007), 19.

158. Abu-Nimer, "Islamic Principles," 68.

159. Quoted in ibid.

160. LaHurd, "The Sinner Will Repent," 292.

161. Saeed Gassama Kalokoh, "What Islam Says about War, Peace and Reconciliation" in *Christian-Muslim Perspectives on War, Peace, and Reconciliation*, ed. A. Cee Temple Anono (Freetown: Council of Churches in Sierra Leone, 2006), 13.

162. Ibid., 12.

163. Willa Boesak, "Truth, Justice, and Reconciliation," in *To Remember and to Heal: Theological and Psychological Reflections on Truth and Reconciliation*, ed. H. Russel Botman and Robin Petersen (Cape Town: Human and Rousseau, 1996), 65–69.

164. Wolfram Kistner, "The Biblical Understanding of Reconciliation," in *To Remember and to Heal: Theological and Psychological Reflections on Truth and Reconciliation*, ed. H. Russel Botman and Robin Petersen (Cape Town: Human and Rousseau, 1996), 89.

165. Nigel Biggar, "The Ethics of Forgiveness and the Doctrine of Just War: A Religious View of Righting Atrocious Wrongs," in *The Religious in Responses to Mass Atrocity: Interdisciplinary Perspectives*, ed. Thomas Brudholm and Thomas Cushman (New York: Cambridge University Press, 2009), 116.

166. Abu-Nimer, "Islamic Principles," 49.

167. Ibid., 55.

168. Ibid.

169. Robert J. Schreiter, *Reconciliation: Mission and Ministry in a Changing Social Order* (Maryknoll, NY: Orbis, 1992).

170. De Gruchy, *Reconciliation*, 205.

171. Marc Gopin, *Between Eden and Armageddon: The Future of World Religions, Violence, and Peacemaking* (New York: Oxford University Press, 2000), 13.

172. Biggar, "Ethics of Forgiveness," 114.

Chapter 6. Traditional Reconciliation Practices

1. Sierra Leone Truth and Reconciliation Commission Act, 2000, pt. 7, no. 2.

2. Modern gacaca was not an example for the Sierra Leone TRC to emulate, since it only began judging and sentencing its first suspects in 2005, long after the TRC had concluded.

3. The ringleaders of the genocide were tried in the International Criminal Tribunal for Rwanda in Arusha, Tanzania.

4. Before colonialism, gacaca dealt with manslaughter, but during the colonial era, manslaughter was heard in the formal court system. See Timothy Longman, "Justice at the Grassroots? Gacaca Trials in Rwanda," in *Transitional Justice in the Twenty-First Century: Beyond Truth versus Justice*, ed. Naomi Roht-Arriaza and Javier Mariezcurrenta (New York: Cambridge University Press, 2006), 209–10.

5. Phil Clark, "Hybridity, Holism, and 'Traditional' Justice: The Case of the Gacaca Courts in Post-genocide Rwanda," *George Washington International Law Review* 39, no. 4 (2007): 779.

6. Vocal critics of gacaca include academics Bert Ingelaere and Lars Waldorf and human rights organizations Human Rights Watch and Amnesty International.

7. Clark, "Hybridity," 778.

8. Bert Ingelaere, "The Gacaca Courts in Rwanda," in *Traditional Justice and Reconciliation after Violent Conflict: Learning from African Experiences*, ed. Luc Huyse and Mark Salter (Stockholm: IDEA, 2008), 57.

9. See Lars Waldorf, "Mass Justice for Mass Atrocity: Rethinking Local Justice as Transitional Justice," *Temple Law Review* 79, no. 1 (2006): 1–87.

10. Ingelaere, "Gacaca Courts," 49.

11. Ibid., 54.

12. Phil Clark, *The Gacaca Courts, Post-genocide Justice and Reconciliation in Rwanda: Justice without Lawyers* (Cambridge: Cambridge University Press, 2010), 6.

13. Ibid., 157.

14. Clark, "Hybridity," 800, 811.

15. Catholics (mainly Hutu) make up 56% of Rwandans, while Protestants (mainly Tutsi) make up 28%.

16. Clark, *Gacaca Courts*, 257, 309.

17. Victor Igreja, "The Politics of Peace, Justice and Healing in Postwar Mozambique: 'Practices of Rupture,'" in *Peace versus Justice? The Dilemma of Transitional Justice in Africa*, ed. Chandra Lekha Sriram and Suren Pillay (Rochester, NY: James Currey, 2010), 277–300.

18. Honwana, "Collective Body," 30–35.

19. Carolyn Nordstrom, *A Different Kind of War Story* (Philadelphia: University of Pennsylvania Press, 1997), 147.

20. Honwana, "Collective Body," 30–35.

21. Hayner, *Unspeakable Truths*, 192–93.

22. Nordstrom, *War Story*, 146.

23. James Ojera Latigo, "Northern Uganda: Tradition-Based Practices in the Acholi Region," in *Traditional Justice and Reconciliation after Violent Conflict*, ed. Huyse and Salter, 104–5.

24. Charles Villa-Vicencio, *Walk with Us and Listen: Political Reconciliation in Africa* (Cape Town: University of Cape Town Press, 2009), 137.

25. According to Latigo, nearly all of the 12,000 LRA returnees have undergone this ceremony to remove the violence of the war. See Latigo, "Northern Uganda," 106.

26. Villa-Vicencio, *Walk with Us*, 138.

27. Latigo, "Northern Uganda," 108.

28. The International Criminal Court has indicted five commanders of the LRA. The first to be brought before the ICC was Dominic Ongwen, second in command to Joseph Kony, who surrendered in the Central African Republic in January 2015.

29. See Berkeley Human Rights Center, "*Forgotten Voices: A Population-Based Survey on Attitudes about Peace and Justice in Northern Uganda* (Berkeley: University of California, 2005).

30. See Berkeley Human Rights Center, *When the War Ends: A Population-Based Survey on Attitudes about Peace, Justice, and Social Reconstruction in Northern Uganda* (Berkeley: University of California, 2007).

31. Tim Allen, "Ritual (Ab)use? Problems with Traditional Justice in Northern Uganda," in *Courting Conflict: Justice, Peace and the ICC in Africa*, ed. Nicholas Waddell and Phil Clark (London: Royal African Society, 2008), 52.

32. Ibid., 47–54.

33. Comfort Ero, "Understanding Africa's Position on the International Criminal Court," in *Transitional Justice Research Collected Essays: Debating International Justice in Africa* (Oxford: Oxford University, 2010), 11–14.

34. Mamoh Taziff Koroma, author of the Manifesto 99 study, interview, July 30, 2007.

35. Alie, "Reconciliation and Traditional Justice," 144.

36. Elisabeth Hoffman, "Reconciliation in Sierra Leone: Local Processes Yield Global Lessons," *Fletcher Forum of World Affairs* 32, no. 2 (2008), 138.

37. Alie, "Reconciliation and Traditional Justice," 140.

38. Stovel, "Long Way Home," 235.

39. Keen, *Conflict and Collusion*, 10.

40. Ibid., 68.

41. Augustine S. J. Park, "Restorative Approaches to Justice: Strategies for Peace in Sierra Leone" (Issues Paper no. 2, Center for International Governance and Justice, Canberra, May 2007), 3.

42. Sierra Leone Truth and Reconciliation Commission, *Witness*, 3B:438.

43. Ibid., 1:58.

44. Manifesto 99, "Traditional Methods," 4.

45. Park, "Restorative Approaches," 4.

46. Manifesto 99, "Traditional Methods," 21.

47. National Forum for Human Rights, "Traditional Methods of Conflict Resolution and Reconciliation," Report of Workshop Hosted for National Rulers/Paramount Chiefs, Freetown, 2001.

48. Ibid.
49. In the Madingo, Soso, and Fullah ethnic groups, the secret societies structures are weak.
50. Park, "Restorative Approaches," 3.
51. Manifesto 99, "Traditional Methods"; National Forum for Human Rights, "Traditional Methods."
52. Park, "Restorative Approaches," 3.
53. Manifesto 99, "Traditional Methods," 29.
54. Shaw, "Rethinking Truth and Reconciliation," 4, 8.
55. Shaw, "Memory Wars," 12.
56. Shaw, "Rethinking Truth and Reconciliation," 9.
57. Shaw, "Memory Wars," 7.
58. Shaw, "Transitional Subjectivities," 7.
59. Shaw, "Rethinking Truth and Reconciliation," 6.
60. Rosalind Shaw, "Memory Frictions: Localizing the Truth and Reconciliation Commission in Sierra Leone," *International Journal of Transitional Justice* 1, no. 2 (2007): 188.
61. Shaw, "Memory Wars," 26.
62. Ibid.
63. Ibid.
64. Ibid., 28.
65. Ibid.
66. Park, "Restorative Approaches," 3.
67. Shaw, "Rethinking Truth and Reconciliation," 11.
68. Shaw, "Transitional Subjectivities," 14.
69. National Forum for Human Rights, "Traditional Methods."
70. For the Kissi to revoke a curse, they must flog a dog and the confessor simultaneously until the dog defecates.
71. Manifesto 99, "Traditional Methods," 42.
72. Ibid., 24.
73. Ibid., 25.
74. Alie, "Reconciliation and Traditional Justice," 137.
75. Manifesto 99, "Traditional Methods," 50.
76. Park, "Restorative Approaches," 11.
77. Alie, "Reconciliation and Traditional Justice," 144.
78. See Mariane Ferme, *The Underneath of Things: Violence, History and the Everyday in Sierra Leone* (Berkeley: University of California Press, 2001).
79. Stovel, "Long Way Home," 253.
80. Alie, "Reconciliation and Traditional Justice," 144.

81. All of the district reconciliation officers recommended the continuation of the program since a number of activities were left undone. See Inter-Religious Council of Sierra Leone, *Report of the Program Coordinator*, Second Biennial General Assembly (Freetown: IRCSL, November 29–30, 2005).

82. Mbayo, interview, July 13, 2007.

83. Ibid.

84. Khanu, "Role," 105.

85. Inter-Religious Council of Sierra Leone, "Summary of the Reports of the District Reconciliation Workshops from November 2003" (Freetown: IRCSL, n.d.), appendix 2, 5.

86. Mbayo, interview, July 13, 2007.

87. Inter-Religious Council of Sierra Leone, "Summary of the Reports," 9.

88. Mbayo, interview, July 13, 2007.

89. Inter-Religious Council of Sierra Leone, *Koinadugu District: Final Report*, Community Based Reconciliation Project (Freetown: IRCSL, n.d.).

90. Inter-Religious Council of Sierra Leone, *Port Loko District: Final Report*, Community Based Reconciliation Project (Freetown: IRCSL, n.d.).

91. Coulter, *Bush Wife*, 355–57.

92. Aisha Fofana Ibrahim, "War's Other Voices: Testimonies by Sierra Leonean Women" (PhD diss., Illinois State University, 2006).

93. Coulter, *Bush Wife*, 346–47.

94. Inter-Religious Council of Sierra Leone, *Moyamba District: Final Report*, Community Based Reconciliation Project (Freetown: IRCSL, n.d.).

95. Inter-Religious Council of Sierra Leone, *Western Area: Final Report*, Community Based Reconciliation Project (Freetown: IRCSL, n.d.).

96. Inter-Religious Council of Sierra Leone, *Kenema District: Final Report*, Community Based Reconciliation Project (IRCSL: Freetown, n.d.).

97. Inter-Religious Council of Sierra Leone, *Kenema District*; Inter-Religious Council of Sierra Leone, *Port Loko District*.

98. Inter-Religious Council of Sierra Leone, *Bonthe District: Final Report*, Community Based Reconciliation Project (Freetown: IRCSL, n.d.).

99. Inter-Religious Council of Sierra Leone, *Bombali District: Final Report*, Community Based Reconciliation Project (Freetown: IRCSL, n.d.).

100. Inter-Religious Council of Sierra Leone, *Bonthe District*.

101. Inter-Religious Council of Sierra Leone, *Bo District: Final Report*, Community Based Reconciliation Project (Freetown: IRCSL, n.d.).

102. Inter-Religious Council of Sierra Leone, *Port Loko District*.

103. Inter-Religious Council of Sierra Leone, *Tonkolili District: Final Report*, Community Based Reconciliation Project (Freetown: IRCSL, n.d.).

104. Mbayo, interview, July 13, 2007.
105. Abdul Kuyateh, "Reconciliation at Work in Kono," *Standard Times*, August 31, 2004.
106. Khanu, interview, July 17, 2007.
107. Mbayo, interview, July 13, 2007.
108. See Inter-Religious Council of Sierra Leone, *Western Area*; Inter-Religious Council of Sierra Leone, *Bo District*.
109. Inter-Religious Council of Sierra Leone, *Kono District: Final Report*, Community Based Reconciliation Project (Freetown: IRCSL, n.d.).
110. Several monuments were built in many districts to mark mass graves, and a national war memorial opened in 2010 in Freetown near the iconic Cotton Tree.
111. Mbayo, interview, July 13, 2007.
112. Pel Koroma, "Sierra Leone: Konos Want to Bury Their Dead," *Concord Times*, January 26, 2009.
113. The program was conceived earlier, but it took years for Caulker to get funding. See Elisabeth Hoffman, "Reconciliation in Sierra Leone," 140.
114. John Caulker, interview, November 16, 2009.
115. Fambul Tok, "Project Summary" (Freetown: Fambul Tok, 2008).
116. Pel Koroma, "Focus on Community Reconciliation in Kono," *Concord Times*, December 23, 2008.
117. Elisabeth Hoffman, "Reconciliation in Sierra Leone," 132.
118. Jina Moore, "Sierra Leone's 'Family Talk' Heals Scars of War," *Christian Science Monitor*, July 7, 2008.
119. In addition to Kailahun, Bonthe and Tonkolili (the hometown of RUF leader, Foday Sankoh) were also included in the pilot phase.
120. *AllAfrica*, "Sierra Leone Ex-combatants Make Peace with Victims," April 4, 2008.
121. Jina Moore, "Sierra Leoneans Look for Peace through Full Truth about War Crimes," *Christian Science Monitor*, July 8, 2008.
122. *AllAfrica*, "Sierra Leone Ex-combatants."
123. Moore, "Sierra Leoneans."
124. Caulker, interview, November 18, 2009.
125. Fambul Tok, "Community Healing in Sierra Leone and the World: Our Second Year" (Freetown: Fambul Tok, 2010), 31.
126. Robert Roche, field program officer, Fambul Tok, correspondence with the author, March 15, 2010.
127. Robert Roche, interview, April 6, 2010.

128. *Augusta Free Press*, "EMU Alumni in Liberia, Sierra Leone Tap Local Resilience and Resourcefulness in Curbing Ebola," January 24, 2015.

129. Elisabeth Hoffman, "Reconciliation in Sierra Leone," 135.

130. Fambul Tok, "Project Summary."

131. Ibrahim Jaffa Condeh, "Fambul Tok Creates Safe Space for Us to Speak Out," *Concord Times*, March 20, 2009.

132. Andy Carl, quoted in Jina Moore, "A Former Rebel Faces the Sierra Leonean Farmer He Maimed," *Christian Science Monitor*, July 9, 2008.

133. Stephen Kauffman, "Sierra Leone: 'Family Talk' Empowers Country to Move Past Civil Conflict," *AllAfrica*, March 25, 2009.

134. Caulker, interview, November 18, 2009.

135. Ibid.

136. Fambul Tok, "Community Healing in Sierra Leone: Our First Year" (Freetown: Fambul Tok, 2009), 15.

137. Ibid.

138. Sara Terry, "Fambul Tok: A Documentary Film about the Power of Forgiveness" (New York: First Run Features, 2011).

139. Caulker, interview, November 18, 2009.

140. See Sierra Leone Truth and Reconciliation Commission, *Witness*, 1:99; and Fambul Tok, "Our First Year," 13.

141. Caulker, interview, November 18, 2009.

142. Fambul Tok, "Our First Year," 4.

143. John Caulker, "Fambul Tok: Reconciling Communities in Sierra Leone," *Accord* 23 (2012), 53.

144. John Paul Lederach, *Building Peace: Sustainable Reconciliation in Divided Societies* (Washington, DC: USIP Press, 1997).

145. Fambul Tok, "Our First Year," 29.

146. Fambul Tok, "Our Second Year," 8.

147. Ibid.

148. Ibid.

149. Pel Koroma, "Fambul Tok Promotes Community Healing," *Concord Times*, September 14, 2009.

150. Fambul Tok, "Our First Year," 19.

151. See Brandon Hamber, "Reparation as Symbol: Narratives of Resistance, Reticence and Possibility in South Africa" (paper presented at Reparations: An Interdisciplinary Examination of Some Philosophical Issues Conference, Queen's University, Kingston, ON, February 6–8, 2004), 24.

152. Libby Hoffman, "How It Works: An In-Depth Look at the Fambul Tok Process," in *Fambul Tok*, Fambul Tok International (New York: Umbrage Editions, 2011), 77–94.

153. Lansana Gberie, "The Redundant Court for Sierra Leone," *New African*, December 1, 2009. This figure was disputed by the Special Court's chief of Outreach and Public Affairs, Peter Andersen, who told me the Court had spent $185 million to date (conversation with the author, February 17, 2010). It is reasonable to assume that since 2010, the Court has spent $105 million, if one accepts that it costs between $35 and $40 million per year to operate the Court. See Colin Waugh, "Charles Taylor," May 31, 2012.

154. Still, one wonders if the structures put in place—the reconciliation committees that mediate disputes that come up daily among the community—will be permanent, as Caulker envisions. The IRC and the Red Cross had assumed the committees they had set up—and the Community Peace Consolidation committees—would take hold permanently and deal with ongoing conflicts, but they have fallen apart.

Chapter 7. Unfinished Business

1. Sierra Leone Truth and Reconciliation Commission, *Witness*, 1:165.
2. Sierra Leone Truth and Reconciliation Commission Act, 2000.
3. Sierra Leone Truth and Reconciliation Commission, *Witness*, 2:204.
4. This was perhaps in response to the criticisms of the South African TRC, which put forward a host of recommendations, including substantial reparations. These were either ignored or rejected by the government of South Africa. While El Salvador had required implementation of the recommendations, it did not mandate a follow-up committee to enforce it.
5. Sierra Leone Truth and Reconciliation Commission, *Witness*, 2:115–224.
6. Government of Sierra Leone, "White Paper."
7. Sierra Leone Working Group on Truth and Reconciliation, "Searching for Truth," 1.
8. Sierra Leone Truth and Reconciliation Commission, *Witness*, 2:119.
9. Ibid., 2:120.
10. Ibid., 2:121. The recommendations for the dissemination of the report fall mostly under the *call on* category, as implementing them would involve nongovernmental actors. For instance, the TRC recommends "the

widest possible dissemination of its Report," including the various versions such as the children's and video versions. It encourages the production of popular versions and summaries in the different local languages, to be produced in consultation with the Human Rights Commission, and the use of the report to promote dialogue in workshops around the country. It also recommends that the contents of the report be incorporated into education programs from the primary through tertiary levels—a *seriously consider* recommendation. It suggests the report, including the appendixes, be made available on the Internet (203–4).

11. The TRC proposed that Parliament enact "without delay" an omnibus bill to address the *imperative* recommendations to be implemented by repeal of existing legislation, which it declined to do.

12. Other subheadings include the Commission and the Special Court, National Vision for Sierra Leone, and Dissemination of the Commission's Report, which are either *seriously consider* or *call on* recommendations and are beyond the scope of this chapter.

13. Sierra Leone Truth and Reconciliation Commission, *Witness*, 2:135–36.

14. Ibid., 2:202–3.

15. Government of Sierra Leone, "White Paper," 12.

16. The National Vision was launched in September 2003 by the TRC. Two hundred fifty contributions were received in the form of poems, plays, paintings, and essays. The TRC recommended the establishment of a trust to oversee the activities of the project.

17. Government of Sierra Leone, "White Paper," 5.

18. Thomas Hull, interview, July 6, 2007.

19. United Nations Integrated Office in Sierra Leone (UNIOSIL), "A Matrix on the Status of Implementation of the Truth and Reconciliation Commission Recommendations," Human Rights and Rule of Law Section, May 2008.

20. The Peace Museum holds the TRC and Special Court archives, memorial garden, and exhibition rooms.

21. The TRC urged Sierra Leone to *seriously consider* the creation of a new constitution that would be the product of a wide and thorough consultative and participatory program, since the current constitution was not the product of a participatory process (Sierra Leone Truth and Reconciliation Commission, *Witness*, 2:122). Since the TRC recognized this would be an arduous process, it did not make the recommendation *imperative* but warned that its not doing so should not be construed as permitting the delay of

other *imperative* recommendations aimed at amending the 1991 Constitution of Sierra Leone.

22. Ibid., 2:126.
23. Government of Sierra Leone, "White Paper," 4.
24. Ibid., 5.
25. Ibid.
26. The Constitutional Review Commission also recommended Parliament review the death penalty every five years. See Republic of Sierra Leone. *Sierra Leone Constitutional Review Commission Report* (Freetown: Republic of Sierra Leone, 2007).
27. Human Rights Commission of Sierra Leone, *The State of Human Rights in Sierra Leone: 2011* (Freetown: HRCSL, 2012), 36.
28. Sierra Leone Truth and Reconciliation Commission, *Witness*, 2:127.
29. Ibid., 2:196–97.
30. Ibid., 2:127.
31. Government of Sierra Leone, "White Paper," 6.
32. US Department of State, *Country Reports on Human Rights Practices for 2006: Sierra Leone* (Washington, DC: Bureau of Democracy, Human Rights, and Labor), 2007.
33. Human Rights Commission of Sierra Leone, *Sierra Leone: 2008*, 59.
34. UNIOSIL, "Matrix," 1.
35. Sierra Leone Truth and Reconciliation Commission, *Witness*, 2:128–29.
36. Government of Sierra Leone, "White Paper," 6.
37. Sabrina Mahtani, "Justice in a Time of Ebola," *Daily Vox*, February 10, 2015.
38. Human Rights Watch, *World Report: Sierra Leone, 2008* (New York: Human Rights Watch 2009), 3.
39. Sierra Leone Truth and Reconciliation Commission, *Witness*, 2:134.
40. US Department of State, *Human Rights Practices for 2005*; US Department of State, *Human Rights Practices for 2006*.
41. Sierra Leone Truth and Reconciliation Commission, *Witness*, 2:132.
42. The publisher later served as the special executive assistant to the president, whom she had lambasted, and in that role railed against journalists who wrote negative stories about him.
43. Mohamed Fofanah, "Sierra Leone: Mixed Reactions to Libel Law Ruling," Inter Press Service, December 7, 2009.
44. Aska Mohamed Sorie Kargbo, "Who Is Molesting Who: The President or the VP?," *Independent Observer*, October 17, 2013.

45. *Guardian*, "Sierra Leone: Journalist Arrested after Questioning Official Ebola Response," November 5, 2014.

46. Sierra Leone Truth and Reconciliation Commission, *Witness*, 2:154.

47. Amanda Vragovich, "Sierra Leone: Freedom of Information Is One Thing, Freedom of Press Is Another," *Think Africa Press*, November 7, 2013.

48. Anti-Corruption Commission of Sierra Leone, Press Release, "Sierra Leone Moves Four Steps Upwards," press release, December 12, 2013.

49. Sierra Leone Truth and Reconciliation Commission, *Witness*, 2:143.

50. Government of Sierra Leone, "White Paper," 6.

51. Ibid., 7.

52. Ibid.

53. Sierra Leone Truth and Reconciliation Commission, *Witness*, 2:140–41.

54. Ibid., 2:142–43.

55. Ibid., 2:144.

56. Human Rights Commission of Sierra Leone, *Sierra Leone: 2011*, 40.

57. Sierra Leone Truth and Reconciliation Commission, *Witness*, 2:145.

58. Ibrahim Tommy and Aruna Kallon, "The Legal Aid Act of Sierra Leone: When Will Implementation Start?," Center for Accountability and Rule of Law, April 1, 2014.

59. Human Rights Commission of Sierra Leone, *Sierra Leone: 2011*, 40.

60. Sierra Leone Truth and Reconciliation Commission, *Witness*, 2:148–49.

61. Ibid., 2:136.

62. Ibid., 2:137.

63. Ibid., 2:150–51.

64. Ibid., 2:151.

65. Government of Sierra Leone, "White Paper," 7–8.

66. Ibid., 8.

67. Sierra Leone Truth and Reconciliation Commission, *Witness*, 2:151.

68. Ibid., 2:153.

69. Ibid., 2:155.

70. UNIOSIL, "Matrix," 5.

71. Ibid., 6.

72. Sierra Leone Truth and Reconciliation Commission, *Witness*, 2:162.

73. *Standard Times*, "Betrayal of Confidence: Whistleblower Exposes Corruption at ACC," January 31, 2015.

74. Sierra Leone Truth and Reconciliation Commission, *Witness*, 2:160.

75. US Department of State, *Country Reports on Human Rights Practices for 2010: Sierra Leone* (Washington, DC: Bureau of Democracy, Human Rights, and Labor), 2011.
76. Sierra Leone Truth and Reconciliation Commission, *Witness*, 2:164.
77. Human Rights Watch, *Sierra Leone: 2009*, 2.
78. *AllAfrica*, "18 Members of US Congress Call for Logging Investigations of Sierra Leone Logging Scandal," December 13, 2011.
79. Sierra Leone Truth and Reconciliation Commission, *Witness*, 2:160.
80. Joseph Hanlon, "Is the International Community Helping to Recreate the Preconditions for War in Sierra Leone?," *Round Table* 94, no. 38 (2005): 465.
81. Laura Marcus-Jones, interview, July 31, 2007.
82. Quoted in International Crisis Group, "Sierra Leone: A New Era of Reform?" Africa Report no. 143, July 31, 2008, 17.
83. Mohamed Suma, interview, December 14, 2009.
84. Human Rights Watch, *Sierra Leone: 2010*, 1. See also *Awareness Times*, "ACC Presents Annual Report to President," July 7, 2010.
85. US Department of State, *Human Rights Practices for 2010*.
86. Abdul Tejan-Cole resigned in May 2010, over security concerns and for government interference, and was replaced by John Fitzgerald Kamara, the former deputy prosecutor of the Special Court.
87. Peter Apps, "Sierra Leone Could Jail Corrupt Foreign Investors," Reuters, November 18, 2009.
88. Anti-Corruption Commission, "The Mayor of the Freetown City Council, His Chief Administrator and Five Others Convicted at the High Court in Freetown," press release, August 10, 2012.
89. Reuters, "Sierra Leone's Top Medical Officer Cleared of Graft," October 25, 2013.
90. Sierra Leone Truth and Reconciliation Commission, *Witness*, 2:176.
91. Ibid., 2:133–34.
92. Josephine Thompson Shaw, contact person with the SLHRC who oversaw TRC implementation, interview, July 1, 2010.
93. Sierra Leone Truth and Reconciliation Commission, *Witness*, 2:177.
94. Human Rights Commission of Sierra Leone, *Sierra Leone: 2008*, 49.
95. Mamie Sulleh and Isata Sowa, "Registration of Customary [Marriage] and Divorce Act and Early/Forced Marriage: Its Implications on Our Girls and Society," Center for Accountability and Rule of Law, July 20, 2012.
96. Sierra Leone Truth and Reconciliation Commission, *Witness*, 2:177–79.
97. Ibid., 2:178.

98. Ibid., 2:176.
99. Josephine Thompson Shaw, interview, July 1, 2010.
100. UNIOSIL, "Matrix," 16.
101. Ibid.
102. Sierra Leone Truth and Reconciliation Commission, *Witness*, 2:178.
103. Ibid., 2:187–88.
104. US Department of State, *Human Rights Practices for 2005*.
105. Sierra Leone Truth and Reconciliation Commission, *Witness*, 2:165.
106. Ibid., 2:166.
107. Government of Sierra Leone, "White Paper," 8.
108. Sierra Leone Truth and Reconciliation Commission, *Witness*, 2:166–67.
109. Foday Jalloh, "APPYA Commends President Koroma of Sierra Leone," *Sierra Express Media*, February 27, 2013.
110. Sierra Leone Truth and Reconciliation Commission, *Witness*, 2:180.
111. Government of Sierra Leone, "White Paper," 10.
112. Ibid., 11.
113. Sierra Leone Truth and Reconciliation Commission, *Witness*, 2:184.
114. Ibid., 2:186.
115. Ibid., 2:187.
116. Government of Sierra Leone, "White Paper," 11.
117. Ibid.
118. Ibid.
119. *Financial Times*, "Special Report: Sierra Leone, This Is Africa," April 2011, 15.
120. Republic of Sierra Leone, Constitutional Review.
121. Hanlon, "War in Sierra Leone," 466.
122. Freedom of Information Advocates Network, "Sierra Leone Portal No Substitute for FOI Law, Advocates Say," January 27, 2012.
123. Sierra Leone Truth and Reconciliation Commission, *Witness*, 2:196.
124. Ibid.
125. Ibid., 2:251–59.
126. Ibid., 2:264.
127. Ibid., 2:198–99.
128. Government of Sierra Leone, "White Paper," 12.
129. *Awareness Times*, "War Victims Get Umbrella Body in Sierra Leone," September 15, 2006.
130. Ibid.
131. See Lyn S. Graybill, "Debt Relief: A Panacea for Sierra Leone," *CSIS Africa Policy Forum*, February 9, 2007.

132. Suma and Correa, "Report and Proposals," 1.
133. Ibid., 10.
134. Ibid., 11.
135. Ibid., 8.
136. Ibrahim Tarawallie, "Sierra Leone: NaCSA Doles Out US $1.3 Million as Micro-grants," *Concord Times*, October 7, 2009.
137. Suma and Correa, "Report and Proposals," 1.
138. Ibid., 9.
139. Ibid.
140. Ibid.
141. Suma, interview, December 14, 2009.
142. Abu Kalokoh, "Support War Victims," *New Citizen*, November 20, 2009.
143. Suma and Correa, "Report and Proposals," 14.
144. Ibid.
145. Government of Sierra Leone (submission to the Universal Periodic Review of the UN Human Rights Council, 11th Session, May 2011), 4.
146. Human Rights Commission of Sierra Leone, *Sierra Leone: 2011*, 55.
147. Relief Web, "Sierra Leone Victims Receive Compensation," Report from International Organization for Migration, press release, June 26, 2012.
148. African Press Organization, "Amputees in Sierra Leone—Victims of Conflict," October 4, 2013.
149. Hayner, *Unspeakable Truths*, 169.
150. Sierra Leone Working Group on Truth and Reconciliation, "Searching for Truth," 17.

Conclusion

1. Ellen Lutz and Kathryn Sikkink, "The Justice Cascade: The Evolution and Impact of Foreign Human Rights Trials in Latin America," *Chicago Journal of International Law* 2 (2001): 1.
2. Diane F. Orentlicher, "Settling Accounts: The Duty to Prosecute Human Rights Violations of a Prior Regime," *Yale Law Journal* 100 (1991): 2537–615.
3. Diane F. Orentlicher, " 'Settling Accounts' Revisited: Reconciling Global Norms with Local Agency," *International Journal of Transitional Justice* 1, no. 1 (2007): 10–22.

4. United Nations, "The Rule of Law and Transitional Justice in Conflict and Post-conflict Societies: Report of the Secretary-General," UN document S/2004/616, August 23, 2004.

5. Argentina had granted amnesties but had them overturned in 2005, paving the way for prosecutions. In Chile, Augusto Pinochet was charged with human rights violations in 2007, despite an earlier amnesty agreement.

6. Priscilla Hayner, *Unspeakable Truths: Transitional Justice and the Challenge of Truth Commissions*, 2nd ed. (New York: Routledge, 2011), 95.

7. Ibid., 138.

8. Alex Boraine highlights four types of truth relevant to the South African Truth and Reconciliation Commission project: objective, factual, forensic; personal, narrative; dialogical; and healing, restorative. See *A Country Unmasked: Inside South Africa's Truth and Reconciliation Commission* (New York: Oxford University Press, 2000), 288–92.

9. Kenneth Roth and Alison Des Forges, "Justice or Therapy?," *Boston Review* (Summer 2002).

10. Helena Cobban, "The Legacies of Collective Violence," *Boston Review* (April/May 2002).

11. David Mendeloff, "Truth-Seeking, Truth-Telling, and Postconflict Peacebuilding: Curb the Enthusiasm?," *International Studies Review* 6 (2004): 363–66.

12. Suzanne Daley, "In Apartheid Inquiry, Agony Is Relived but Not Put to Rest," *New York Times*, July 17, 1997.

13. Chapman, "Perspectives," 76.

14. Shaw, "Rethinking Truth and Reconciliation," 7.

15. Shaw, "Memory Frictions," 202–3.

16. Eduard Gonzalez, truth commission specialist with the International Center for Transitional Justice, quoted in BBC World Service Trust and Search for Common Ground, "Building a Better Tomorrow," 14.

17. David Crane, quoted in Sierra Leone Working Group on Truth and Reconciliation, "Searching for Truth," 10.

18. There are eighteen cases before the ICC in eight African countries.

19. Hayner, *Unspeakable Truths*, 105.

20. Penfold, "Is This Justice?"

21. Lansana Gberie, "Trial of a 'War Hero,'" *Znet*, March 10, 2006.

22. Beth K. Dougherty, "Right-Sizing International Criminal Justice: The Hybrid Experiment at the Special Court for Sierra Leone," *International Affairs* 80, no. 2 (2004): 311–28.

23. Cobban analyzed the costs of retributive justice versus restorative justice and determined that each trial at the International Criminal Tribunal for Rwanda cost $42,300,000, while each amnesty case before the South African TRC, where perpetrators received amnesty in exchange for truth, cost $4,290. See Cobban, *Amnesty after Atrocity?*, 209.

24. The actual cost is difficult to determine. The annual budgets on the Special Court website are not accurate, according to Peter Andersen, the Court's former chief of Outreach and Public Affairs, since budgets often fell short of fundraising goals (Peter Andersen, conversation with the author, November 23, 2013).

25. Stephen Rapp, quoted in Owen Bowcott and Monica Mark, "Charles Taylor Found Guilty of Abetting Sierra Leone War Crimes," *Guardian*, April 26, 2012.

26. Sierra Leone Truth and Reconciliation Commission, *Witness*, 1:170.

27. Ibid., 2:235.

28. John Braithwaite, "Restorative Justice: Assessing an Immodest Theory and a Pessimistic Theory" (review essay prepared for University of Toronto law course, "Restorative Justice: Theory and Practice in Criminal Law and Business Regulation," 1997, 3, quoted in Jennifer J. Llewellyn and Robert Howse, "Institutions for Restorative Justice: The South African Truth and Reconciliation Commission," *University of Toronto Law Journal* 49, no. 3 (1999): 372.

29. Hun Joon Kim and Kathryn Sikkink, "Explaining the Deterrence Effect of Human Rights Trials," *International Studies Quarterly* 54, no. 4 (2010): 953.

30. Kathryn Sikkink and Carrie Booth Walling, "The Impact of Human Rights Trials in Latin America," *Journal of Peace Research* 44, no. 4 (2007): 437.

31. Kim and Sikkink, "Deterrence Effect," 939–63.

32. Jack Snyder and Leslie Vinjamuri, "Trials and Errors: Principle and Pragmatism in Strategies of International Justice," *International Security* 28, no. 3 (2003–04): 43.

33. Minow, "Making History," 180.

34. There is a burgeoning literature that seeks to develop the empirical basis for claims about the alleged successes of transitional justice mechanisms. See Oskar N. T. Thoms, Roland Paris, and James Ron, "The Effects of Transitional Justice Mechanisms: A Summary of Empirical Research Findings and Implications for Analysts and Practitioners" (working paper,

University of Ottawa Centre for International Policy Studies, ON, 2008); and Hugo Van der Merwe, Victoria Baxter, and Audrey R. Chapman, eds., *Assessing the Impact of Transitional Justice: Challenges for Empirical Research* (Washington, DC: USIP Press, 2008). For critiques of theorizing about transitional justice in the absence of verifiable proof, see Eric Brahm, "Uncovering the Truth: Examining Truth Commission Success and Impact," *International Studies Perspectives* 8 (2007): 16–35; David Mendeloff, "Trauma and Vengeance: Assessing the Psychological and Emotional Effects of Post-conflict Justice," *Human Rights Quarterly* 31, no. 3 (2009): 592–623; and Mendeloff, "Truth-Seeking," 355–80.

35. Francis Deng, quoted in Villa-Vicencio, *Walk with Us*, 140.

36. Orentlicher, "'Settling Accounts' Revisited," 20.

37. Peter Walker, "Charles Taylor War Crimes Trial—The Verdict," *Guardian*, April 26, 2012.

38. Thomas Brudholm, "On the Advocacy of Forgiveness after Mass Atrocities, " in *The Religious in Responses to Mass Atrocity: Interdisciplinary Prospects*, ed. Thomas Brudholm and Thomas Cushman (Cambridge: Cambridge University Press, 2009): 124–53.

39. Vamik Volkan, "Transgenerational Transmissions and Chosen Traumas: An Aspect of Large-Group Identity," *Group Analysis* 34 (March 2001): 79–97.

40. The war, however, did inflame ethnic/regional tensions. President Kabbah blamed the north for the war, since RUF rebel leader Foday Sankoh hailed from that region, and suggested the north apologize to the south and east.

41. The election in 2007 indicated a softening of regional alliances; the Western Area, especially Freetown, which historically had been loyal to the SLPP, transferred its support to the APC. SLPP candidates in Kailahun, traditionally the SLPP heartland, performed only marginally better than the APC, and the new People's Movement for Democratic Change party cut across all regional lines in garnering support.

42. Cynthia Sampson posits that religious leaders can be especially effective in conflicts not marked by religious divisions. See Sampson, "Religion and Peacebuilding," 309.

43. Ted Robert Gurr, "Containing Internal War in the Twenty-First Century," in *From Reaction to Conflict Prevention: Opportunities for the UN System*, ed. Fen Osler Hampson and David M. Malone (Boulder: Lynne Rienner, 2002), 48.

44. Human Rights Watch, "We'll Kill You," 9.

45. Susan Dwyer, "Reconciliation for Realists," *Ethics and International Affairs* 13, no. 1 (1999): 81–98.

46. Howard Zehr, *Changing Lenses: A New Focus for Crime and Justice* (Waterloo, ON: Herald Press, 1990).

47. Shaw, "Rethinking Truth and Reconciliation," 4.

48. Sierra Leone Truth and Reconciliation Commission, *Witness*, 3B:464.

49. Tim Kelsall, "Truth, Lies, Ritual," 378–80.

50. According to Jamesina King, commissioner of the Human Rights Commission, "Most people already knew what happened" (King, interview, July 13, 2007).

51. In some instances there was confusion about who was committing the offenses, as soldiers often masqueraded as rebels and vice versa.

52. Quoted in Andre du Toit, "The Moral Foundations of the South African Truth and Reconciliation Commission: Truth as Acknowledgment and Justification as Recognition," in *Truth v. Justice: The Morality of Truth Commissions*, ed. Robert I. Rotberg and Dennis Thompson (Princeton, NJ: Princeton University Press, 2000), 132.

53. Anthropologists refer to the Krio adage, *Tok haf lef haf* (talk half, leave half) as a cultural justification for withholding information.

54. This confirms the importance of track-two actors as valuable intermediaries between those at the top and those at the bottom. See Lederach, *Building Peace*.

55. Keen, *Conflict and Collusion*, 73.

56. Stovel, "Long Way Home," 17.

57. Abu-Nimer, *Nonviolence and Peacebuilding in Islam: Theory and Practice*. (Gainesville: University of Florida Press, 2003), 27.

58. Philpott, *Just and Unjust*, 54.

59. John Braithwaite and Valerie Braithwaite, "Shame, Shame Management and Regulation," in *Shame Management through Reintegration*, ed. Eliza Ahmed, Nathan Harris, John Braithwaite, and Valerie Braithwaite (Cambridge: Cambridge University Press, 2002), quoted in Keen, *Conflict and Collusion*, 301.

60. Francis Deng, quoted in Villa-Vicencio, *Walk with Us*, 140.

61. Ogulu Odama, Catholic bishop of Gulu (Uganda), quoted in Villa-Vicencio, *Walk with Us*, 141.

62. Brandon Hamber and Richard Wilson, "Symbolic Closure through Memory, Reparation and Revenge in Post-conflict Societies," *Journal of Human Rights* 1, no. 1 (2002): 36.

63. Walter R. Fisher, *Human Communication as Narration: Toward a Philosophy of Reason, Value, and Action* (Columbia: University of South Carolina Press, 1987), 67, quoted in Teresa Godwin Phelps, *Shattered Voices: Language, Violence, and the Work of Truth Commissions* (Philadelphia: University of Pennsylvania Press, 2004), 58.

64. Roland Barthes, "Introduction to the Structural Analysis of Narratives," in *Image, Music, Text*, trans. Stephen Heath (London: Fontana, 1987), 79, cited in Phelps, *Shattered Voices*, 58.

65. Hayden White, *The Content of the Form: Narrative Discourse and Historical Representation* (Baltimore: Johns Hopkins University Press, 1987), 1, quoted in Phelps, *Shattered Voices*, 58.

66. See Elaine Scarry, *The Body in Pain: The Making and Unmaking of the World* (Oxford: Oxford University Press, 1985).

67. Coulter, *Bush Wife*, 47.

68. Keen, *Conflict and Collusion*, 293–94.

69. Lederach, *Building Peace*.

70. Keen, *Conflict and Collusion*, 296.

71. Daly and Sarkin, *Reconciliation*, 17.

72. John Caulker, interview, November 16, 2009.

73. On the distinction between individual reconciliation and national unity and reconciliation, see Tristan Borer, "Reconciling South Africa or South Africans?," *African Studies Quarterly* 8, no. 1 (2004): 19–38.

74. Daly and Sarkin, *Reconciliation*, 98.

75. Michael Jackson, *In Sierra Leone* (Durham, NC: Duke University Press, 2004), 72.

76. Ibid.

77. Louis Kriesberg, "Changing Forms of Coexistence," in *Reconciliation, Justice, and Coexistence*, ed. Mohammed Abu-Nimer (New York: Lexington Books, 2001), 48.

78. Sierra Leone Truth and Reconciliation Commission, *Witness*, Transcripts of TRC Public Hearings, CD-ROM, appendix 3, 133.

79. Lome Peace Accord, art. 28.

80. Shaw, "Memory Frictions," 197.

81. In 2005, Shaw had cited statistics from South Africa that indicated 60% of victims there felt worse after testifying, implying that this was, or would be, the case for Sierra Leonean victims (Shaw, "Rethinking Truth and Reconciliation," 7). But in an article published two years later, she conceded that no one in the group of testifying victims she was later able to interview claimed to have felt worse after testifying, and all but one said he or she had

felt better. Still, she never corrected her thesis that testifying publicly was inappropriate and harmful to victims. See Shaw, "Memory Frictions," 203.

82. Gearoid Millar, "Truth-Telling in Sierra Leone," 486–94.

83. Rama Mani argues that as much attention should be placed on the need for distributive (economic) justice as on the need for legal justice. See Rama Mani, *Beyond Retribution: Seeking Justice in the Shadow of War* (Cambridge: Polity Press, 2002).

84. John Caulker of Forum of Conscience (and Fambul Tok), Mohamed Suma of the Sierra Leone Court Monitoring Project (renamed CARL), and Jusu Jaka of the Amputees and War Wounded Association, among others whom I interviewed.

85. Mohammed Wusu Sankoh, testimony, May 1, 2003, Port Loko, in Sierra Leone Truth and Reconciliation Commission, *Witness*, transcripts of TRC Public Hearings, CD ROM, appendix 3, 42.

86. Kadiath Fofanah, testimony, April 25, 2003, Freetown, in Sierra Leone Truth and Reconciliation Commission, *Witness*, transcripts of TRC Public Hearings, CD ROM, appendix 3, 142.

87. Villa-Vicencio, *Walk with Us*, 164.

88. Abu-Nimer, *Nonviolence and Peacebuilding*, 49.

89. Ibid., 57.

90. Keen, *Conflict and Collusion*, 172.

91. Inter-Religious Council, *Report of the Secretary General*, 6.

92. Appleby, *Ambivalence of the Sacred*.

93. Hilary Hurd, "The Inter-Religious Council of Sierra Leone (IRCSL) as Peace-Facilitator in Sierra Leone (1991–Present)" (master's thesis, St. John's College, University of Cambridge, 2014), 91, 101.

94. Keen, *Conflict and Collusion*, 172.

95. Alimamy Koroma, IRCSL/CCSL presentation to the TRC Thematic Hearing, May 9, 2003, *Witness*, transcripts of TRC Public Hearings, CD Rom, appendix 3, 66. He also made a presentation on behalf of the IRC and Council of Churches in Sierra Leone, on August 1, 2003, titled "Promoting Reconciliation and National Reintegration and Reparation."

96. Alimamy Koroma, interview, April 21, 2010.

97. Huyse, "Introduction," 6.

98. Mahmood Mamdani, *When Victims Become Killers: Colonialism, Nativism, and the Genocide in Rwanda* (Princeton, NJ: Princeton University Press, 2001), 277.

BIBLIOGRAPHY

Abu-Nimer, Mohammed. "Islamic Principles of Nonviolence and Peacebuilding." In *Nonviolence and Peacebuilding in Islam: Theory and Practice*, edited by Mohammed Abu-Nimer, 48–84. Gainesville: University of Florida Press, 2003.

———. *Nonviolence and Peacebuilding in Islam: Theory and Practice*. Gainesville: University of Florida Press, 2003.

———, ed. *Reconciliation, Justice, and Coexistence: Theory and Practice*. Lanham, MD: Lexington Books, 2001.

Adeyemi, Temitope. "Summary of the Strategic Roll-Out Plan for Implementation of the Three Gender Acts." Sierra Leone Court Monitoring Project, March 20, 2009.

Africa News Service. "Amputees to Take Part in Reconciliation Hearings." September 6, 2002.

African Press Organization. "Amputees in Sierra Leone—Victims of Conflict." October 4, 2013.

Ahmed, Eliza, Nathan Harris, John Braithwaite, and Valerie Braithwaite, eds. *Shame Management through Reintegration*. Cambridge: Cambridge University Press, 2002.

Ainley, Kirsten, Simone Datzberger, Rebekka Friedman, and Chris Mahoney. *Ten Years On: Transitional Justice in Post-conflict Sierra Leone*. Report and analysis of a conference held at Goodenough College, London, December 2012. London: London School of Economics, 2013.

Alie, Joe A. D. "Reconciliation and Traditional Justice: Tradition-Based Practices of the Kpaa Mende in Sierra Leone." In Huyse and Salter, *Traditional Justice and Reconciliation after Violent Conflict*, 123–46.

AllAfrica. "18 Members of US Congress Call for Logging Investigations of Sierra Leone Logging Scandal." December 13, 2011.

———. "Sierra Leone Ex-combatants Make Peace with Victims." April 4, 2008.

———. "Sierra Leone: 'Forced Marriage' Conviction a First." February 26, 2009.

Allen, Tim. "Ritual (Ab)use? Problems with Traditional Justice in Northern Uganda." In *Courting Conflict: Justice, Peace and the ICC in Africa*, edited by Nicholas Waddell and Phil Clark, 47–54. London: Royal African Society, 2008.

Amnesty International. "Rwanda: Reports of Killings and Abductions by the Rwandese Patriotic Army, April–August 1994." Index no. AFR 47/016/1994. October 20, 1994.

Amstutz, Mark. "Restorative Justice, Political Forgiveness, and the Possibility of Political Reconciliation." In *The Politics of Past Evil: Religion, Reconciliation, and the Dilemmas of Transitional Justice*, edited by Daniel Philpott, 151–88. Notre Dame, IN: University of Notre Dame, 2006.

Anono, A. Cee Temple, ed. *Christian-Muslim Perspectives on War, Peace, and Reconciliation.* Freetown: Council of Churches in Sierra Leone, 2006.

Anti-Corruption Commission of Sierra Leone. "The Mayor of the Freetown City Council, His Chief Administrator and Five Others Convicted at the High Court in Freetown." Press Release. August 10, 2012.

———. "Sierra Leone Moves Four Steps Upwards." Press Release. December 12, 2013.

Appleby, R. Scott. *The Ambivalence of the Sacred: Religion, Violence, and Reconciliation.* Lanham, MD: Rowman and Littlefield, 2000.

Apps, Peter. "Sierra Leone Could Jail Corrupt Foreign Investors." Reuters, November 18, 2009.

Arzt, Donna E. "Views on the Ground: The Local Perception of International Criminal Tribunals in the Former Yugoslavia and Sierra Leone." *Annals of the American Academy of Political and Social Science* 603, no. 226 (2006): 226–38.

Augusta Free Press. "EMU Alumni in Liberia, Sierra Leone Tap Local Resilience and Resourcefulness in Curbing Ebola." January 24, 2015.

Awareness Times. "ACC Presents Annual Report to President." July 7, 2010.

———. "War Victims Get Umbrella Body in Sierra Leone." September 15, 2006.

Barthes, Roland. "Introduction to the Structural Analysis of Narratives." In *Image, Music, Text*, translated by Stephen Heath. London: Fontana, 1987.

BBC World Service Trust and Search for Common Ground. "Building a Better Tomorrow: A Survey of Knowledge and Attitudes for Transitional Justice in Sierra Leone." August 2008, 1–37.

Bennett, Richard. "The Evolution of the Sierra Leone Truth and Reconciliation Commission." In *Truth and Reconciliation in Sierra Leone: A Compilation of Articles on the Sierra Leone Truth and Reconciliation Commission.* Freetown: United Nations Mission in Sierra Leone, 2001.
Berewa, Solomon. "Addressing Impunity Using Divergent Approaches: The Truth and Reconciliation Commission and the Special Court." In *Truth and Reconciliation in Sierra Leone: A Compilation of Articles on the Sierra Leone Truth and Reconciliation Commission.* Freetown: United Nations Mission in Sierra Leone, 2001.
Berkeley Human Rights Center. *Forgotten Voices: A Population-Based Survey on Attitudes about Peace and Justice in Northern Uganda.* Berkeley: University of California, 2005.
———. *When the War Ends: A Population-Based Survey on Attitudes about Peace, Justice, and Social Reconstruction in Northern Uganda.* Berkeley: University of California, 2007.
Biggar, Nigel. "The Ethics of Forgiveness and the Doctrine of Just War: A Religious View of Righting Atrocious Wrongs." In *The Religious in Responses to Mass Atrocity: Interdisciplinary Perspectives,* edited by Thomas Brudholm and Thomas Cushman, 105–23. New York: Cambridge University Press, 2009.
Boersch-Supan, Johanna. "What the Communities Say: The Crossroads between Integration and Reconciliation: What Can Be Learned from the Sierra Leone Experience?" Master's thesis, St. Cross College, Oxford University, 2008.
Boesak, Willa. "Truth, Justice, and Reconciliation." In *To Remember and to Heal: Theological and Psychological Reflections on Truth and Reconciliation,* edited by H. Russel Botman and Robin Petersen, 65–69. Cape Town: Human and Rousseau, 1996.
Boraine, Alex. *A Country Unmasked: Inside South Africa's Truth and Reconciliation Commission.* New York: Oxford University Press, 2000.
Borer, Tristan. "Reconciling South Africa or South Africans?" *African Studies Quarterly* 8, no. 1 (2004): 19–38.
Botman, H. Russel, and Robin Petersen, eds. *To Remember and to Heal: Theological and Psychological Reflections on Truth and Reconciliation.* Cape Town: Human and Rousseau, 1996.
Bowcott, Owen, and Monica Mark. "Charles Taylor Found Guilty of Abetting Sierra Leone War Crimes." *Guardian,* April 26, 2012.
Brahm, Eric. "Uncovering the Truth: Examining Truth Commission Success and Impact." *International Studies Perspectives* 8 (2007): 16–35.

Braithwaite, John. "Restorative Justice: Assessing an Immodest Theory and a Pessimistic Theory," review essay prepared for University of Toronto law course, 'Restorative Justice: Theory and Practice in Criminal Law and Business Regulation,' 1997, 1–100.

Braithwaite, John, and Valerie Braithwaite. "Shame, Shame Management and Regulation." In *Shame Management through Reintegration,* edited by Eliza Ahmed, Nathan Harris, John Braithwaite, and Valerie Braithwaite, 3–72. Cambridge: Cambridge University Press, 2002.

Bronkhorst, Daan. *Truth and Reconciliation: Obstacles and Opportunities for Human Rights.* Amsterdam: Amnesty International Dutch Section, 1995.

Brudholm, Thomas. "On the Advocacy of Forgiveness after Mass Atrocities." In *The Religious in Responses to Mass Atrocity: Interdisciplinary Prospects,* edited by Thomas Brudholm and Thomas Cushman, 124–53. London: Cambridge University Press, 2009.

Brudholm, Thomas, and Thomas Cushman, eds. *The Religious in Responses to Mass Atrocity: Interdisciplinary Prospects.* London: Cambridge University Press, 2009.

Campaign for Good Governance. *Opinion Poll Report on the TRC and Special Court.* Freetown: Campaign for Good Governance, 2003.

Carlson, Khristopher, and Dyan Mazurana. *From Combat to Community: Women and Girls of Sierra Leone.* Washington, DC: Women Waging Peace, 2004.

Caulker, John. "Fambul Tok: Reconciling Communities in Sierra Leone." *Accord* 23 (2012): 52–54.

Chapman, Audrey R. "Perspectives on the Role of Forgiveness in the Human Rights Violations Hearings." In *Truth and Reconciliation in South Africa: Did the TRC Deliver?,* edited by Audrey R. Chapman and Hugo van der Merwe, 66–89. Philadelphia: University of Pennsylvania Press, 2008.

Chapman, Audrey R., and Bernard Spong, eds. *Religion and Reconciliation in South Africa: Voices of Religious Leaders.* Philadelphia: Templeton Press, 2003.

Chapman, Audrey R., and Hugo van der Merwe. *Truth and Reconciliation in South Africa: Did the TRC Deliver?* Philadelphia: University of Pennsylvania Press, 2008.

Clark, Phil. *The Gacaca Courts, Post-genocide Justice and Reconciliation in Rwanda: Justice without Lawyers.* Cambridge: Cambridge University Press, 2010.

———. "Hybridity, Holism, and 'Traditional' Justice: The Case of the Gacaca Courts in Post-genocide Rwanda," *George Washington International Law Review* 39, no. 4 (2007): 765–838.

Cobban, Helena. *Amnesty after Atrocity? Healing Nations after Genocide and War Crimes.* Boulder: Paradigm, 2007.
———. "The Legacies of Collective Violence." *Boston Review*, April/May 2002.
Concord Times. "Sierra Leone Women Sidelined in Upcoming Campaign." June 29, 2007.
Condeh, Ibrahim Jaffa. "Fambul Tok Creates Safe Space for Us to Speak Out." *Concord Times,* March 20, 2009.
Conflict Transformation Working Group. "Building Peace from the Ground Up: A Call to the U.N. for Stronger Collaboration with Civil Society." New York: CTWG, 2002.
Coulter, Chris. *Being a Bush Wife: Women's Lives through War and Peace in Northern Sierra Leone.* Uppsala: Uppsala University, 2006.
Crimes of War Education Project. Website. www.crimesofwar.org.
Daley, Suzanne. "In Apartheid Inquiry, Agony Is Relived but Not Put to Rest." *New York Times,* July 17, 1997.
Daly, Erin, and Jeremy Sarkin. *Reconciliation in Divided Societies: Finding Common Ground.* Philadelphia: University of Pennsylvania Press, 2006.
De Greiff, Pablo, ed. *The Handbook of Reparations.* New York: Oxford University Press, 2006.
De Gruchy, John W. *Reconciliation: Restoring Justice.* Minneapolis: Fortress Press, 2002.
Denney, Lisa, and Aisha Fofana Ibrahim. "Violence against Women in Sierra Leone: How Women Seek Redress." London: Overseas Development Institute, December 2012.
Denov, Myriam S. "Wartime Sexual Violations: Assessing a Human Security Response to War-Affected Girls in Sierra Leone." *Security Dialogue* 37, no. 3 (2006): 319–42.
Des Forges, Alison. *Leave None to Tell the Story: Genocide in Rwanda.* New York: Human Rights Watch, 1999.
Dougherty, Beth K. "Right-Sizing International Criminal Justice: The Hybrid Experiment at the Special Court for Sierra Leone." *International Affairs* 80, no. 2 (2004): 311–28.
———. "Searching for Answers: Sierra Leone's Truth and Reconciliation Commission." *African Studies Quarterly* 8, no. 1 (2004): 39–55.
Duggan, Colleen, and Adila Abusharaf. "Reparation of Sexual Violence in Democratic Transitions: The Search for Gender Justice." In *The Handbook of Reparations,* edited by Pablo de Greiff, 623–49. New York: Oxford University Press, 2006.

Du Toit, Andre. "The Moral Foundations of the South African Truth and Reconciliation Commission: Truth as Acknowledgment and Justification as Recognition." In *Truth v. Justice: The Morality of Truth Commissions*, edited by Robert I. Rotberg and Dennis Thompson, 122–40. Princeton, NJ: Princeton University Press, 2000.

Dwyer, Susan. "Reconciliation for Realists." *Ethics and International Affairs* 13, no. 1 (1999): 81–98.

Eaton, Shana. "Sierra Leone: The Proving Ground for Prosecuting Rape as a War Crime." *Georgetown Journal of International Law* 35, no. 4 (2004): 873–919.

Ero, Comfort. "Understanding Africa's Position on the International Criminal Court." In *Transitional Justice Research Collected Essays: Debating International Justice in Africa*, 11–14. Oxford: Oxford University Press, 2010.

European Union Election Observation Mission. "Final Report: Presidential, Parliamentary and Local Council Elections, November 17, 2012," February 20, 2013.

Fambul Tok. "Community Healing in Sierra Leone and the World: Our Second Year." Freetown: Fambul Tok, 2010.

———. "Community Healing in Sierra Leone: Our First Year." Freetown: Fambul Tok, 2009.

———. *Fambul Tok*. New York: Umbrage Editions, 2011.

———. "Project Summary." Freetown: Fambul Tok, 2008.

Ferme, Mariane. *The Underneath of Things: Violence, History and the Everyday in Sierra Leone*. Berkeley: University of California Press, 2001.

Ferme, Mariane, and Danny Hoffman. "Hunter Militias and the International Human Rights Discourse in Sierra Leone and Beyond." *Africa Today* 50, no. 4 (2004): 73–95.

Financial Times. "Special Report: Sierra Leone, This Is Africa." April 2011.

Fisher, Walter R. *Human Communication as Narration: Toward a Philosophy of Reason, Value, and Action*. Columbia: University of South Carolina Press, 1987.

Fofanah, Mohamed. "Sierra Leone: Mixed Reactions to Libel Law Ruling." Inter Press Service, December 7, 2009.

Foullah, L. A., and Macsood Gibril Sesay. "Peaceful Co-existence in a Multireligious Society." Freetown: Council of Churches in Sierra Leone, 2006.

Freedom of Information Advocates Network. "Sierra Leone Portal No Substitute for FOI Law, Advocates Say." January 27, 2012.

Gabel, Katy, and Courtney Hess. "Sierra Leone: Women Aim for the Presidency by 2012." *AllAfrica*, October 28, 2007.
Gberie, Lansana. "Briefing: The Special Court of Sierra Leone." *African Affairs* 102, no. 409 (2003): 637–48.
———. *A Dirty War in West Africa: The RUF and the Destruction of Sierra Leone.* Bloomington: Indiana University Press, 2005.
———. "The Redundant Court for Sierra Leone." *New African*, December 1, 2009.
———, ed. *Rescuing a Fragile State: Sierra Leone 2002–2008*. Waterloo, ON: Wilfrid Laurier University Press, 2009.
———. "Trial of a 'War Hero.'" *Znet*, March 10, 2006.
Gelfand, Lauren. "As Sentencing Approaches, Cynicism about Sierra Leone Tribunal Lingers." *World Politics Review*, July 12, 2007.
Gevisser, Mark. "The Ultimate Test of Faith." *Mail and Guardian*, April 12, 1996.
Goldblatt, Beth, and Sheila Meintjes. "Gender and the Truth and Reconciliation Commission." Submission to the South African Truth and Reconciliation Commission, 2006.
Gopin, Marc. *Between Eden and Armageddon: The Future of World Religions, Violence, and Peacemaking.* New York: Oxford University Press, 2000.
———. "Forgiveness as an Element of Conflict Resolution in Religious Cultures: Walking the Tightrope of Reconciliation and Justice." In *Reconciliation, Justice, and Coexistence: Theory and Practice,* edited by Mohammed Abu-Nimer, 87–99. New York: Lexington Books, 2001.
Government of Sierra Leone. Submission to the Universal Periodic Review of the UN Human Rights Council, 11th Session, May 2011.
———. "White Paper on the Report of the Truth and Reconciliation Commission," June 27, 2005.
Graybill, Lyn S. "The Contribution of the Truth and Reconciliation Commission toward the Promotion of Women's Rights in South Africa." *Women's Studies International Forum* 24, no. 1 (2001): 1–10.
———. "Debt Relief: A Panacea for Sierra Leone." *CSIS Africa Policy Forum*, February 9, 2007.
———. "Honoring the Voices of Children at the Truth and Reconciliation Commission." *Iris* 39 (Fall 1999): 32–35.
———. "Pardon, Punishment, and Amnesia: Three African Post-conflict Methods." *Third World Quarterly* 25, no. 6 (2004): 1117–30.
———. *Truth and Reconciliation in South Africa: Miracle or Model?* Boulder: Lynne Rienner, 2002.

Griffiths, Courtenay. "Interview with Taylor's Lead Counsel Courtenay Griffiths QC in the Hague." By Angela Stavrianou. *Monitor* 40 (October–November 2009): 13–17.

Guardian. "Sierra Leone: Journalist Arrested after Questioning Official Ebola Response." November 5, 2014.

Gupta, Sulakshana. "Stephen Rapp: Obama's Point Man on War Crimes." *Time International*, September 14, 2009.

Gurr, Ted Robert. "Containing Internal War in the Twenty-First Century." In *From Reaction to Conflict Prevention: Opportunities for the UN System*, edited by Fen Osler Hampson and David M. Malone, 41–62. Boulder: Lynne Rienner, 2002.

Halpern, Jodi, and Harvey M. Weinstein. "Rehumanizing the Other: Empathy and Reconciliation." *Human Rights Quarterly* 26 (2004): 561–83.

Hamber, Brandon. "Reparation as Symbol: Narratives of Resistance, Reticence and Possibility in South Africa." Paper presented at Reparations: An Interdisciplinary Examination of Some Philosophical Issues Conference, Queen's University, Kingston, ON, February 6–8, 2004.

Hamber, Brandon, and Richard Wilson. "Symbolic Closure through Memory, Reparation and Revenge in Post-conflict Societies." *Journal of Human Rights* 1, no. 1 (2002): 35–53.

Hampson, Fen Osler, and David M. Malone, eds. *From Reaction to Conflict Prevention: Opportunities for the UN System*. Boulder: Lynne Rienner, 2002.

Hanlon, Joseph. "Is the International Community Helping to Recreate the Preconditions for War in Sierra Leone?" *Round Table* 94, no. 38 (2005): 459–72.

Hayner, Priscilla. *Unspeakable Truths: Confronting State Terror and Atrocity*. New York: Routledge, 2001.

———. *Unspeakable Truths: Transitional Justice and the Challenge of Truth Commissions*. 2nd ed. New York: Routledge, 2011.

Hirsch, John L. *Sierra Leone: Diamonds and the Struggle for Democracy*. Boulder: Lynne Rienner, 2001.

Hoffman, Elisabeth. "Reconciliation in Sierra Leone: Local Processes Yield Global Lessons." *Fletcher Forum of World Affairs* 32, no. 2 (2008): 129–41.

Hoffman, Libby [Elisabeth]. "How It Works: An In-Depth Look at the Fambul Tok Process." In *Fambul Tok*, 77–94. New York: Umbrage Editions, 2011.

Honwana, Alcinda. "The Collective Body: Challenging Western Concepts of Trauma and Healing." *Track Two* 8, no. 1 (1999): 30–35.

———. "Sealing the Past, Facing the Future: Trauma Healing in Rural Mozambique." *Accord* 3 (1998): 75–80.
Horovitz, Sigall. "Transitional Criminal Justice in Sierra Leone." In *Transitional Justice in the Twenty-First Century: Beyond Truth versus Justice*, edited by Naomi Roht-Arriaza and Javier Mariezcurrenta, 43–69. New York: Cambridge University Press, 2006.
Human Rights Commission of Sierra Leone. *The State of Human Rights in Sierra Leone: 2008*. Freetown: HRCSL, 2009.
———. *The State of Human Rights in Sierra Leone: 2011*. Freetown: HRCSL, 2012.
Human Rights Watch. "Justice in Motion: The Trial Phase of the Special Court for Sierra Leone." *Human Rights Watch* 17, no. 14-A (2005): 1–46.
———. "We'll Kill You If You Cry: Sexual Violence in the Sierra Leone Conflict." *Human Rights Watch* 15, no. 1-A (2003): 1–75.
———. *World Report: Sierra Leone, 2008*. New York: Human Rights Watch, 2009.
———. *World Report: Sierra Leone, 2009*. New York: Human Rights Watch, 2010.
Humphreys, Macartan, and Jeremy Weinstein. "What the Fighters Say: A Survey of Ex-combatants in Sierra Leone." CGSD Working Paper 20, Columbia Global Centers, Columbia University, New York, August 2004.
Huntington, Samuel P. *The Third Wave: Democratization in the Late Twentieth Century*. Norman: University of Oklahoma Press, 1991.
Hurd, Hilary. "The Inter-Religious Council of Sierra Leone (IRCSL) as Peace-Facilitator in Sierra Leone (1991–Present)." Master's thesis, St. John's College, University of Cambridge, 2014.
Huyse, Luc. "Introduction: Tradition-Based Approaches in Peacemaking, Transitional Justice and Reconciliation Policies." In Huyse and Salter, *Traditional Justice and Reconciliation after Violent Conflict*, 1–21.
Huyse, Luc, and Mark Salter, eds. *Traditional Justice and Reconciliation after Violent Conflict: Learning from African Experiences*. Stockholm: IDEA, 2008.
Ibrahim, Aisha Fofana. "War's Other Voices: Testimonies by Sierra Leonean Women." PhD diss., Illinois State University, 2006.
Igreja, Victor. "The Politics of Peace, Justice and Healing in Post-war Mozambique: 'Practices of Rupture.'" In *Peace versus Justice? The Dilemma of Transitional Justice in Africa*, edited by Chandra Lekha Sriram and Suren Pillay, 277–300. Rochester, NY: James Currey, 2010.

Ingelaere, Bert. "The Gacaca Courts in Rwanda." In Huyse and Salter, *Traditional Justice and Reconciliation after Violent Conflict,* 25–59.

International Center for Transitional Justice. "The Sierra Leone Truth and Reconciliation Commission: Reviewing Its First Year." New York: ICTJ, 2004.

International Crisis Group. "Sierra Leone after Elections: Politics as Usual?" July 15, 2002.

———. "Sierra Leone: A New Era of Reform?" Africa Report no. 143, July 31, 2008, 1–38.

———. "Sierra Leone's Truth and Reconciliation Commission: A Fresh Start?," December 20, 2002.

———. "The Special Court for Sierra Leone: Promises and Pitfalls of a 'New Model.'" Report no. 16, August 4, 2003.

Inter-Religious Council of Sierra Leone. Communique. February 25, 1999.

———. *Bo District: Final Report.* Community Based Reconciliation Project. Freetown: IRCSL, n.d.

———. *Bombali District: Final Report.* Community Based Reconciliation Project. Freetown: IRCSL, n.d.

———. *Bonthe District: Final Report.* Community Based Reconciliation Project. Freetown: IRCSL, n.d.

———. *Kenema District: Final Report.* Community Based Reconciliation Project. Freetown: IRCSL, n.d.

———. *Koinadugu District: Final Report.* Community Based Reconciliation Project. Freetown: IRCSL, n.d.

———. *Kono District: Final Report.* Community Based Reconciliation Project. Freetown: IRCSL, n.d.

———. *Moyamba District: Final Report.* Community Based Reconciliation Project. Freetown: IRCSL, n.d.

———. *Port Loko District: Final Report.* Community Based Reconciliation Project. Freetown: IRCSL, n.d.

———. *Report of the Program Coordinator.* Second Biennial General Assembly. Freetown: IRCSL, November 29–30, 2005.

———. *Report of the Secretary General.* Freetown: IRCSL, 2003.

———. "Summary of the Reports of the District Reconciliation Workshops from November 2003." Freetown: IRCSL, n.d.

———. *Tonkolili District: Final Report.* Community Based Reconciliation Project. Freetown: IRCSL, n.d.

———. *Western Area: Final Report.* Community Based Reconciliation Project. Freetown: IRCSL, n.d.

Irinnews. "Fighting Gender-Based Violence in Sierra Leone." November 6, 2013.

———. "Sex Crimes Up amid Ebola Outbreak in Sierra Leone." February 4, 2015.

———. "Sierra Leone: Fighting Gender Bias Ahead of Elections." June 13, 2007.

Jackson, Michael. *In Sierra Leone*. Durham, NC: Duke University Press, 2004.

Jalloh, Foday. "APPYA Commends President Koroma of Sierra Leone." *Sierra Express Media,* February 27, 2013.

Johnston, Douglas, and Cynthia Sampson. *Religion, the Missing Dimension of Statecraft*. New York: Oxford University Press, 1994.

Kabbah, Ahmad Tejan. "Unity, Freedom and Justice." Address to the Nation on the Occasion of the Thirty-Ninth Anniversary of Sierra Leone's Independence, Freetown, Sierra Leone, April 27, 2000.

Kalokoh, Abu. "Support War Victims." *New Citizen*, November 20, 2009.

Kalokoh, Saeed Gassama. "What Islam Says about War, Peace and Reconciliation." In *Christian-Muslim Perspectives on War, Peace, and Reconciliation,* edited by A. Cee Temple Anono, 8–14. Freetown: Council of Churches in Sierra Leone, 2006.

Kamara, Santigie. "Human Rights Issues." *Standard Times,* April 9, 2010.

Kamara, Tom. *Sierra Leone: A Search for Peace against the Odds*. Geneva: UNHCR, 2000.

Kaplan, Robert. "The Coming Anarchy: How Scarcity, Crime, Over-Population and Diseases Are Rapidly Destroying Our Planet." *Atlantic Monthly,* February 1994, 44–76.

Kargbo, Aska Mohamed Sorie. "Who Is Molesting Who: The President or the VP?" *International Observer,* October 17, 2013.

Kauffman, Stephen. "Sierra Leone: 'Family Talk' Empowers Country to Move Past Civil Conflict." *AllAfrica,* March 25, 2009.

Keen, David. *Conflict and Collusion in Sierra Leone*. Oxford: James Currey, 2005.

Kelsall, Michelle Staggs, and Shanee Stepakoff. "'When We Wanted to Talk about Rape': Silencing Sexual Violence at the Special Court for Sierra Leone." *International Journal for Transitional Justice* 1, no. 3 (2007): 355–74.

Kelsall, Tim. *Culture under Cross-Examination: International Justice and the Special Court for Sierra Leone*. New York: Cambridge University Press, 2009.

———. "Truth, Lies, Ritual: Preliminary Reflections on the Truth and Reconciliation Commission in Sierra Leone." *Human Rights Quarterly* 27, no. 2 (2005): 361–91.

Kendall, Sara, and Michelle Staggs. "Silencing Sexual Violence: Recent Developments in the CDF Case at the Special Court for Sierra Leone." War Crimes Studies Center, University of California at Berkeley, 2005.

Khadduri, Majid. *The Islamic Conception of Justice.* New York: Johns Hopkins University Press, 1984.

Khanu, Moses Benson. "The Role of the Inter-Religious Council in the Sierra Leone Peace Process (1977–2003)." Master's thesis, Fourah Bay College, 2005.

Kim, Hun Joon, and Kathryn Sikkink, "Explaining the Deterrence Effect of Human Rights Trials." *International Studies Quarterly* 54, no. 4 (2010): 939–63.

King, Jamesina. "Gender and Reparations in Sierra Leone: The Wounds of War Remain Open." In *What Happened to the Women? Gender and Reparations for Human Rights Violations,* edited by Ruth Rubio-Marin, 246–83. New York: Social Science Research Council, 2006.

Kistner, Wolfram. "The Biblical Understanding of Reconciliation." In *To Remember and to Heal: Theological and Psychological Perspectives on Truth and Reconciliation,* edited by H. Russel Botman and Robin Petersen, 79–95. Cape Town: Human and Rousseau, 1996.

Koroma, Pel. "Fambul Tok Promotes Community Healing." *Concord Times,* September 14, 2009.

———. "Focus on Community Reconciliation in Kono." *Concord Times,* December 23, 2008.

———. "Sierra Leone: Konos Want to Bury Their Dead." *Concord Times,* January 26, 2009.

Kriesberg, Louis. "Changing Forms of Coexistence." In *Reconciliation, Justice, and Coexistence: Theory and Practice,* edited by Mohammed Abu-Nimer, 47–64. New York: Lexington Books, 2001.

Kuyateh, Abdul. "Reconciliation at Work in Kono." *Standard Times,* August 31, 2004.

LaHurd, Carol Shersten. "So That the Sinner Will Repent: Forgiveness in Islam and Christianity." *Dialog* 35, no. 4 (1996): 287–92.

Lampman, Jane. "Faith's Unbreakable Force." *Christian Science Monitor,* December 23, 1999.

Latigo, James Ojera. "Northern Uganda: Tradition-Based Practices in the Acholi Region." In Huyse and Salter, *Traditional Justice and Reconciliation after Violent Conflict,* 85–120.

Lederach, John Paul. *Building Peace: Sustainable Reconciliation in Divided Societies.* Washington, DC: USIP Press, 1997.

Little, David. "The Power of Organization: Alimamy Koroma." In *Peacemakers in Action: Profiles of Religion in Conflict Resolution,* edited by David Little, 278–301. New York: Cambridge University, 2007.

Llewellyn, Jennifer J., and Robert Howse. "Institutions for Restorative Justice: The South African Truth and Reconciliation Commission." *University of Toronto Law Journal* 49, no. 3 (1999): 355–88.

Lome Peace Accord. July 7, 1999.

Longman, Timothy. "Justice at the Grassroots? Gacaca Trials in Rwanda." In *Transitional Justice in the Twenty-First Century: Beyond Truth versus Justice,* edited by Naomi Roht-Arriaza and Javier Mariezcurrenta, 206–28. New York: Cambridge University Press, 2006.

Lutz, Ellen, and Kathryn Sikkink. "The Justice Cascade: The Evolution and Impact of Foreign Human Rights Trials in Latin America." *Chicago Journal of International Law* 2 (2001): 1–34.

Mahtani, Sabrina. "Justice in a Time of Ebola," *Daily Vox,* February 10, 2015.

Mamdani, Mahmood. *When Victims Become Killers: Colonialism, Nativism, and the Genocide in Rwanda.* Princeton, NJ: Princeton University Press, 2001.

Manifesto 99. "Traditional Methods of Conflict Management/Resolution of Possible Complementary Value to the Proposed Sierra Leone Truth and Reconciliation Commission." Freetown, 2002.

Mani, Rama. *Beyond Retribution: Seeking Justice in the Shadow of War.* Cambridge: Polity Press, 2002.

Marks, Susan Collins. *Watching the Wind: Conflict Resolution during South Africa's Transition to Democracy.* Washington, DC: USIP Press, 2000.

McKay, Susan, and Dyan Mazurana. *Where Are the Girls? Girls in Fighting Forces in Northern Uganda, Sierra Leone and Mozambique: Their Lives during and after War.* Montreal: International Center for Human Rights and Democratic Developments, 2004.

Mendeloff, David. "Trauma and Vengeance: Assessing the Psychological and Emotional Effects of Post-conflict Justice." *Human Rights Quarterly* 31, no. 3 (2009): 592–623.

———. "Truth-Seeking, Truth-Telling, and Postconflict Peacebuilding: Curb the Enthusiasm?" *International Studies Review* 6 (2004): 355–80.

Mertus, Julie. "The War Crimes Tribunal: Triumph of the 'International Community,' Pain of the Survivors." *Mind and Human Interaction* 8, no. 1 (1997): 47–57.

Millar, Gearoid. "Assessing Local Experiences of Truth-Telling in Sierra Leone: Getting to 'Why' through a Qualitative Case Study Analysis." *International Journal of Transitional Justice* 4, no. 3 (2010): 477–96.

Minow, Martha. "Making History or Making Peace: When Prosecutions Should Give Way to Truth Commissions and Peace Negotiations." *Journal of Human Rights* 7, no. 2 (2008): 174–85.

Moore, Jina. "A Former Rebel Faces the Sierra Leonean Farmer He Maimed." *Christian Science Monitor*, July 9, 2008.

———. "Sierra Leoneans Look for Peace through Full Truth about War Crimes." *Christian Science Monitor*, July 8, 2008.

———. "Sierra Leone's 'Family Talk' Heals Scars of War." *Christian Science Monitor,* July 7, 2008.

Nairobi Declaration on Women's and Girls' Right to a Remedy and Reparation, 2007.

National Forum for Human Rights. "Traditional Methods of Conflict Resolution and Reconciliation." Report of Workshop Hosted for National Rulers/Paramount Chiefs, Freetown, 2001.

No Peace Without Justice. *Making Justice Count: Assessing the Impact and Legacy of the Special Court for Sierra Leone in Sierra Leone and Liberia.* Survey. New York: No Peace Without Justice, 2013.

Nordstrom, Carolyn. *A Different Kind of War Story.* Philadelphia: University of Pennsylvania Press, 1997.

———. *Girls and Warzones: Troubling Questions.* Uppsala: Life and Peace Institute, 1997.

Nowrojee, Binaifer. "Making the Invisible War Crime Visible: Post-conflict Justice for Sierra Leone's Rape Victims." *Harvard Human Rights Journal* 18 (2005): 85–105.

———. "'Your Justice Is Too Slow': Will the ICTR Fail Rwandan's Rape Victims?" Occasional Paper 10, United Nations Research Institute for Social Development, November 2005.

O'Flaherty, Michael. "Sierra Leone's Peace Process: The Role of the Human Rights Community." *Human Rights Quarterly* 26 (2004): 29–62.

Orentlicher, Diane F. "Settling Accounts: The Duty to Prosecute Human Rights Violations of a Prior Regime." *Yale Law Journal* 100, no. 8 (1991): 2537–615.

———. "'Settling Accounts' Revisited: Reconciling Global Norms with Local Agency." *International Journal of Transitional Justice* 1, no. 1 (2007): 10–22.

Park, Augustine S. J. "'Other Inhumane Acts': Forced Marriage, Girl Soldiers and the Special Court for Sierra Leone." *Social and Legal Studies* 15, no. 3 (2006): 315–37.

———. "Restorative Approaches to Justice: Strategies for Peace in Sierra Leone." Issues Paper No. 2, Center for International Governance and Justice, Canberra, May 2007.

Penfold, Peter. *Atrocities, Diamonds and Diplomacy: The Inside Story of the Conflict in Sierra Leone.* Barnsley, UK: Pen and Sword Books, 2012.

———. "Faith in Resolving Sierra Leone's Bloody Conflict." *Round Table* 94, no. 382 (2005): 549–57.

———. "An Interview with Peter Penfold." By Lansana Gberie. *African Affairs* 104, no. 414 (2005): 117–25.

———. "Is This Justice? Sierra Leone's Special Court Drags On." *Znet*, January 20, 2005.

———. "The Special Court for Sierra Leone: A Critical Analysis." In *Rescuing a Fragile State: Sierra Leone 2002–2008,* edited by Lansana Gberie, 53–72. Waterloo, ON: Wilfrid Laurier University Press, 2009.

Pham, J. Peter. "Lazarus Rising: Civil Society and Sierra Leone's Return from the Grave." *International Journal of Not for Profit Law* 7, no. 1 (2004): 49–75.

———. "Liberia and Sierra Leone: A Study of Comparative Human Rights Approaches by Civil Society Actors." *Interdisciplinary Journal of Human Rights Law* 1, no. 1 (2006): 69–105.

Phelps, Teresa Godwin. *Shattered Voices: Language, Violence, and the Work of Truth Commissions.* Philadelphia: University of Pennsylvania Press, 2004.

Philpott, Daniel. *Just and Unjust Peace: An Ethic of Political Reconciliation.* New York: Oxford University Press, 2012.

———, ed. *The Politics of Past Evil: Religion, Reconciliation, and the Dilemmas of Transitional Justice.* Notre Dame, IL: University of Notre Dame Press, 2006.

———. "Religion, Reconciliation, and Transitional Justice: The State of the Field." SSRC Working Paper, October 17, 2007.

———. "When Faith Meets History: The Influence of Religion on Transitional Justice." In *The Religious in Responses to Mass Atrocity: Interdisciplinary Perspectives,* edited by Thomas Brudholm and Thomas Cushman, 174–212. London: Cambridge University Press, 2009.

Physicians for Human Rights. *War-Related Sexual Violence in Sierra Leone: A Population Based Assessment.* New York: Physicians for Human Rights, 2002.

Post-Conflict Reintegration for Development and Empowerment (PRIDE). *Ex-combatant Views of the Truth and Reconciliation Commission and the Special Court in Sierra Leone.* Freetown: PRIDE, September 12, 2002.

Prunier, Gerard. *The Rwanda Crisis*. New York: Columbia University Press, 1995.

Relief Web. "Sierra Leone Victims Receive Compensation." Report from International Organization for Migration. Press Release. June 26, 2012.

Religion and Ethics Newsweekly. "Sierra Leone: Truth and Reconciliation." January 10, 2003.

Religions for Peace. Commission on Conflict Transformation. Eighth World Assembly, Kyoto, Japan, August 2006.

Republic of Sierra Leone. *Sierra Leone Constitutional Review Commission Report*. Freetown: Republic of Sierra Leone, 2007.

Reuters. "Sierra Leone's Top Medical Officer Cleared of Graft." October 25, 2013.

Revolutionary United Front. "Footpaths to Democracy: Toward a New Sierra Leone." 1995.

Richards, Paul. *Fighting for the Rain Forest: War, Youth, and Resources in Sierra Leone*. Portsmouth, NH: Heinemann, 1996.

Roht-Arriaza, Naomi, and Javier Mariezcurrenta, eds. *Transitional Justice in the Twenty-First Century: Beyond Truth versus Justice*. New York: Cambridge University Press, 2006.

Rotberg, Robert I., and Dennis Thompson, eds. *Truth v. Justice: The Morality of Truth Commissions*. Princeton, NJ: Princeton University Press, 2000.

Roth, Kenneth, and Alison Des Forges. "Justice or Therapy?" *Boston Review* (Summer 2002).

Rubio-Marin, Ruth, ed. *What Happened to the Women? Gender and Reparations for Human Rights Violations*. New York: Social Science Research Council, 2006.

Sampson, Cynthia. "Religion and Peacebuilding." In *Peacemaking in International Conflict: Methods and Techniques*, edited by I. William Zartman, 273–323. Washington, DC: USIP Press, 2007.

———. "'To Make Real the Bond between Us All': Quaker Conciliation during the Nigerian Civil War." In *Religion, the Missing Dimension of Statecraft*, edited by Douglas Johnston and Cynthia Sampson, 88–118. New York: Oxford University Press, 1994.

Sawyer, Edward. "Restoration, Retribution, Post-conflict Development: Grassroots Perceptions of Transitional Justice in Sierra Leone." Undergraduate thesis, Newcastle University, March 2006.

Sawyer, Edward, and Tim Kelsall. "Truth vs. Justice? Popular Views on the Truth and Reconciliation Commission and the Special Court for Sierra Leone." *Online Journal of Peace and Conflict Resolution* 7, no. 1 (2007): 36–68.

Scarry, Elaine. *The Body in Pain: The Making and Unmaking of the World.* Oxford: Oxford University Press, 1985.
Schabas, William A. "The Relationship between Truth Commissions and International Courts: The Case of Sierra Leone." *Human Rights Quarterly* 25 (2003): 1035–66.
———. "The Sierra Leone Truth and Reconciliation Commission." In *Transitional Justice in the Twenty-First Century: Beyond Truth versus Justice,* edited by Naomi Roht-Arriaza and Javier Mariezcurrenta, 21–42. New York: Cambridge University Press, 2006.
———. "A Synergistic Relationship: The Sierra Leone Truth and Reconciliation Commission and the Special Court for Sierra Leone." *Criminal Law Forum* 15, no. 1–2 (2004): 3–54.
Schreiter, Robert J. *Reconciliation: Mission and Ministry in a Changing Social Order.* Maryknoll, NY: Orbis, 1992.
Schuler, Corrina. "Sierra Leone's 'See No Evil' Pact." *Christian Science Monitor,* September 15, 1999.
Sesay, Amadu. "Does One Size Fit All? The Sierra Leone Truth and Reconciliation Commission Revisited." Discussion Paper 36, Uppsala, Nordiska Afrikainstitutet, 2007.
Shaw, Rosalind. "Memory Frictions: Localizing the Truth and Reconciliation Commission in Sierra Leone." *International Journal of Transitional Justice* 1, no. 2 (2007): 183–207.
———. "Memory Wars: Commissioning Truth and Reconciliation in Sierra Leone." Unpublished paper, n.d.
———. "Rethinking Truth and Reconciliation Commissions: Lessons from Sierra Leone." USIP Special Report 130, February 2005.
———."Transitional Subjectivities: Reconciling Ex-combatants in Northern Sierra Leone." Unpublished paper, n.d.
Sierra Leone Truth and Reconciliation Commission Act, 2000.
Sierra Leone Truth and Reconciliation Commission. *Witness to Truth: Report of the Sierra Leone Truth & Reconciliation Commission.* Vols. 1, 2, 3A, 3B, and CD-ROM. Accra: Graphic Packaging, 2004.
Sierra Leone Working Group on Truth and Reconciliation. "Searching for Truth and Reconciliation in Sierra Leone: An Initial Study of the Performance and Impact of the Truth and Reconciliation Commission." Freetown, 2006.
Sikkink, Kathryn, and Carrie Booth Walling. "The Impact of Human Rights Trials in Latin America." *Journal of Peace Research* 44, no. 4 (2007): 427–45.

Smock, David R, ed. "Religious Contributions to Peacemaking: When Religion Brings Peace, Not War." *Peaceworks* no. 55 (January 2006).
Snyder, Jack, and Leslie Vinjamuri. "Trials and Errors: Principle and Pragmatism in Strategies of International Justice." *International Security* 28, no. 3 (2003–2004): 5–44.
Special Court for Sierra Leone. "Guilty Verdict in the Trial of the AFRC Accused." Press Release. June 20, 2007.
Special Court for Sierra Leone. Office of the Prosecutor. Press Release. February 25, 2009.
Special Court for Sierra Leone Statute, January 16, 2002.
Sriram, Chandra Lekha, and Suren Pillay, eds. *Peace versus Justice? The Dilemma of Transitional Justice in Africa.* Rochester, NY: James Currey, 2010.
Standard Times. "Betrayal of Confidence: Whistleblower Exposes Corruption at ACC." January 31, 2015.
———. "Coalition of Women's Organisations in Sierra Leone Writes Attorney General and Minister of Justice." March 2, 2009.
———. "President Koroma Consoles 11,000 War Widows." April 1, 2010.
Stovel, Laura. "Long Way Home: Building Reconciliation and Trust in Postconflict Sierra Leone." PhD diss., Simon Fraser University, 2006.
Strachan, Harold. Letter to the editor. *Mail and Guardian,* July 25, 1997.
Sulleh, Mamie, and Isata Sowa. "Registration of Customary [Marriage] and Divorce Act and Early/Forced Marriage: Its Implications on Our Girls and Society." Center for Accountability and Rule of Law (CARL), July 20, 2012.
Suma, Mohamed, and Cristian Correa. "Report and Proposals for the Implementation of Reparations in Sierra Leone." New York: International Center for Transitional Justice, December 2009.
Tarawallie, Ibrahim. "Sierra Leone: NaCSA Doles Out US $1.3 Million as Micro-grants." *Concord Times,* October 7, 2009.
Teale, Lotta. "Addressing Gender-Based Violence in the Sierra Leone Conflict: Notes from the Field." *African Journal on Conflict Resolution* 9, no. 2 (2009): 69–90.
———. "The Gender Bills: An Update." Sierra Leone Court Monitoring Project, March 26, 2007.
———. "Sierra Leone Passes the Gender Bills into Law." *Monitor* 24 (June 2007): 11–12.
TerraViva News. "Sierra Leone: No End to Rape." December 15, 2004.
Terry, Sara. "Fambul Tok: A Documentary Film about the Power of Forgiveness." New York: First Run Features, 2011.

Thoms, Oskar N. T., Roland Paris, and James Ron. "The Effects of Transitional Justice Mechanisms: A Summary of Empirical Research Findings and Implications for Analysts and Practitioners." Working Paper, University of Ottawa Centre for International Policy Studies, ON, 2008.

Toft, Monica Duffy, Daniel Philpott, and Timothy Samuel Shah. *God's Century: Resurgent Religion and Global Politics*. New York: W. W. Norton, 2011.

Tommy, Ibrahim, and Aruna Kallon. "The Legal Aid Act of Sierra Leone: When Will Implementation Start?" Center for Accountability and Rule of Law, April 1, 2014.

Turay, Thomas Mark. "Civil Society and Peacebuilding: The Role of the Inter-Religious Council of Sierra Leone." *Accord* 9 (2000): 50–53.

Tutu, Desmond. *No Future without Forgiveness*. New York: Doubleday, 1999.

UNAIDS. *Global Report: UNAIDS Report on the Global Epidemic*. Geneva: UNAIDS, 2010.

UNICEF. Global Databases, Education: Adult Literacy. October 2015.

———. Global Databases, Education: Secondary Net Attendance Ratio— Percentage. October 2015.

United Nations. "The Rule of Law and Transitional Justice in Conflict and Post-conflict Societies: Report of the Secretary-General." UN document S/2004/616, August 23, 2004.

United Nations Integrated Office in Sierra Leone (UNIOSIL). "A Matrix on the Status of Implementation of the Truth and Reconciliation Commission Recommendations." Human Rights and Rule of Law Section, May 2008.

UN News Service. "UN Names Local Lawyer to Top Post in Court Trying War Crimes in His Homeland." September 8, 2009.

USAID Office of Women in Development. "Gender Matters." Information Bulletin no. 9 (December 2000).

US Department of State. *Country Reports on Human Rights Practices for 2005: Sierra Leone*. Washington, DC: Bureau of Democracy, Human Rights, and Labor, 2006.

———. *Country Reports on Human Rights Practices for 2006: Sierra Leone*. Washington, DC: Bureau of Democracy, Human Rights, and Labor, 2007.

———. *Country Reports on Human Rights Practices for 2010: Sierra Leone*. Washington, DC: Bureau of Democracy, Human Rights, and Labor, April 8, 2011.

Van der Merwe, Hugo, Victoria Baxter, and Audrey R. Chapman, eds. *Assessing the Impact of Transitional Justice: Challenges for Empirical Research*. Washington, DC: USIP Press, 2008.

Vendley, William. "Exploring Strategies to Enhance Interfaith Cooperation for Sustainable Peace: The Experience of Religions for Peace." Paper presented at the United Nations Conference on Interfaith Cooperation for Peace, New York, June 2005.

Verwoerd, Wilhelm. "Forgiving the Torturer but Not the Torture." *Sunday Independent*, December 14, 1998.

Villa-Vicencio, Charles. *Walk with Us and Listen: Political Reconciliation in Africa.* Cape Town: University of Cape Town Press, 2009.

Vincent, Robert. "Punishment and Forgiveness in Sierra Leone—A Response to Peter Penfold." *Observer*, November 3, 2002.

Volkan, Vamik. "Transgenerational Transmissions and Chosen Traumas: An Aspect of Large-Group Identity." *Group Analysis* 34 (March 2001): 79–97.

Vragovich, Amanda. "Sierra Leone: Freedom of Information Is One Thing, Freedom of Press Is Another." *Think Africa Press,* November 7, 2013.

Waddell, Nicholas, and Phil Clark, eds. *Courting Conflict: Justice, Peace and the ICC in Africa.* London: Royal African Society, 2008.

Waldorf, Lars. "Mass Justice for Mass Atrocity: Rethinking Local Justice as Transitional Justice." *Temple Law Review* 79, no. 1 (2006): 1–87.

Walker, Peter. "Charles Taylor War Crimes Trial—The Verdict." *Guardian*, April 26, 2012.

Waugh, Colin. "Charles Taylor—The Long Wait for Justice Almost at an End." African Arguments, May 31, 2012.

White, Hayden. *The Content of the Form: Narrative Discourse and Historical Representation.* Baltimore: Johns Hopkins University Press, 1987.

Wilson, Richard. *The Politics of Truth and Reconciliation in South Africa: Legitimizing the Post-apartheid State.* Cambridge: Cambridge University Press, 2001.

———. "Reconciliation and Revenge in Post-apartheid South Africa: Rethinking Legal Pluralism and Human Rights." Paper presented at the Truth and Reconciliation Commission Conference on Commissioning the Past, University of Witwatersrand, Johannesburg, June 1999.

World Bank. *Education in Sierra Leone: Present Challenges, Future Opportunities.* Africa Human Development Series. In collaboration with the Ministry of Education, Science and Technology of Sierra Leone. Washington, DC: World Bank, 2006.

Zartman, I. William, ed. *Peacemaking in International Conflict: Methods and Techniques.* Washington, DC: USIP Press, 2007.

Zehr, Howard. *Changing Lenses: A New Focus for Crime and Justice.* Waterloo, ON: Herald Press, 1990.

Zehr, Howard, and Harry Mika. "Fundamental Concepts of Restoration Justice." *Contemporary Justice Review* 1, no. 1 (1998): 47–55.

Zeigler, Sara L., and Gregory Gilbert Gunderson. "The Gendered Dimensions of Conflict's Aftermath: A Victim-Centered Approach to Compensation." *Ethics and International Affairs* 20, no. 2 (2006): 171–92.

INDEX

Aberdeen Amputee Camp, 41
Abidjan Peace Accord, 9, 11, 26, 34, 216n.4
Abuja Accord, 11
Acholi, 130, 131, 132
'adl, 123–24
AFRC. *See* Armed Forces Revolutionary Council
African Development Bank, 117
African Methodist Episcopal Church, 106
African Minerals, 172
All Africa Conference of Churches (AACC), 13, 16
All Peoples Congress (APC), 7–8, 65, 166, 170. *See also* Koroma, Ernest Bai
All Political Parties Youth Association, 170
amnesty
  Abidjan Accord and, 216n.4
  disagreements about, 26, 31–32
  knowledge of, 72
  Lome Peace Accord and, 2, 10, 27–28, 31, 34, 43, 72, 221n.76
  Mozambique and, 129
  prosecutions after, 256n.5
  South Africa and, 81, 222n.92
  Uganda and, 131
  United Nations on, 27–28, 32, 216n.4
amputees
  complaints by, 176
  Kabbah, Ahmad Tejan, promises to, 41
  on prosecutions, 89
  reparations to, 63, 174
  TRC, recommendations on, 63
Amputees (organization), 176
Anglican Church, 100
Annan, Kofi, 182
Anti-Corruption Act, 165, 166–67
Anti-Corruption Commission (ACC)
  amendment on whistleblowers, 165
  Asset Declarations Defaulters list, 165
  Conteh, Abu Bakarr, as advisory committee member, 117
  Dove, Reuben on, 118
  Kamara, Joseph Fitzgerald, head of, 167
  Koroma, Abdul Karim on, 117–18
  leaks within, 165
  Marcus-Jones, Laura on, 166
  Nabieu, Francis on, 118

285

Anti-Corruption Commission (*cont.*)
  prosecutions by, 167
  Samuels, Henry on, 118
  Sierra Leone Court Monitoring
    Project, on independence of,
    167
  Tejan-Cole, Abdul, head of, 167
  TRC recommendations on, 166
Anti-Human Trafficking Act, 168
APC. *See* All Peoples Congress
Armed Forces Revolutionary
    Council (AFRC)
  conscription, forced, 188
  coup, 9, 19, 32, 200
  crimes, 54
  —amnesty for, 31
  —apology, lack of, 44
  —gender, 54
  —number of, 44
  RUF alliance, 10
  at Special Court
  —gender crimes, prosecution of,
    54–57
  —indictments, 33, 56
  —sentences, 111
  —trials, 49
  —verdicts, 87
  See also Koroma, Johnny Paul
Arusha Peace Accord, 16

Bah, Ibrahim, 26
Bangura, A. A.
  on AFRC defendants' sentences,
    111
  churches, critique of, 120–21
  on forgiveness, Muslim view, 100
  on punishment, Muslim view, 100
  on youth, needs of, 116
Bangura, Mohamed, 50

Bao, Augustine, 47
Barnett, Marie
  on forgiveness, 106
  on perpetrators, behavior of,
    106
  on Special Court, criticisms, 111
  on TRC recommendations, 113
  on victims, value of speaking,
    107
  on women, compensation to,
    116
Barnett, Tom
  churches, critique of, 121
  on forgiveness, 103, 122
  —Muslim view, 100
  Special Court, criticisms of,
    111–12
  on TRC
  —criticisms, 110
  —Muslim support, 100
  —recommendations, 116
  —victims, value to, 107
  on victims
  —expectations of, 116
  —reluctance to testify, 107
Battle of Badr, 101
BBC/Search for Common Ground,
    86–88, 92, 94
Berewa, Solomon, 41
Biguzzi, George
  on civil war, dealing with causes,
    105
  on healing, group aspect, 149–50
  on IRC, postwar, 120
  on TRC
  —cleric as chair, 98
  —recommendations, 113
  —repentance, lack of, 105
  —and Special Court, 114

Bill and Melinda Gates Foundation, 167
Bockerie, Sam, 33, 50, 113
Boersch-Supan, Johanna, 88–90
Boesak, Allan, 14
Boraine, Alex, 41
Brainard, Prince Charles
  on amputees, assistance to, 115
  on confession, 102
  —reasons for lack of, 104–5
  on forgiveness, 102
  —and reconciliation, difference between, 102–3
  on punishment, 111
  Special Court, value of, 111
  TRC recommendations, 115
bush wives, 54, 56, 60–61, 90, 142, 228n.56. *See also* forced marriage

Campaign for Good Governance, 79–80
Carew, Alfred, 49
Catalyst for Peace, 147, 200
Catholic Bishops Conference of the Gambia and Sierra Leone, 102
Catholic Church, 17, 97, 213n.43
Caulker, John
  on chiefs, 148
  on confession, 146
  Fambul Tok, director, 145
  Forum of Conscience, founder, 145, 149
  on justice, Western approach, 150
  on reconciliation, bottom-up approach, 196
  on TRC, critique, 145, 149
  TRC Working Group, founder, 145

CDF. *See* Civil Defense Forces
Centre for Accountability and the Rule of Law (CARL), 69
chiefs, 35, 133–34, 135, 140, 143, 144, 148, 172, 193
Chikane, Frank, 14
Child Rights Act, 62, 66, 168–70
Child Rights Coalition, 168
Chissano, Joaquim, 14
Christ Apostolic Church, 104
Christianity
  on forgiveness, 121–23, 124
  on justice, 124–25
  —economic, 199
  on punishment, 124–25
  on reconciliation, 121, 124–25
  on reparations, 125
Church of the Brotherhood of the Cross and Star, 20
Church of God of Prophecy Mission, 102
Church World Service, 144
Civil Defense Forces (CDF)
  acknowledgment, lack of, 43–44, 60, 73
  civilians, targeting of, 8
  code of conduct, 50
  confessions, 143, 148
  conscription, forced, 188
  crimes
  —against AFRC/RUF, 10
  —amnesty for, 31
  —gender, 54
  —numbers of, 44, 50, 60
  Kabbah, Ahmad Tejan, reliance on, 9
  at Special Court
  —gender crimes, non-prosecution of, 56, 57, 58

Civil Defense Forces (*cont.*)
—indictments, 33
—legal defense, 51
—non-prosecution of gender crimes, 56, 57, 58
—trials, 49
youth in, 42, 74
See also Norman, Samuel Hinga
civil war
causes of, 83, 84, 116, 196
—chiefs, behavior of, 133–34, 140
—corruption, 117, 118, 133, 154, 166, 196, 197
—ethnic dimension, lack of, 190
—ideology, lack of, 190
—religious basis, lack of, 189
—youth, neglect of, 116, 170
crimes during, 9, 10, 20–21, 23, 54, 134
culture, impact on, 133, 146
justice sector, destruction of during, 92
longevity of, 190
memorial, 144–45
public aspect, 84
Coalition of War Disabled in Sierra Leone, 176
Cole, Abdul Tejan, 167
Commission for the Consolidation of Peace, 10, 27–28
Commission for the Management of Strategic Resources. *See* Mineral Resources Commission
compensation. *See* reparations
Conakry Peace Accord, 19
Conciliation Services, 148

Constitution, TRC recommendations on
amendments, 156, 161
customary law, 162–63
death penalty, 157
discriminatory sections, repeal of, 63
emergency powers, 158
freedom of expression, 160
paramilitary forces, 163
Constitutional Review Commission (1990), 161
Constitutional Review Commission (2007), 65, 157, 172, 251n.26
Conteh, Abu Bakarr
ACC, advisory board member, 117
on corruption, 118
on forgiveness, example of Mohammed, 101
during invasion of Freetown, 21–22
on punishment, 101
on reconciliation in Islam, 101
on TRC recommendations, 115
Corporal Punishment Act, 168
corruption
as cause of war, 117, 118, 133, 166
of chiefs, 133
church leaders and, 118
Foday-Khabenje, Aiah D. on, 118–19
Khazali, Paul on, 117
Koroma, Abdul Karim on, 117
Large, Bankole on, 119
ongoing, 179
perceptions of, 166
Quran on, 117

religious leaders on, 117–19
remuneration, low, as explanation for, 162
Salia, Sahr Kemoore on, 118
Simbo, Billy on, 118
Transparency International Index and, 160
See also Anti-Corruption Commission
Council of Churches in Sierra Leone, 17, 97, 119, 144
Council of Elders, 135
Council of Elders and Religious Leaders, 27
Crane, David, on Special Court
  benefit of simultaneous institutions, 81, 185
  children, not indicting, 43, 221n.73
  forced marriages, 55
  independence of, 43
  indictments, 55
  Norman, Samuel Hinga, refusal to let him testify at TRC, 76
  polling and, 49
curandeiro, 130

Danforth, John, 13
DDR (disarmament, demobilization, and reintegration programs), 29, 42, 68, 75, 98, 116, 139, 176, 193, 221n.70
Desay, Daniel
  on amputees, assistance to, 115
  on confession, benefit to perpetrators, 108
  on TRC
  —participation, low, 114
  —reconciliation ceremonies, 108
  —recommendations, 115
Dhlakama, Afonso, 14
Domestic Violence Act, 62, 65, 66
Dove, Reuben
  on Anti-Corruption Commission, 118
  on forgiveness
  —without apology, 103, 122
  —Muslim view, 100
  on Special Court, criticisms, 112
  on TRC, value to victims, 107

Ebola, 66, 147, 159, 160
ECOMOG. *See* Economic Community of West African States Monitoring Group
Economic Community of West African States (ECOWAS), 26, 113
Economic Community of West African States Monitoring Group (ECOMOG), 10, 20, 21, 24, 27, 33, 54, 60, 113
ECOWAS. *See* Economic Community of West African States
Education Act of 2004, 169
Ekemode, M. O.
  on forgiveness, 104
  on TRC
  —cleric as chair, 98–99
  —recommendations, 113
Eshun-Baiden, Nematta, 65
ethnic groups
  Creoles, 78, 109, 135
  Fullah, 78, 140, 245n.49
  Kissi, 78, 136

ethnic groups (*cont.*)
  Kono, 140, 144
  Koranko, 78, 140, 142
  Limba, 121, 135, 140
  Loko, 78, 136, 140
  Mandingo, 140, 245n.49
  Mende, 91, 109, 121, 140, 142, 189
  Sherbro, 78, 140
  Soso, 78, 245n.49
  Temne, 3, 91, 109, 121, 136, 140, 189
  Yalunka, 140
Evangelical Fellowship for Sierra Leone, 17, 97
Evangelical Lutheran Church, 100
Executive Outcomes, 8, 9, 10, 225n.8
Ex-service Wounded in Action Personnel Organization, 176
Extractive Industries Transparency Commission, 172
Eyadema, Gnassingbe, 26

Fambul Tok, 3, 63, 145–52
  Catalyst for Peace, funding from, 200
  ceremonies, 147–50, 194, 195
  consultations for, 146
  cost, 151–52
  development projects, 150–51, 195
  local ownership of, 201
  radio listening clubs, 149
  reconciliation committees, 148–49
  reparations, 151
  restorative justice, example of, 150
  tradition, deviations from, 148
  women and, 147, 148
  youth and, 148–49
  See also Caulker, John
Family Support Units, 59
Federation of Muslim Women's Associations of Sierra Leone, 17, 97, 99
50/50 (NGO), 65
Finnoh, Tamba, 41
Foday-Khabenje, Aiah D.
  on corruption, 118–19
  on forgiveness, Christian view, 104
  on Special Court
  —death of key figures, 113
  —Norman, Samuel Hinga, prosecution of, 113
  —prosecution, lack of for UNAMSIL and ECOWAS, 113
  on TRC
  —recommendations, 115
  —testifying, value to perpetrators, 108
  —victims, expectations of, 116
"Footpaths to Democracy," 23
forced marriage, 54, 56, 61, 62
  Crane on, 55–56
  criminalization of, 62, 66
  prosecutions of, 56
  See also bush wives
Fornah, Usman
  on civil war, addressing causes of, 112
  on culture of silence, 105–6
  on faith community, advocacy role, 120
  on forgiveness, 104, 122

—Christ as example, 104
on reconciliation, priority over
 justice, 39, 112
on Special Court
—contemporaneous with TRC, 114
—misunderstandings of, 114
on TRC
—cleric as chair, 98
—recommendations, 113, 117
—reconciliation ceremonies, 108
—role within, 34, 105
—vs. Special Court, 112
on War Victims Fund, 116–17
Forum of Conscience, 38, 145, 149
Freedom of Information Act, 160
Freetown Central Mosque, 102
Frelimo, 13, 129

gacaca, 127–29, 201
gamba, 129
Ganda, Joseph, 17, 21
gender bills, 62, 65–66, 168
General Peace Accord
 (Mozambique), 14
Ghaffaar, 122
ghufran, 122
Golley, Omrey, 26
Goncalves, Jaime, 14
Gowan, Yakubu, 13
Griffiths, Courtenay, 50
gumo tong ("bending of the spears"), 131

Habre, Hissene, 185
Hollis, Brenda, 49, 91
Holy Trinity Church, 20
HRCSL. *See* Human Rights
 Commission of Sierra Leone

Hudud, 123
Human Rights Commission of
 Sierra Leone (HRCSL)
on Child Rights Act, 168
on corporal punishment, 168
on courts, local, 162
commissioners
—appointment of, 156
—Khanu, Moses, 11, 65, 118
—King, Jamesina, 61
—youth representatives, lack of, 170
on detention, arbitrary, 158
Koroma, Alimamy on, 201
and TRC recommendations
—conference on status of, 156
—for HRCSL, 155–56
—matrix of implementation, 156
White Paper on, 156
on women in government, 65
Human Rights Committee, 34
Human Rights Watch, 54, 58, 159, 190
Humper, Joseph
on apology, lack of, 105
bishop, United Methodist
 Church, 38
on forgiveness, 40, 103, 122
during invasion of Freetown, 22
IRC president, 34, 38, 99
on Sierra Leone as "laboratory," 112
SLPP connections, 36
on Special Court
—differences from TRC, 1, 38
—misunderstandings about, 114
—value of, 112
as TRC chair, 34, 38, 98, 99

Humper, Joseph (*cont.*)
—criticisms of, 36, 99, 112, 219n.47
on TRC, criticisms of
—funding, 112
—Special Court, competition with, 112
—time constraints, 105
—on TRC recommendations, 113, 115
Humphreys, Macartan, and Weinstein, Jeremy, 75–78
Hutu, 55, 128

ICC. *See* International Criminal Court
ICTR. *See* International Criminal Tribunal for Rwanda
immunity. *See* amnesty
Interfaith Mediation Committee, 12
International Center for Transitional Justice, 81, 177–78
International Conflict Group, 35
International Convention on the Rights of the Child, 168
International Covenant on Civil and Political Rights, 159
International Criminal Court (ICC), xii–xiii, 33, 80, 81, 131, 181, 185
International Criminal Tribunal for Rwanda (ICTR), 181, 185
cost of, 186, 257n.23
gender crimes, handling of, 53, 54, 55, 56, 57, 59
location, 57
prosecutions, one-sided, 55

International Human Rights Group, 81
International Labor Organization, 169
International Monetary Fund, 172
Inter-Religious Council (IRC)
AFRC coup, response to, 19, 199
on amnesty, 26, 31, 35, 192
co-option of leaders, 119–20
critiques by
—Bangura, A. A., 120–21
—Barnett, Tom, 121
—Biguzzi, George, 120
—Khanu, Moses, 120
—Koroma, Abdul Karim, 120
—Koroma, Alimamy, 200–201
"experience-sharing" sessions, 38–39
founding, 17–18, 97, 200
goals, 17–18
Humper, Joseph, president of, 99
invasion of Freetown, warning to government, 20
Kabbah, Ahmad Tejan, meeting with, 19, 24, 199
Khanu, Moses, founding member of, 18
Koroma, Alimamy, leader of, 17
Koroma, Johnny Paul, meeting with, 19
Lome Peace Accord
—promotion of, 28
—role in, 2, 26–28
member organizations, 97
reconciliation activities, sponsorship of, 110, 141–44, 194, 195, 249n.154

Sankoh, Foday
—meeting with, 19, 24–25
—rebuffed by, 29
Special Court
—simultaneous with TRC, problems with, 123
—support for, 123
Taylor, Charles, appeal to, 26
TRC
—assistance to, 34
—support for, 123
—workshops on recommendations, 115
war memorial, establishment of, 144–45
World Conference of Religions for Peace, support from, 200
invasion of Freetown, 10, 20, 37
IRC. *See* Inter-Religious Council
Islam
 on corruption, 117
 on forgiveness, 99–100, 101, 122–23, 124
 —apology as prerequisite for, 122–23
 on justice, 123–25
 —economic, 125, 199
 —and reparations, 122, 125
 —as restorative, 125
 —as right relationships, 125
 on punishment, 123, 124–25
 on reconciliation, 124

Jaka, Jusu, 41
Jetley, Vija, 25
Jow, Ajaaratou Satang, 35, 36, 59
Judicial and Legal Services Commission, 161, 162

justice
 distributive (economic), 67–69, 94, 125, 179, 199, 231n.113, 261n.83. *See also* reparations
 restorative
 —in Christianity and Islam, 123–25, 188, 193–94
 —economic aspects, 198
 —elements of, xiii
 —popular preferences for, 5, 87–88, 125, 186–87
 —religious preferences for, 39, 125
 —in Sierra Leone, 183–84
 —vs. retributive justice, xi–xii, 5, 38, 87–88, 93–94, 95, 131, 186–87, 257n.23
 —and traditional conflict resolution methods, 127–32
 —and TRC, 38
 —Tutu on, 4, 39
 —and *ubuntu*, xii, xiii, 5
 —*See also* Fambul Tok
 retributive
 —and deterrence, 187
 —elements of, xiii
 —in South Africa, 4
 —and Special Court, 38
 —Western preference for, 181–82, 186–87
Jusu-Sheriff, Yasmin, 35, 36, 48, 81–82

Kabbah, Ahmad Tejan
 AFRC coup against, 19
 amputees, promises to, 41
 apology, lack of, 45, 102
 CDF, reliance on, 9
 civil war, announces end of, 11

Kabbah, Ahmad Tejan (*cont.*)
  death penalty, 157
  ECOMOG, restores to power, 10, 20
  election victory in 1996, 9
  exile, return from, 10
  Ganda, Joseph, relationship with, 21
  gender bills and, 65
  IRC, meeting with, 19, 20, 24
  Lome Peace Accord, signing of, 10
  marriage, as example of religious tolerance, 18, 98
  on TRC
  —international control of, 36
  —need for, 32
  UN, request to establish Special Court, 29, 33, 80
Kairos Document, 15
Kamajors, 8, 11, 29, 112, 143. *See also* Civil Defense Forces
Kamara, Abdul, 197
Kamara, Buya, 178
Kamara, Ibrahim, 177
Kamara, John, 36
Kamara, Joseph Fitzgerald, 49, 167
Kampbell, Solomon
  on corruption, 118
  on forgiveness, 104, 122
  on punishment, 111
  on Special Court, 111
Kargbo, Franklyn, 35
Karim, Abdul Babatunde
  on confession, lack of, 105
  on IRC reconciliation activities, 110
  on TRC

  —cleric as chairman, 99
  —criticisms, 110
Kassim, Saimihafu, 25
Kelsall, Tim
  on culture of secrecy, 6, 192
  on Special Court, criticisms
  —international law at odds with local understandings, 50–51
  —payment to witnesses, 51
  on TRC
  —criticisms of, 3–4, 42, 191, 198
  —reconciliation ceremonies, 4, 44–45, 191
Khanu, Moses
  on confession, public, 109
  Human Rights Commission, commissioner on, 11, 109
IRC
  —co-founder of, 17
  —director of, 17, 109
  —on reconciliation activities, 141
  on leaders, religious
  —co-option of, 120
  —timidity of, 11, 120
  on Lome Accord, 26–27
  on RUF, meeting with, 24
  on TRC, reconciliation ceremonies, 44
Khazali, Paul, 117
King, Jamesina, 61, 62, 64, 67
Konteh, Joseph
  on apology, 103–4, 122
  on forgiveness
  —Joseph, as example of, 101, 103
  —Muslim view, 100
  —independent of TRC, 109

on TRC recommendations, 113, 119
Koroma, Abdul Karim
  on Anti-Corruption Commission, 117–18
  on apology, 102
  on corruption, 117–18
  on forgiveness
  —of child rebels, 102
  —in Quran, 101, 102
  on IRC, postwar, 120
  on justice, 102
  on local courts, preference for, 113
  on Special Court, legacy of, 113
  on TRC
  —cleric as chairman, 99
  —recommendations, 117
  —SATRC, comparison with, 107
  —victims, worthless to, 107
  on Tutu, Desmond, 99
Koroma, Alimamy
  on amnesty, 35
  APC government, minister in, 201
  arrest of, 19
  Council of Churches in Sierra Leone, general secretary, 17, 200
  on Human Rights Commission, 201
  and IRC
  —Lome Peace Accord, role in, 26, 28
  —Sankoh, Foday, meeting with, 25
  —secretary general of, 17
  —success of, 18, 200

Koroma, Ernest Bai
  apologies from, 45
  assets, declaration of, 165
  death penalty, commutation of sentences, 157
  logging, ban on, 165
  "rat," called by press, 160
  state of emergency, imposition of, 159
  War Victims Trust Fund, launching of, 178
Koroma, Johnny Paul
  AFRC chairman, selection as, 9
  Commission for the Consolidation of Peace, appointment to, 10, 27
  death of, 33, 50
  IRC, meeting with, 19
  Peace Task Force, establishment of, 11, 29
  Special Court, indictment by, 29
Koroma, Tamba
  on TRC recommendations, 113, 119
  on youth, needs of, 116
Kpomgbo, James, 188

Large, Bankole
  on confession, public, 106
  on corruption, 119
  on forgiveness
  —in absence of TRC, 108–9
  —Muslim view, 99–100
  on Special Court and TRC
  —on sequencing, 114
  —simultaneous institutions, 113–14
  —value of both, 112
Law Reform Commission, 162

Legal Aid Act, 162
Liberia
  civil war in, 12
  Inter-Religious Council of, 12
  IRC delegation to RUF, 26
  RUF invasion from, 7
  TRC, recommendations on, 171
  truth commission in, 183, 185
Linhobello, Antonio, 19
Lome Peace Accord
  amnesty in, 2, 10, 31–32, 34, 43, 72, 93
  collapse of, 10–11, 33, 34
  criticisms of, 27–28
  on Human Rights Commission, 154
  signing of, 2, 10, 26–27, 28, 38
  on Special Fund for War Victims, 173
  on TRC, 32
  on women, 58
Lord's Resistance Army, 130, 131, 132, 133
Lynch, J. O. P.
  on forgiveness, Muslim and Christian views, 100
  during invasion of Freetown, 22–23
  on Special Court, criticisms
  —concurrent with TRC, 114
  —misunderstandings about, 114
  —sequencing and TRC, 114
  on TRC recommendations, 113, 115

Mahdi, Mariatu, 17, 99, 106–7
Mandela, Nelson, 45
Manifesto 99
  polling by, 71–73, 74, 78
  traditional conflict methods, report on, 132–33, 134, 139
Mansary, Tamba, 144–45
Marah, Milton
  on confession, public, 109–10
  on forgiveness, 104, 122
  on punishment, 112
  on Special Court, timing of, 114, 120
  on TRC
  —criticisms of, 110
  —recommendations, 113, 120
  —on women testifying, 108
Marcus-Jones, Laura, 36, 166
mato oput, 130
Mbayo, Mabel
  on IRC, reconciliation activities, 110, 141, 143–44
  on TRC, 141
  on war memorial, 144
Meindy, John
  on apology, 102
  TRC, recommendations of, 113
  on women, cultural barriers to testifying, 107
Melrose, Joseph, 18, 27
memorial, war, 144–45
Mercy Ships, 177
Millar, Gearoid, 90–91
Millenium Challenge Corporation, 160
Mineral Resources Commission (Commission for the Management of Strategic Resources), 10, 27
Mines and Mineral Act, 172
Ministry of Mineral Resources (Mines and Mineral Resources), 171, 172, 173

Ministry of Social Welfare, Gender, and Children's Affairs, 59, 63
Ministry of Youth and Sports, 170
Missionary Church of Africa, 104
Momoh, Joseph, 12
Mozambique
 Christian Council of, 14
 curandeiros in, 130
 Frelimo, 13, 129
 gamba in, 129
 peacemakers in, 13–14
 reconciliation in, 3, 132
 Renamo, 14, 129
 and Sant'Egidio, 14, 16
 truth commission in, 185
Muslim Brotherhood Islamic Mission, 17, 97

Nabieu, Francis
 on Anti-Corruption Commission, 118
 on forgiveness, Muslim and Christian views, 100
 on God, Muslim and Christian views, 100
 on Special Court's refusal to let Norman, Samuel Hinga, testify at TRC, 113
 on TRC
 —recommendations, 113, 119
 —reconciliation ceremonies, 108
NaCSA. *See* National Commission for Social Action
Nairobi Declaration on Women's and Girls' Rights to Reparation, 67
National Christian Evangelical Mission, 117
National Commission for Democracy and Human Rights, 34
National Commission for Social Action (NaCSA), 81, 173, 174, 175, 176, 177
National Forum for Human Rights, 34, 35, 49, 217n.26
National Patriotic Front of Liberia, 210n.1
National Peace Accord (South Africa), 15
National Provisional Ruling Council (NPRC)
 amputations by, 9
 CDF/*Kamajors*, relationship with, 8
 coup by, 7–8
 Executive Outcomes and, 8
National Resistance Army (Uganda), 131
National Security Council, 171
National Vision for Sierra Leone, 155
National Youth Commission, 170
Naude, Beyers, 14
Nigeria
 Abuja Accord, signed in, 11
 ECOMOG and, 10
 peacemakers in, 13
 Quakers in, 13
 TRC statement-taking in, 37
No Peace Without Justice, 91–94
Norman, Samuel Hinga, 33, 44, 47–48, 50, 51, 60, 76, 94, 112–13
Norwegian Church Aid, 26
NPRC. *See* National Provisional Ruling Council

nyouo tong gweno ("stepping on the egg"), 130–31

OAU. *See* Organization of African Unity
Ocampo, Moreno, 81
OHCHR. *See* UN Office of the High Commissioner of Human Rights
Ojukwu, Emeka, 13
Okelo, Francis G., 19, 20, 24, 27–28
Open Government Partnership, 160
"Operation Pay Yourself," 9–10
Operational Support Division, 163–64
Organization of African Unity (OAU), 13

peacemaking, religious, 17–18, 201
  examples of, 12–16
  tools of, 15–16, 125–26
  See also Inter-Religious Council
Peace Museum, 156, 250n.20
Peace Task Force, 11, 29
Penfold, Peter, 19, 21, 28, 33, 49, 50, 76, 186
Pentecostal Churches Council, 17, 97
People's Movement for Democratic Change (PMDC), 65
Philpott, Daniel
  on forgiveness, Islamic teaching, 123
  on "liberal peace," xiii
  on reconciliation, Christian and Muslim texts, 193–94
  on restorative justice, religious involvement, 39

Physicians for Human Rights, 54
PMDC. *See* People's Movement for Democratic Change
Political Parties Registration Act, 164–65
Political Parties Registration Commission, 165
polls
  BBC World Service Trust/Search for Common Ground, 86–88, 92, 94
  Boersch-Supan, Johanna, 88–90
  Campaign for Good Governance, 79–80
  Humphreys and Weinstein, 75, 77–78
  Manifesto 99, 71–73, 74, 78
  Millar, Gearoid, 90–91
  No Peace Without Justice, 91–94
  PRIDE, 73–75, 77, 137
  problems with, 71, 137
  Sawyer, Edward, 82–83
  Sesay, Amadu, 83–86
  Sierra Leone Truth and Reconciliation Working Group, 80–82
  summary of, 95–96
Poros, M. Perez, 19
Post-conflict Reintegration Initiatives for Development and Empowerment (PRIDE)
  Humphreys and Weinstein, collaboration with, 75
  polling by, 73–75, 77, 137
  on TRC and Special Court, relationship, 46
Project for Christians and Muslims (PROCMURA), 213n.42

Promotion of National Unity and
    Reconciliation Act (South
    Africa), 46
Public Order Act, 159–60

Qisas, 123
Quakers, 13

Raffaeli, Mario, 14
rahmah, 124
Rainbow Center, 67
Randall, F. T. C.
    on combatants, former, 116
    on forgiveness
    —in absence of apology, 103
    —Christ as example, 103
rape
    ceremonies, cleansing for, 130, 135
    conviction, first in Sierra Leone for, 226n.31
    during civil war, 10, 20, 54, 83
    Fambul Tok and, 147
    law, customary and, 57, 140
    marital, 62
    post–civil war, 66, 67
    prosecution of, at Special Court, 54–58, 62
    testimony at TRC on, 60
    TRC final report on, 54
Rapp, Stephen, 52, 56, 186
reconciliation
    vs. justice, xi–xii, 1–2, 4–5
    and religion, 16, 121, 125, 193–94
    See also justice: restorative
Red Cross, 134, 249n.154
Registration of Customary Marriage and Divorce Act, 65, 66–67, 168

Religions for Peace. *See* World Conference of Religions for Peace
Renamo, 14, 129
reparations
    amounts received, 68–69, 176–78
    community, 174
    criticisms of, 176–77
    expectations for, 198–99
    in Fambol Tok, 151
    in gacaca, 128
    importance of, 67–68, 90, 91, 136
    in Islam, 122
    in Rwanda, 128
    in South Africa, 12, 184
    symbolic, 174–75
    in Uganda, 130, 131
    in traditional conflict-resolution, 135, 136
    TRC final report, recommendations for, 173–78
    truth commissions, often ignored by, 68, 136, 151, 184
    views on, 75, 87, 90, 91, 94, 95
    by War Victims Trust Fund, 176–78
    to women, 63, 68–69
Revolutionary United Front (RUF)
    and Abidjan Accord, 9
    amnesty for, 9, 31, 143
    amputations by, 9
    confessions by, 44, 143
    crimes committed
    —gender, 54–57
    —number of, 44, 50
    defeat of, 33
    forcible recruitment by, 74, 189
    ideology of, 23, 133, 166
    invasion of Freetown, 9, 20

Revolutionary United Front (*cont.*)
  IRC, meeting with, 24–25
  Liberian roots of, 7, 146
  and Lome Accord, 26–27
  as political party, 9
  religion, position on, 23
  and Special Court
  —hearings, lack of remorse at, 40
  —indictments, 33, 56
  —prosecutions, 49, 54–57
  TRC, on selection committee, 217n.26
  UN peacekeepers, abduction of, 10, 29
  women in, 61
  youth in, 42, 74
  See also Taylor, Charles
Riccardi, Andrea, 14
Robertson, Geoffrey, 47, 48
Rogbalen Mosque, 21
RUF. *See* Revolutionary United Front
Rustenburg statement, 15
Rwanda. *See gacaca*; International Criminal Tribunal for Rwanda

Salia, Sahr Kemoore, 118
Samuels, Henry
  on Anti-Corruption Commission, 118
  on forgiveness, Muslim view, 100
  on president, lack of apology, 102
  on TRC
  —cleric as chairman, 99
  —hearings, acknowledgment at, 102
  —recommendations, 113
Sandi, Paul, 115
Sankoh, Foday
  AFRC, deputy chair, appointed, 9
  amnesty for, 31
  arrest of, 11
  death of, 29, 33, 50, 113
  demonstration at home, 11, 29
  IRC
  —meeting with, 19, 24
  —release of abducted children, negotiated, 24–25
  —turn against, 28
  Jackson, Jesse on, 216n.3
  Mineral Resources Commission, appointment to, 10, 27
  on religion, 23
  RUF, leader of, 7
  Saquee, Adama and, 143
  Special Court, indictment by, 29
  See also Revolutionary United Front
Sant'Egidio, 14, 16
Saquee, Adama, 143–44
SATRC. *See* South African Truth and Reconciliation Commission
Sawyer, Edward, 82–83
Schabas, William, 35, 36, 37, 45–46, 185
secret societies, 133, 135, 142
Sesay, Amadu, 83–86
Sesay, Unisa, 81
Sessay, Issa, 42
Sexual Offenses Act, 66, 168
Shaw, Josephine Thompson, 168
Shaw, Rosalind
  on apology, verbal, 89, 137, 139, 192
  on behavior, change in, 4
  on culture of secrecy, 6, 136–37, 198

on polling, problems with, 137
on TRC
—confession, lack of, 43–44
—criticisms of, 3–4, 184, 198
—popular support for, 35, 42, 82, 136
—testimony, unwillingness to provide, 61, 77, 137–38
—trauma, from testifying, 184, 198, 260n.81
—victims, expectation of material benefits from testifying, 198
Shura, 101
Sierra Leone Army (Sierra Leone Armed Forces), 8, 9, 31, 33, 54, 73, 143, 158, 163, 189
Sierra Leone Association of Journalists, 160
Sierra Leone Broadcasting Service, 149
Sierra Leone Court Monitoring Project, 50, 157, 167
Sierra Leone Muslim Congress, 17, 97
Sierra Leone Muslim Missionaries Union, 17, 97
Sierra Leone Peoples Party (SLPP)
and corruption, 166
election, 1996, 9
election defeat, 2007 and 2012, 166
Humper, Joseph, ties to, 99
and TRC, support for, 37
See also Kabbah, Ahmad Tejan
Sierra Leone Police, 59, 159, 163
Sierra Leone Truth and Reconciliation Commission (TRC)
commissioners, 35, 36, 217n.19
confessions, limited, 43–44, 190, 191
cost of, 80, 152, 186
criticisms of, 35–37, 80–82
—centralized, 79, 110, 149
—confessions, inability to solicit, 89, 105, 113, 141, 143, 191
—contemporaneous with Special Court, 77, 80, 85, 107, 113–14, 192
—distance, 149, 195
—financial problems, 35–36, 37, 81, 192
—international control, 81
—knowledge, lack of, 61–62, 72, 87, 107
—official, 141, 145, 149
—participation, low, 76–77
—pro-SLPP, 36
—reparations, inadequate, 91, 116, 117, 198–99
—staff, unqualified, 35
—time constraints, 85, 105, 107, 110, 141–42, 149, 192
—tradition, under-reliance on, 81, 110
gender crimes, 58–62
hearings, 37, 39, 40, 44, 190, 191
—on children, 37, 42–43
—closed, 37, 60
—event, 37
—institutional, 37
—thematic, 197–98
—on women, 37, 41, 59–60
IRC assistance to, 34, 141
and Lome Peace Accord, 32
mandate, 1–2, 32, 38, 39–40, 77, 153
National Vision Program, 155

302   Index

Sierra Leone Truth and
    Reconciliation Commission
    (*cont.*)
Norman, Samuel Hinga and, 44,
    48, 76
public opinion. *See* polls
recommendations. *See*
    Sierra Leone Truth and
    Reconciliation Commission
    final report: recommendations
reconciliation ceremonies at, 44,
    45, 108, 132, 136, 138, 191
salaries, 36
SATRC as model, 32, 38, 81
selection panel for, 99, 217n.26
and Special Court
—contemporaneous with, 38, 77,
    81
—differences between, 1–2, 38
—relationship to, 45–48, 76–77,
    85, 107
statements
—number of, 37, 58, 186, 218n40
—from perpetrators, 37, 43, 76,
    113, 191
—from women, 58, 60
statement-taking, 37, 79, 142
traditional conflict-resolution
    methods and, 72, 84–85,
    132–33, 134, 139
unique features of, 153, 155,
    191–92
victim-perpetrator mediation, 44,
    191
Sierra Leone Truth and
    Reconciliation Commission
    Act (TRC Act), 34, 47, 48, 81,
    127, 173

on follow-up committee, 155–56
on Human Rights Commission,
    155
on recommendations,
    implementation of, 64, 153
on Special Fund for War Victims,
    173
on women, 58
Sierra Leone Truth and
    Reconciliation Commission
    final report, 2, 37, 44, 82, 115
on abuses, number of, 44
as advocacy tool, 82, 198
on apology and forgiveness, 40
on chiefs, 134
children's version, 37–38
copies, limited number of, 115
on faith institutions, 12
on gender crimes, 54, 60
on Kabbah, criticism of, 45
recommendations, 153–79
—amputees, 63
—Anti-Corruption Commission,
    166, 171
—arrest and detention, arbitrary,
    157–58
—assets, disclosure of by public
    officials, 165
—attorney general and minister
    of justice, separation of, 161
—awareness of, 87, 115
—categorization of, 154
—child labor, 169–70
—children, 167–70
—code of conduct, 161–62, 164
—Constitution, 156, 163, 250n.21
—corporal punishment, 168
—corruption, 164, 166

—customary law, 63–64, 162–63
—death penalty, 156
—education, 64, 169, 174
—election reform, 64, 164–65, 170
—emergency powers, 158–59
—external actors, 171
—freedom of expression, 159–60
—freedom of information, 160
—government response to. *See* White Paper
—health care, 63, 174
—Human Rights Commission, 154–55, 170
—human rights training, 159
—judicial reform, 161–62
—micro-credit, 174
—mineral resources, 171–73
—mining licenses, 171
—National Youth Commission, 170
—orphanages, 168–69
—paramilitary forces, 163
—pensions, 63, 174
—procurement, 165
—reconciliation activities, ongoing, 175
—religious leaders on, 115–19
—remuneration, 162
—reparations, 173–78
—sex trafficking, 168
—skills training, 174
—transparency, 165
—war monument, 175
—whistle-blowers, 165
—women, 63–65
—youth, 170
secondary school edition, 38

on Special Court, relationship with, 45, 46–47
on statements, numbers of, 60, 76
Sierra Leone Truth and Reconciliation Commission (TRC) Working Group, 34, 145, 149
Sierra Leone Truth and Reconciliation Working Group, 80–82, 145
Sillah, Ahmed Tejan
on apology, lack of from President Kabbah, 112
on forgiveness, 102
IRC, co-founder of, 17
on punishment, 111
on Special Court, value of, 111
on TRC recommendations, 115, 116
Simbo, Billy
on apology, 105
on corruption, 118
on culture of secrecy, 119
on forgiveness
—in absence of apology, 103, 122
—independent of TRC, 109
—value to victims, 103
on Khanu, Moses, serving on HRC, 118
on Special Court
—criticisms of, 111, 112–13
—and prosecution of Norman, Samuel Hinga, and Taylor, Charles, 112–13
—value of, 111
on TRC

Simbo, Billy (*cont.*)
—perpetrators, few confessions from, 105
—recommendations, 113
—women victims, value to, 108
Sisters of Charity, 21
SLPP. *See* Sierra Leone Peoples Party
sobels, 8
Society for Democratic Initiatives, 172
Sooka, Yasmin Louise, 35, 59
South African Council of Churches, 14, 15
South African Truth and Reconciliation Commission (SATRC)
    amnesty, 81
    Boraine, Alex on, 41
    criticisms of, xi–xii, 40, 85–86, 99, 184, 188
    on gender, 53, 59
    as model, xi–xii, 32–33, 38, 39, 42, 59, 81, 98
    Schabas, William on, 46
    and Sierra Leone TRC, differences, 33, 81
Southern Sudan Liberation Movement, 13
Special Court for Sierra Leone (SCSL)
    convictions, 33–34, 216n.11
    cost of, 51–52, 80, 93, 111, 123, 152, 186–87, 224n.121, 249n.153, 257n.24
    and Crane, David, 43, 55, 76, 185
    criticisms of, 49–51, 93, 123, 187
    death of indictees, 33
    funding, 35–36, 79
    gender crimes, 54–58, 60, 62
    ICTR, comparison to, 55, 56
    indictments, 29, 33, 42, 43, 55, 76, 77
    legacy, 57, 62
    mandate, 1–2, 33, 43
    Norman prosecution, 112–13
    outreach, 49
    public opinion. *See* polls
    religious leaders on, 110–13, 123
    salaries, 49
    staff, 49–50, 79, 93
    statute authorizing, 55
    suspicions, about using TRC testimony, 43
    witnesses
    —experiences at, 57–58
    —payments to, 51
    and TRC
    —contemporaneous with, 38, 77, 80, 81, 123, 185
    —differences with, 1–2, 38
    —Norman, Samuel Hinga, refusal to let testify at, 44, 50, 60, 76, 113
    —relationship to, xi, 4, 5, 45–48, 77, 181
    US support, 33, 80
Special Fund for War Victims. *See* War Victims Trust Fund
Speck, D. M.
    on Special Court, value of, 110–11
    on TRC, recommendations, 115
St. Anthony's Catholic Church, 32
Statute of the Special Court, 55
Stevens, Siaka, 11, 12, 163
Strasser, Valentine, 7
Sudan, 13, 185

Sudanese Inter-Religious Council, 13
Suma, Mohamed, 50, 69, 167
Sumana, Samuel, 165
Supreme Islamic Council, 17, 97
Swaray, Fomba Abubakar
  on forgiveness
  —Islamic view, 101
  —example of Joseph, 101
  on Shura, 101

taba, 122
Taylor, Charles, 7, 26, 33, 34, 50, 51, 89, 91, 92, 113, 171, 186, 188, 210n.1
T'azir, 123
Teale, Lotta, 62
Tejan-Cole, Abdul, 167
Tejan-Kellah, Amie, 67
Thompson, John Bankole, 47
Torto, Sylvanus, 36
tradition
  compatibility with religion, 3, 5–6, 201–2
  and conflict-resolution methods
  —Annan, Kofi on, 182
  —criticisms of, 139–40, 148, 201
  —in Mozambique, 129–30
  —punitive aspects, 139–40
  —and restorative justice, 194–95
  —in Rwanda, 127–29
  —in Sierra Leone, 135–36
  —TRC, failure to use, 81, 84–85, 132–33, 134
  —in Uganda, 130–32
Transparency International, 160
Trauma Center for Victims of Violence and Torture, 184

TRC Act. *See* Sierra Leone Truth and Reconciliation Commission Act
TRC Working Group. *See* Sierra Leone Truth and Reconciliation Commission Working Group
Truth and Reconciliation Working Group. *See* Sierra Leone Truth and Reconciliation Working Group
truth commissions
  advantages of, 41, 93–94, 183, 197
  in Africa, 32–33, 185
  criticisms of, 3, 184
  funding, 217n.20
  prosecutions after, 183
  reassessment by international community, 182–83
  recommendations, implementation of, 178
  United Nations and, 182, 185–86
  worldwide, 32–33
Tutsi, 55, 127, 128
Tutu, Desmond
  criticisms of, xi, 40, 85–86, 98
  on restorative justice, 5, 39
  South African Council of Churches and, 14
  on *ubuntu*, vii, 4, 5
  See also South African Truth and Reconciliation Commission

ubuntu, xii, xiii, 4, 5
Uganda
  Acholi, 130, 131, 132
  ICC and, 185
  Lord's Resistance Army, 130, 131–32

Uganda (*cont.*)
  National Resistance Army, 131
  rituals in
  —*gumo tong* ("bending of the spears"), 131
  —*mato oput*, 130
  —*nyouo tong gweno* ("stepping on the egg"), 130–31
Uganda Peoples Defense Force, 131
UNAMSIL. *See* United Nations Mission in Sierra Leone
UNDP. *See* United Nations Development Program
UN Human Development Index, 51, 176
UNICEF, 37–38, 42, 65
UNIOSL. *See* United Nations Integrated Office for Sierra Leone
United Brethren in Christ Church, 103
United Council of Imams, 17, 97
United Democratic Front (South Africa), 14–15
United Nations
  on amnesty
  —in Abidjan Accord, 216n.4
  —in Lome Accord, 27–28, 32
  retributive justice, preference for, xiii
  Special Court, establishment of, 33
  truth commissions, reassessment of, 182
United Nations Development Program (UNDP), 35, 36, 51, 110, 141

United Nations Integrated Office for Sierra Leone (UNIOSL), 16, 169
United Nations International Covenant on Civil and Political Rights, 157, 158–59
United Nations Mission in Sierra Leone (UNAMSIL), 10–11, 29, 33, 35, 36, 54, 60, 98, 113, 163
Universal Declaration of Human Rights, 126
UN Observer Mission in Sierra Leone, 20, 25
UN Office of the High Commissioner of Human Rights (OHCHR), 35, 36, 72, 80, 81, 132, 217n.26
UN Peacebuilding Fund, 176, 178
UN Resolution 1315, 33
UN Women, 178

Varney, Howard, 178–79
Vendley, William, 16
victim-offender mediation, 44
Vincent, Robin, 38, 47
Vine Memorial Baptist Church, 99
Vision for the Blind, 176

War Victims Trust Fund (Special Fund for War Victims), 69, 116, 173, 175, 176–78
War Wounded, 176
WCRP. *See* World Conference of Religions for Peace
West African Methodist Church, 110
West Side Boys, 11

White Paper (White Paper on the Report of the Truth and Reconciliation Commission)
  on arbitrary arrest and detention, 158
  on attorney general and minister of justice, separation of, 161
  on death penalty, 157
  on emergency powers, 158–59
  on external actors, 171
  on follow-up committee, 155
  on Human Rights Council, 156
  on implementation, promise to, 175
  on mining, 172
  on National Youth Commission, 170
  on paramilitary forces, 163–64
  on women, 64–67
Winter, Renate, 62
Women's Forum, 65
Women's Task Force on the Role of Women in the TRC and Special Court, 55, 59, 225n.11
World Bank, 65, 117
World Council of Churches, 13, 15, 16
World Conference of Religions for Peace, 2, 16, 17, 26, 97, 200
World Council of Churches, 13, 15, 16

Zuppi, Mateo, 14

LYN S. GRAYBILL

is an expert in the role of religious and cultural

resources in international ethics and human rights practices.

The author of *Truth and Reconciliation in South Africa: Miracle or Model?*

and *Religion and Resistance Politics in South Africa*, she has taught

at universities in Virginia, Georgia, and West Africa.

www.ingramcontent.com/pod-product-compliance
Ingram Content Group UK Ltd.
Pitfield, Milton Keynes, MK11 3LW, UK
UKHW021252180426
11946UKWH00004B/93